ATLAS OF
AMERICAN HISTORY

ATLAS OF
AMERICAN HISTORY

JAMES TRUSLOW ADAMS
Editor in Chief

R. V. COLEMAN
Managing Editor

NEW YORK

CHARLES SCRIBNER'S SONS

1943

Foreword

Discovery, exploration, frontier posts, settlement, territorial organization, extension of communication—this, repeated time after time, has, to a large degree, been the history of the United States.

Thus, much of our history is concerned with places; and to understand *what* happened, we must also know *where* it happened.

Yet, to locate many places commonly mentioned in our factual histories has heretofore called for reference to scores of widely separated books, atlases or original maps, often difficult of access and seldom at hand when needed, clumsy to handle—and generally not available in the average library.

The preparation and publication of the *Dictionary of American History* pointed the need for a concise, easy to use, carefully thought out, authoritative atlas of American history. The editors and scholars associated with the production of the earlier work accordingly set themselves the task of making an atlas which would present our geographical history as completely and as readily as the *Dictionary of American History* presents our written history.

The plan and scope of the work received long and careful editorial consideration. It was the judgment of the editors that the need was for maps that would interpret our history through the location of places as they actually existed and exactly where they existed at a given time. Graphs, diagrams and other nonexact pictorial interpretations were, in general, to be avoided as having no place in this Atlas.

That the maps should proceed chronologically was obvious. That the areas and periods dealt with in each map should be entities was desirable. That each map should gear in with the preceding and succeeding maps was important. The intent was to so arrange the maps that, as the pages turned, the development of the country would become more clear and take on a new meaning and significance.

The decision as to what places to show on each map was arrived at by a number of approaches. The standard histories and source materials

Foreword

were indexed. Contemporary maps were examined. Partly on the basis of frequency of reference to a place, and partly on the basis of whether a place was sufficiently important historically to be shown, the locations were made on rough drafts—subject to criticism and revisions.

Then the supervision of each map was assigned to an historian or group of historians familiar with the period and area involved. The supervisor added or eliminated or criticized, and thus the map progressed. But no map was finished until it had been considered in connection with the related maps—to the end that each should supplement the other. From the rough drafts—often worn to tatters by revision—the finished drawings were made.

Every map in this work has been drawn in our editorial offices, under the direct supervision of the editors for factual presentation, and of Mr. Appleton for cartographic presentation—and in every case subject to the final approval of the supervisors.

In general the maps are based upon the best and latest government surveys, but with adjustments to earlier maps in case physical changes have occurred, such as rivers cutting new channels or reefs forming where formerly no reefs existed.

Sixty-four historians actively supervised the drawing of the 147 plates which appear in this Atlas. Many others advised and assisted. Thus, the exact location of Fort Ross was directed by Prof. E. O. Essig of the University of California. Stella Drumm, of the Missouri Historical Society, advised regarding locations on the Missouri River. Prof. R. L. Meriwether, of the University of South Carolina, aided in locations relating to Kings Mountain. Painstaking research, sometimes on the ground, went into the location of many places.

To enable the user of the Atlas to find, easily and quickly, the place which he is looking for, a place index has been made a part of the volume. Where was Kaskaskia? Logstown? Fallen Timbers? South Pass? or any one of the hundreds of other historically important places now lost from our maps or buried under a mass of other names? The index carries the reader instantly to the map or maps where these places are shown. There he sees not only the location of the place, but its relation to other historically important places of the same time.

For those who wish to trace a particular subject from period to period and from area to area, the chronological arrangement of the maps, together with the index, will prove helpful. For example, suppose the reader is interested in following the advance of the frontier: Through the Index, and from map to map, he will see the falling back of the Indians, the establishment of trading posts, the growth of settlements, the formation of territories and the organization of states.

An illustration of the importance of geographical knowledge in our history may be found in so well known a story as that of Boone's blazing the trail to Kentucky. Every schoolchild thinks he knows it. But does he know it? Boone started from the Sycamore Shoals of the Watauga. (Only the local historians now know the spot, yet, there, in 1775, was held a great treaty by which the Cherokee Indians ceded to the Transylvania Company the vast territories of Kentucky and part of Tennessee.) Boone went across the Long Island of Holston. (That location is not readily found on present-day maps, yet it was a landmark in the history of the early southwest.) He passed through Moccasin Gap. (This appears only on the most detailed maps.) He went over Clinch River and Powell Mountain to Cumberland Gap and on into Kentucky. Some of these places are shown on several maps in the Atlas, and all are shown with the route indicated on Plate 62. To see not only the route, but its relation to other routes (shown on other maps) coming down from Virginia and up from Carolina enables one to understand the importance of what Boone did, and why he did it when he did it.

The organization and admittance of states is treated as a part of our western development, yet every territory is brought into being in its proper area and proper period and every new state is admitted, with the dates given in each case, and with the changes in area of each territory or state clearly shown.

In the making of this Atlas, as in the making of all works of this sort, the question of where to stop has been a problem. Many more maps could have been made—and there was often the wish to make them. Many places could have been shown which are not shown, and there was often the inclination to show them. The editors can only hope that they have shown, and have shown in their proper relationship, those places having importance in our history in so far as that history had significance in our national development. Strictly local history, if one can say what is local history as differentiated from national history, had to be passed by. That a question may be raised as to why one place is shown and another not, the editors recognize full well and can only say that they have made the best decisions they could.

Throughout, the intent has been to provide a sufficient number of maps to avoid overcrowding any area. Where a relatively congested area has appeared in an otherwise general map, that area has been treated in broad outline on the general map and then given a separate map in which the details are shown without crowding. The test which the editors themselves applied was whether every location could readily be found without resort to guides on the margins of the maps. Accordingly, it is the belief of the editors that the grid (cross-section) method of indexing has properly been omitted.

As our task nears completion, we wish to express our appreciation of the contribution made by the members of the Advisory Council, who have given most generously of their time and knowledge in helping to plan the work as a whole.

To the Supervisors we are deeply indebted not only for advice and criticism in connection with the drawing of their particular maps, but also for their patience and understanding as the work progressed and each map had to be revised time after time in order to bring it into proper relationship with other maps dealing in part with related periods and areas.

We also desire to express special appreciation of the service of LeRoy H. Appleton, the Chief Cartographer, for his skillful and beautiful presentation of the subject matter of each map, either as drawn by his own pen or as a result of his direction of others. The drawing of maps is an art, to an extent not often realized. It is our belief that Mr. Appleton has set a new standard for maps as drawn in America—in their clarity, their balance of letter and line, and their artistic quality.

Back of each map and back of the work as a whole, lies an immense amount of careful, patient work. To those who, through the two years in which the Atlas was being prepared, faithfully worked out the details, we wish to extend our thanks: To Thomas Robson Hay, Associate Editor, for his constant oversight and particularly for his help on the Civil War maps; to Arthur S. Bryant, Assistant Cartographer, whose sure and experienced hand appears in almost every map; to E. Graham Platt, who was associated with the work throughout; to Marion G. Barnes, whose careful checking, from the making of the rough drafts of the maps to the completion of the Index, has saved us from many a possible error.

Finally, as Editor in Chief, I wish to express my personal and deep indebtedness to R. V. Coleman, Managing Editor. Not only has he supervised the entire work and seen that threads did not become tangled in what became an increasingly complex task, but he did much more. His knowledge of American history, not merely in its broad outlines but in its local details in all sections, has been of immense help in enabling us so to plan the maps and their relations to one another that instead of a series of disjointed plates they form an articulated whole which, in its unity, tells the story of the growth of the nation.

It is the earnest hope, as it has been the constant effort, of all those who have shared in the preparation of this work, that it may prove to be a genuinely useful aid to the better understanding and more correct interpretation of our national story. In scope and plan we have endeavored not only to provide the professional scholar with a new and accurate tool for his research, but also to help the students and readers in high schools, colleges and the home to gain access to that geographical material relating to our history, which is so essential but which hitherto has been difficult or impossible for them to obtain. We can only trust that we have in part, at least, succeeded in accomplishing the task to which we set ourselves.

JAMES TRUSLOW ADAMS

Feb. 8, 1943

The intent in Plate I is to show the area of the United States as it appeared, topographically, in, say, 1491—without a known name or a single identifying description. To give the desired effect both the caption and the border have been omitted from the face of the map and the plate itself has been placed on a hinge to further the sense of unity. The map was drawn by Mr. Appleton under the supervision of Lloyd Arnold Brown.

PLATE 1

Topography
of the
United States

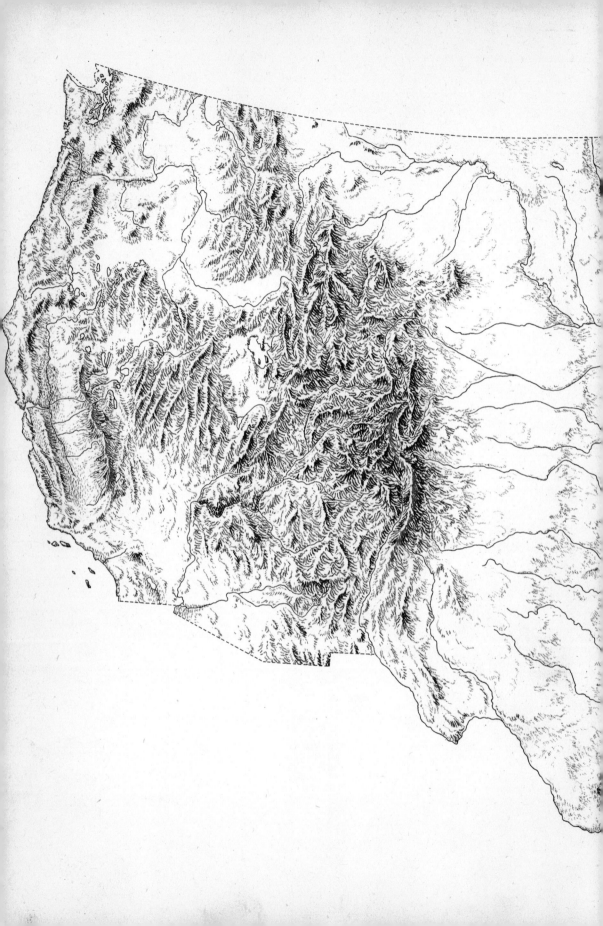

PLATE 1

Topography
of the
United States

PLATE 2

Forests
of the
United States

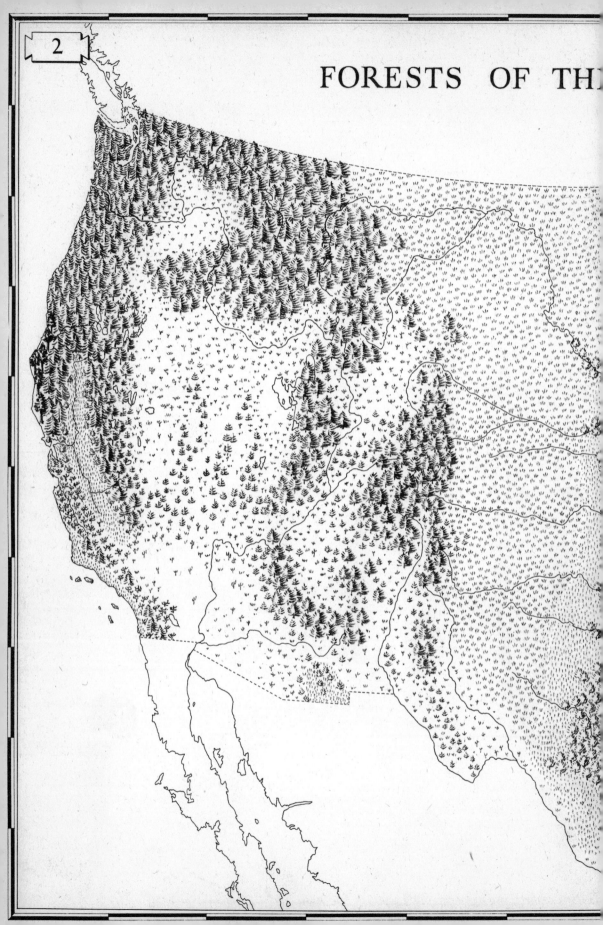

UNITED STATES

Drawn under the supervision of LLOYD A. BROWN

PLATE 3

Forests
of the
United States

PLATE 4

Discovery
of America

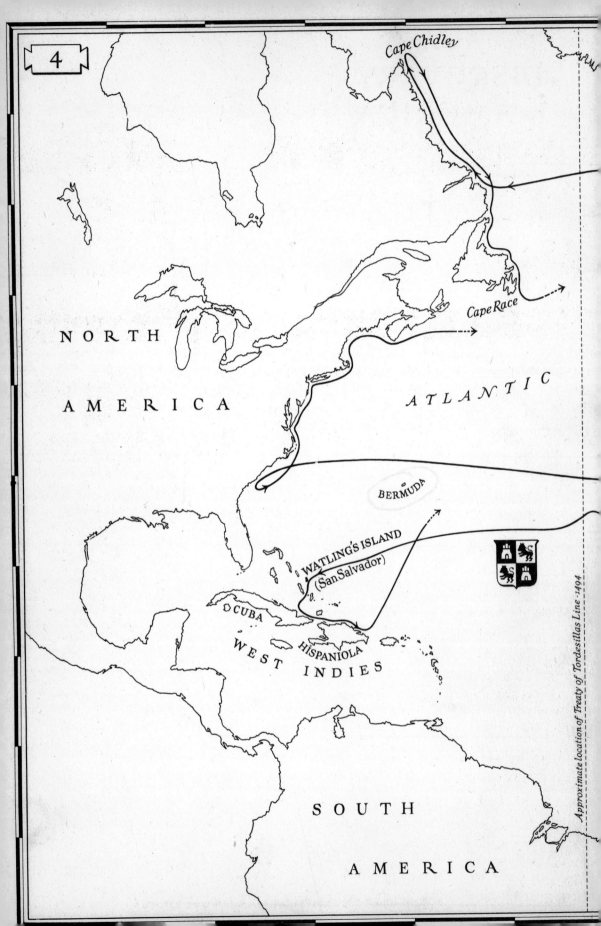

4

Cape Chidley

NORTH

AMERICA

Cape Race

ATLANTIC

BERMUDA

WATLING'S ISLAND
(San Salvador)

CUBA

WEST
INDIES

HISPANIOLA

SOUTH

AMERICA

Approximate location of Treaty of Tordesillas Line 1494

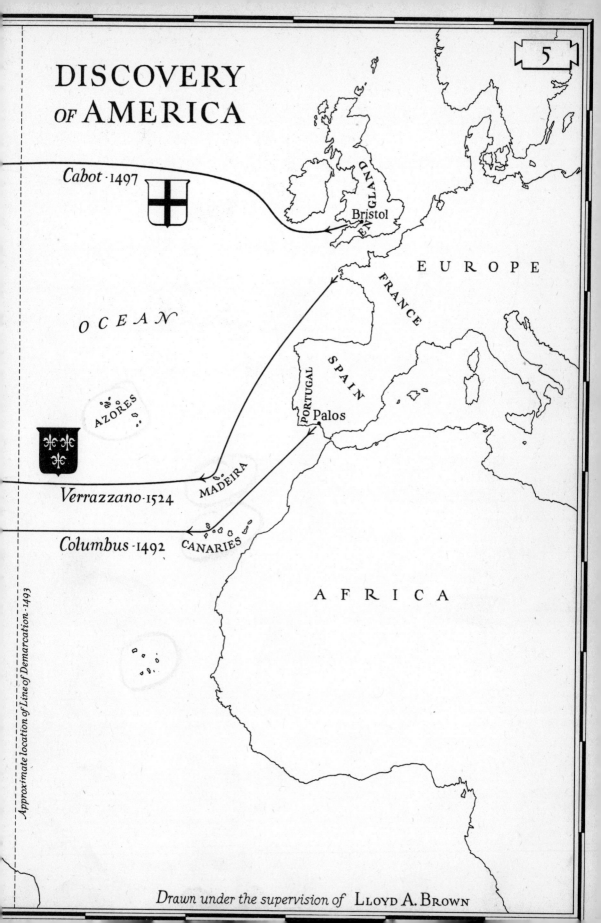

DISCOVERY
OF AMERICA

Cabot ·1497

Bristol

ENGLAND

EUROPE

FRANCE

OCEAN

SPAIN

PORTUGAL

AZORES

Palos

Verrazzano·1524

MADEIRA

Columbus ·1492

CANARIES

AFRICA

Approximate location of Line of Demarcation·1493

Drawn under the supervision of LLOYD A. BROWN

PLATE 5

Discovery
of America

PLATE 6

Sixteenth Century
Spanish Explorations

SIXTEENTH CENTURY

(Arkansas River)

QUIVI[RA]

Grand Cañon
(Colorado River)
Cardenas
(Little Colorado River)
Tusayan (Hopi)
Tovar
Jemez
Taos
Cibola (Zuni)
Tiguex
Cicuye (Pecos)
(Canadian River)
Acoma (Acuco)
QUERECHOS
(Gila River)
Army Returns
Chichilticalli
(Pecos River)
(Brazos River)
Melchior Diaz
Suya
(Colorado River)
Arizpe
Sonora
Ures
(Rio Grande)
Batuco
Yaquimi
Fuerte
Santa Barbara
Sinaloa
PACIFIC OCEAN
(Rio Grande)
Culiacan
San Blas
Tampico
Compostela
Mexico City

Juan Ponce de Leon · 1513
Panfilo de Narvaez · 1528
Alvar Nunez Cabeza de Vaca · 1528-1536
Hernando de Soto · 1539-1542
Luis de Moscoso · 1542-1543
Francisco Vazquez de Coronado · 1540-1542
      Principal Route
      Subsidiary Explorations
Hernando de Alarcon · 1540
Beltran-Espejo Expedition · 1582-1583

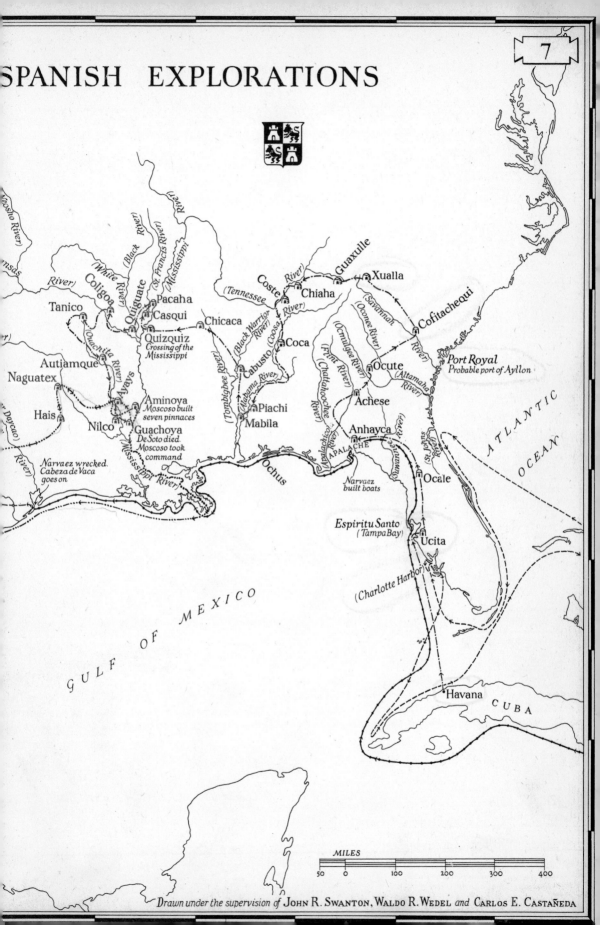

SPANISH EXPLORATIONS

(Arkansas River)
(Poisho River)
(White River)
(Black River)
(St. Francis River)
(Mississippi River)
(Tennessee River)

Guaxulle

Xualla

Coste

Chiaha

Cofitachequi

Coligoa

Pacaha

Tanico

Casqui

Chicaca

(Savannah River)

(Oconee River)

(Ocmulgee River)

Quizquiz
Crossing of the Mississippi

Coca

Coste
(Coosa River)

Port Royal
Probable port of Ayllon

(Ouachita River)

(Black Warrior River)

Cabusto

Ocute

(Altamaha River)

Autiamque

Naguatex

(Alabama River)

Piachi

Achese

Hais

Arkays

Nilco

Aminoya
Moscoso built seven pinnaces

Mabila

Anhayca

(St. Johns River)

Ocale

(Doycao River)

Guachoya
De Soto died. Moscoso took command

APALACHE

Narvaez wrecked. Cabeza de Vaca goes on

(Mississippi River)

Ochus

Narvaez built boats

(Suwannee River)

ATLANTIC OCEAN

Espiritu Santo (Tampa Bay)

Ucita

(Charlotte Harbor)

GULF OF MEXICO

Havana

CUBA

MILES
50 0   100   200   300   400

Drawn under the supervision of JOHN R. SWANTON, WALDO R. WEDEL *and* CARLOS E. CASTAÑEDA

PLATE 7

Sixteenth Century
Spanish Explorations

PLATE 8

Florida
French and Spanish
Settlements

1562-1588

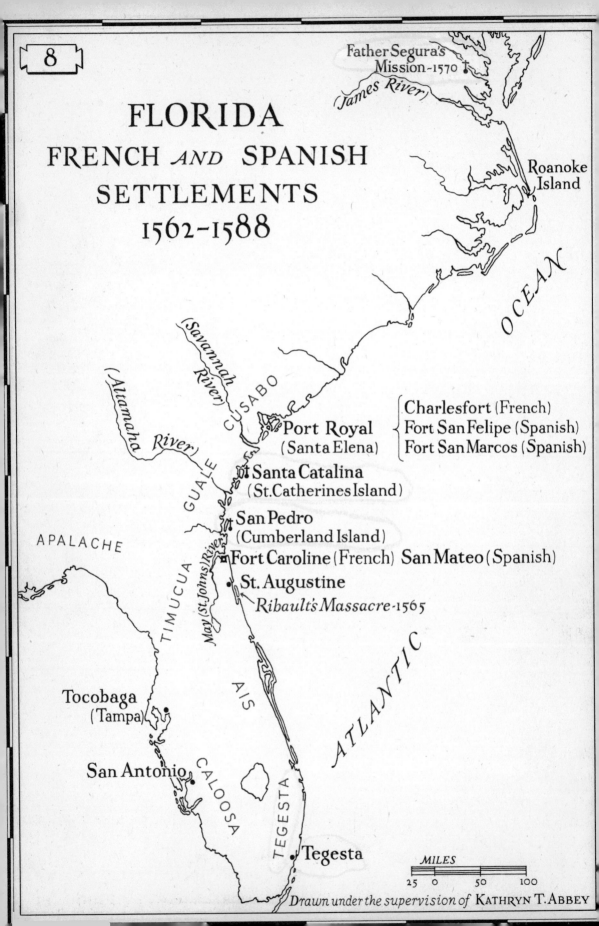

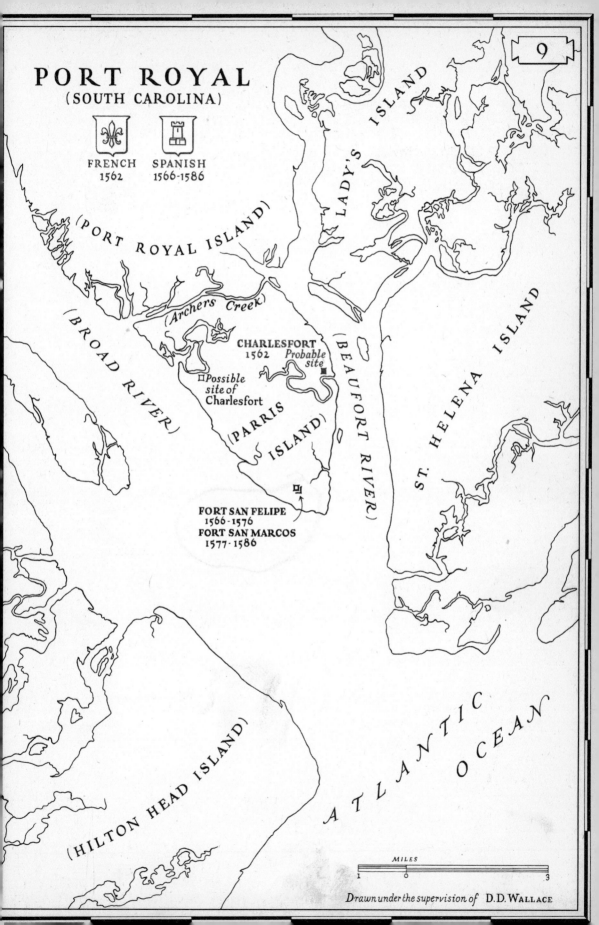

PORT ROYAL
(SOUTH CAROLINA)

FRENCH 1562 SPANISH 1566-1586

9

(PORT ROYAL ISLAND)

LADY'S ISLAND

(BROAD RIVER)

(Archers Creek)

CHARLESFORT
1562 *Probable site*

☐ *Possible site of Charlesfort*

(PARRIS ISLAND)

(BEAUFORT RIVER)

ST. HELENA ISLAND

FORT SAN FELIPE
1566-1576
FORT SAN MARCOS
1577-1586

(HILTON HEAD ISLAND)

ATLANTIC OCEAN

MILES
1 0 3

Drawn under the supervision of D.D.WALLACE

PLATE 9

Port Royal

(*South Carolina*)

PLATE 10

Roanoke Island
Colonies

1584-1591

ROANOKE ISLAND
COLONIES
1584-1591

10

(Chowan River)

CHAWONOAC

WEAPEMEOC

(ALBEMARLE SOUND)

ROANOKE
English Settlement

MORATUC

HATORASCK

Moratuc (Roanoke) River

DASAMONQUEPEUC

ISLAND

SECOTAN

(Pamlico River)

AQUASEOGOC

CROATOAN

(PAMLICO SOUND)

WOCOCON

O C E A N

(Neuse River)

A T L A N T I C

MILES

5   0   10   20

Drawn under the supervision of C. C. CRITTENDEN

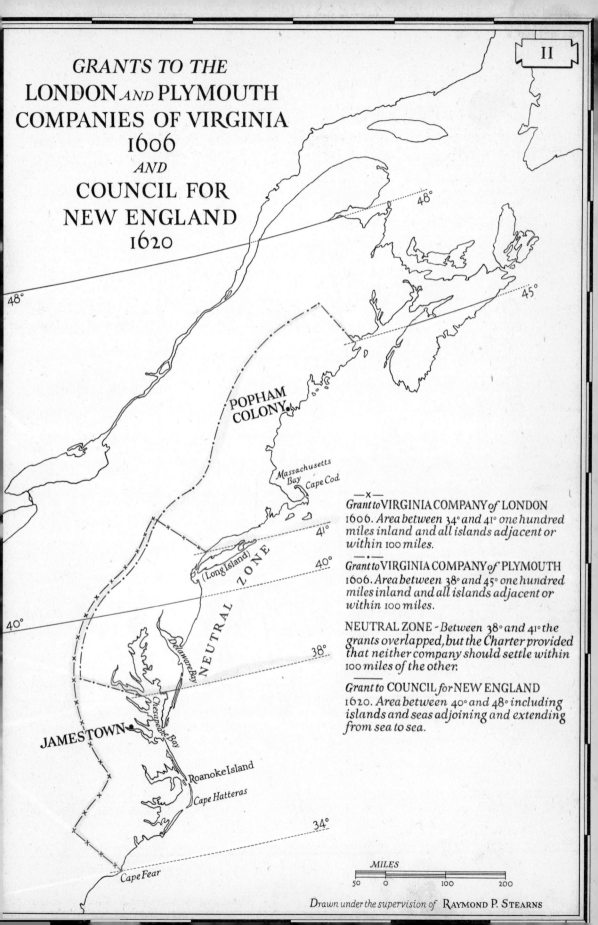

GRANTS TO THE
LONDON *AND* PLYMOUTH
COMPANIES OF VIRGINIA
1606
AND
COUNCIL FOR
NEW ENGLAND
1620

48°

48°

45°

POPHAM COLONY

Massachusetts Bay

Cape Cod

40°

(Long Island)

40°

NEUTRAL ZONE

40°

Delaware Bay

38°

Chesapeake Bay

JAMESTOWN

Roanoke Island

Cape Hatteras

34°

Cape Fear

— x —
Grant to VIRGINIA COMPANY *of* LONDON 1606. *Area between 34° and 41° one hundred miles inland and all islands adjacent or within 100 miles.*

— • —
Grant to VIRGINIA COMPANY *of* PLYMOUTH 1606. *Area between 38° and 45° one hundred miles inland and all islands adjacent or within 100 miles.*

NEUTRAL ZONE - *Between 38° and 41° the grants overlapped, but the Charter provided that neither company should settle within 100 miles of the other.*

Grant to COUNCIL *for* NEW ENGLAND 1620. *Area between 40° and 48° including islands and seas adjoining and extending from sea to sea.*

MILES
50   0   100   200

Drawn under the supervision of RAYMOND P. STEARNS

PLATE 11

Grants to the
London and Plymouth
Companies of Virginia

1606

and Council for
New England

1620

PLATE 12

Jamestown

1607–1619

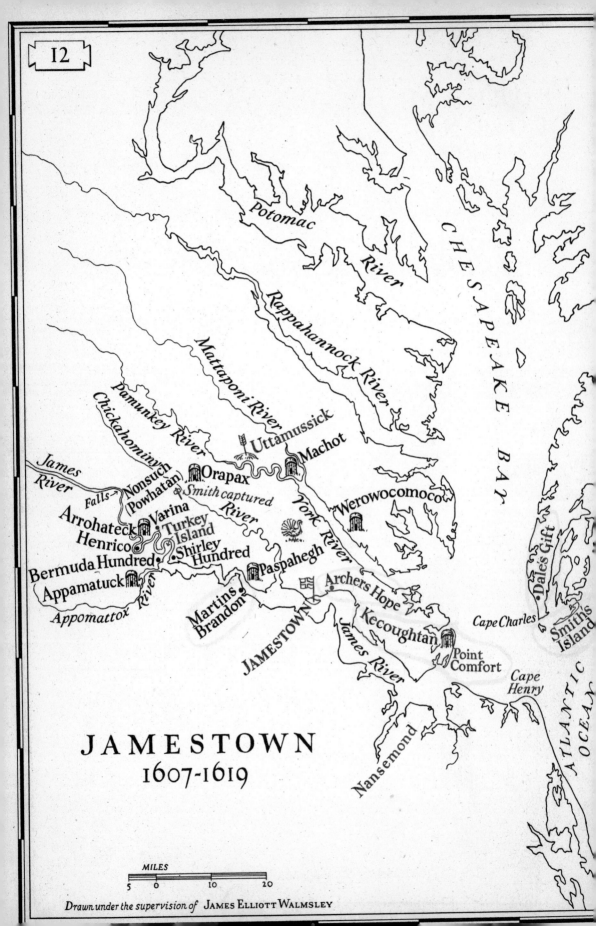

JAMESTOWN
1607-1619

CHESAPEAKE BAY

Potomac River

Rappahannock River

Mattaponi River

Pamunkey River

Chickahominy

James River

Falls

Nonsuch (Powhatan)

Orapax

Uttamussick

Machot

Smith captured

River

Werowocomoco

York River

Arrohateck

Varina

Turkey Island

Henrico

Shirley Hundred

Bermuda Hundred

Appamatuck

Appomattox River

Paspahegh

Martins Brandon

Archers Hope

JAMESTOWN

Kecoughtan

James River

Cape Charles

Dale's Gift

Smiths Island

Point Comfort

Cape Henry

ATLANTIC OCEAN

Nansemond

MILES

5   0   10   20

Drawn under the supervision of JAMES ELLIOTT WALMSLEY

POPHAM COLONY
1607-1608
(MAINE)

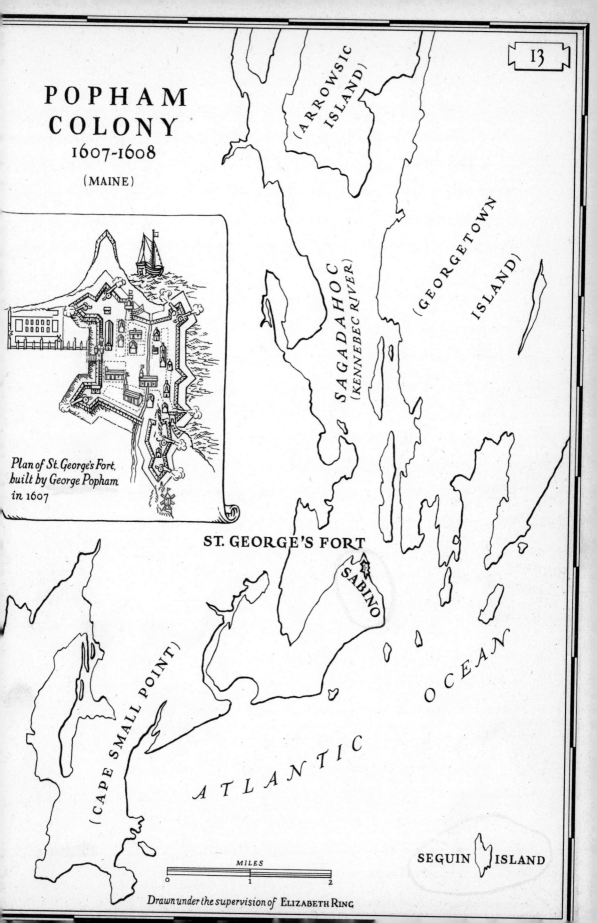

Plan of St. George's Fort,
built by George Popham
in 1607

(ARROWSIC ISLAND)

(GEORGETOWN ISLAND)

SAGADAHOC
(KENNEBEC RIVER)

ST. GEORGE'S FORT

SABINO

(CAPE SMALL POINT)

ATLANTIC OCEAN

SEGUIN ISLAND

MILES
0   1   2

Drawn under the supervision of ELIZABETH RING

PLATE 13

Popham
Colony

1607–1608

PLATE 14

Plymouth
Plantation

1620–1630

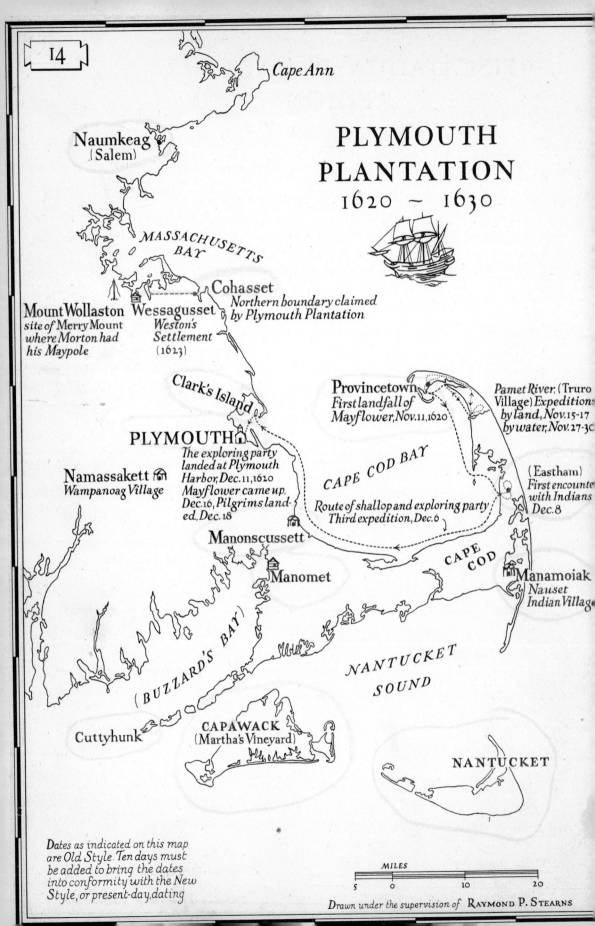

14

PLYMOUTH PLANTATION
1620 – 1630

Cape Ann

Naumkeag
(Salem)

MASSACHUSETTS BAY

Cohasset

Mount Wollaston
site of Merry Mount where Morton had his Maypole

Wessagusset
Weston's Settlement (1623)

Northern boundary claimed by Plymouth Plantation

Clark's Island

Provincetown
First landfall of Mayflower, Nov. 11, 1620

Pamet River, (Truro Village) Expeditions by land, Nov. 15-17 by water, Nov. 27-30

PLYMOUTH
The exploring party landed at Plymouth Harbor, Dec. 11, 1620 Mayflower came up, Dec. 16, Pilgrims landed, Dec. 18

Namassakett
Wampanoag Village

CAPE COD BAY

Route of shallop and exploring party Third expedition, Dec. 6

(Eastham)
First encounter with Indians Dec. 8

Manonscussett

Manomet

CAPE COD

Manamoiak
Nauset Indian Village

(BUZZARD'S BAY)

NANTUCKET SOUND

Cuttyhunk

CAPAWACK
(Martha's Vineyard)

NANTUCKET

Dates as indicated on this map are Old Style. Ten days must be added to bring the dates into conformity with the New Style, or present-day, dating

MILES

5   0   10   20

Drawn under the supervision of RAYMOND P. STEARNS

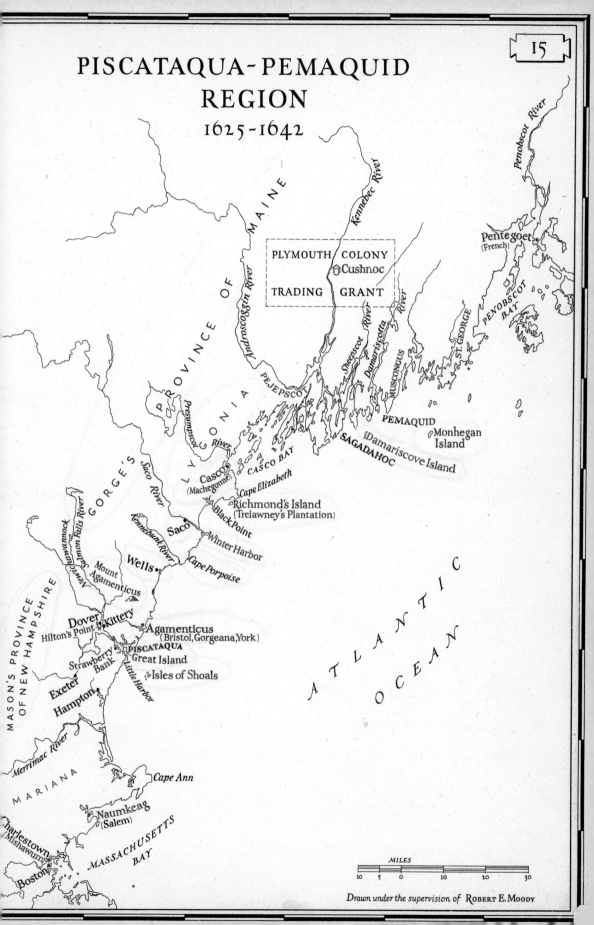

PISCATAQUA-PEMAQUID
REGION
1625-1642

PLYMOUTH   COLONY
⌂ Cushnoc
TRADING   GRANT

Penobscot River

Pente goet ·
(French)

Kennebec River

PENOBSCOT BAY

PROVINCE OF MAINE

Androscoggin River

ST. GEORGE

PEJEPSCOT

Sheepscot River

Damariscotta River

MUSCONGUS

Presumpscot River

L Y G O N I A

PEMAQUID

Monhegan Island

Casco
(Machegonne)

CASCO BAY

Damariscove Island

SAGADAHOC

Cape Elizabeth

GORGE'S

Saco River

Richmond's Island
(Trelawney's Plantation)

Black Point

Kennebunk River

Saco

Winter Harbor

Wells

Mount
Agamenticus

Cape Porpoise

A T L A N T I C

Newichawannock

Salmon Falls River

Dover

Kittery

Hilton's Point

Agamenticus
(Bristol, Gorgeana, York)

PISCATAQUA

Strawberry
Bank

Great Island

O C E A N

Little Harbor

MASON'S PROVINCE
OF NEW HAMPSHIRE

Exeter

Isles of Shoals

Hampton

Merrimac River

MARIANA

Cape Ann

Naumkeag
(Salem)

Charlestown
(Mishawum)

MASSACHUSETTS
BAY

Boston

MILES

10   5   0   10   20   30

Drawn under the supervision of ROBERT E. MOODY

PLATE 15

Piscataqua-Pemaquid Region

1625–1642

PLATE 16

Massachusetts Bay

1630–1642

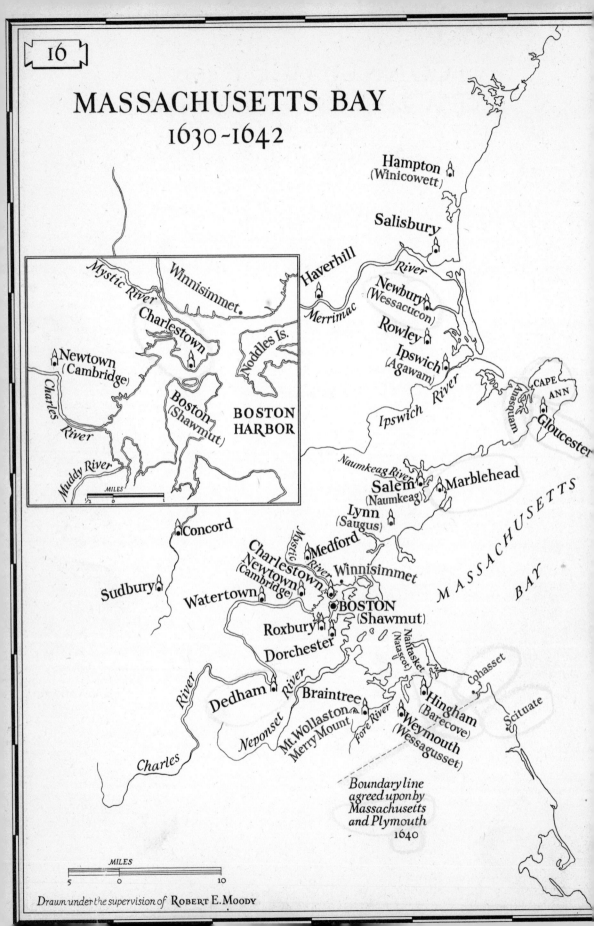

MASSACHUSETTS BAY
1630-1642

Hampton
(Winicowett)

Salisbury

Haverhill

River

Newbury
(Wessacucon)

Merrimac

Rowley

Ipswich
(Agawam)

Ipswich River

Anasquam

CAPE ANN

Gloucester

Naumkeag River

Salem
(Naumkeag)

Marblehead

Lynn
(Saugus)

Concord

Medford

Charlestown
Newtown
(Cambridge)

Winnisimmet

MASSACHUSETTS BAY

Sudbury

Watertown

Mystic River

BOSTON
(Shawmut)

Roxbury

Dorchester

River

Dedham

Braintree

Nantasket
(Natascot)

Cohasset

Hingham
(Barecove)

Scituate

Neponset River

Mt.Wollaston
Merry Mount

Fore River

Weymouth
(Wessagusset)

Charles

Boundary line
agreed upon by
Massachusetts
and Plymouth
1640

Inset: BOSTON HARBOR

Mystic River

Winnisimmet

Charlestown

Noddles Is.

Newtown
(Cambridge)

Charles River

Boston
(Shawmut)

BOSTON HARBOR

Muddy River

MILES
½   0   1

MILES
5   0   10

Drawn under the supervision of ROBERT E. MOODY

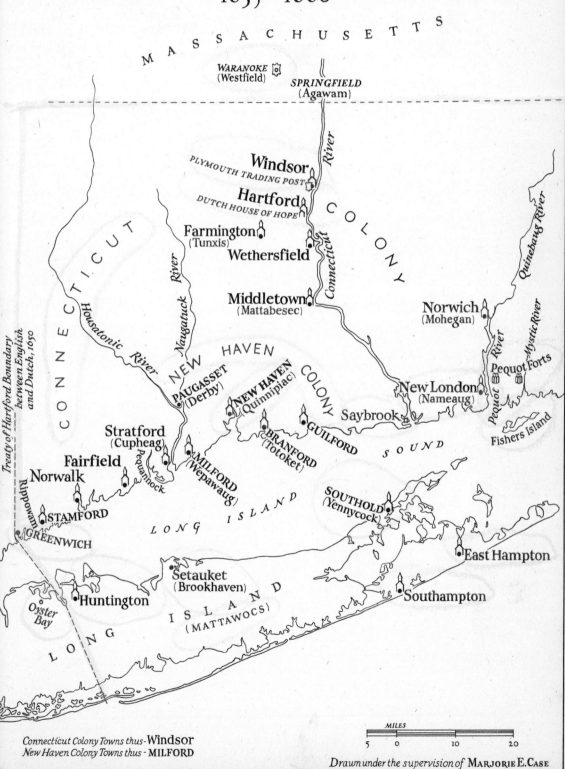

CONNECTICUT AND NEW HAVEN COLONIES
1635 – 1660

MASSACHUSETTS

WARANOKE (Westfield)

SPRINGFIELD (Agawam)

CONNECTICUT River

Windsor

PLYMOUTH TRADING POST

Hartford

DUTCH HOUSE OF HOPE

Farmington (Tunxis)

Wethersfield

CONNECTICUT COLONY

Middletown (Mattabesec)

Norwich (Mohegan)

Quinebaug River

Mystic River

Pequot River

Pequot Forts

New London (Nameaug)

Fishers Island

CONNECTICUT

Housatonic River

Naugatuck River

NEW HAVEN COLONY

Treaty of Hartford Boundary between English and Dutch, 1650

PAUGASSET (Derby)

NEW HAVEN (Quinnipiac)

BRANFORD (Totoket)

GUILFORD

Saybrook

SOUND

Stratford (Cupheag)

MILFORD (Wepawaug)

Pequannock

Fairfield

Norwalk

Rippowam

SOUTHOLD (Yennycock)

LONG ISLAND

STAMFORD

GREENWICH

East Hampton

Setauket (Brookhaven)

Southampton

Oyster Bay

Huntington

LONG ISLAND (MATTAWOCS)

Connecticut Colony Towns thus - Windsor
New Haven Colony Towns thus - MILFORD

MILES
5   0   10   20

Drawn under the supervision of MARJORIE E. CASE

PLATE 17

Connecticut and
New Haven Colonies

1635–1660

PLATE 18

Rhode Island
and
Providence
Plantations

1636–1665

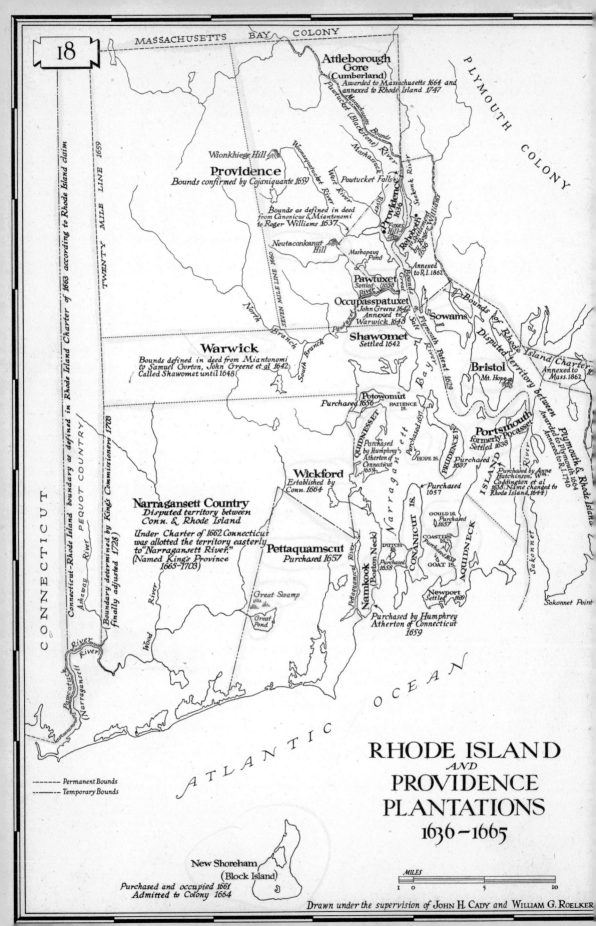

18

MASSACHUSETTS BAY COLONY

PLYMOUTH COLONY

Attleborough Gore (Cumberland)
Awarded to Massachusetts 1664 and
annexed to Rhode Island 1747

Wionkhiege Hill

Providence
Bounds confirmed by Cojaniquante 1659

Pawtucket (Blackstone) River

Pawtucket Falls

Bounds as defined in deed
from Canonicus & Miantonomi
to Roger Williams 1637

Neutaconkanut Hill

Mashapaug Pond

Providence 1636

Rehoboth settled by Roger Williams 1636

Foxes Hill

Annexed to R.I. 1862

Pawtuxet
Settled 1638

Sowams

Occupasspatuxet
John Greene 1642
Annexed to Warwick 1648

Shawomet
Settled 1642

Bounds of Rhode Island Charter

Disputed territory between

Plymouth Patent 1629

Bristol
Mt. Hope
Annexed to Mass. 1862

Warwick
Bounds defined in deed from Miantonomi
to Samuel Gorton, John Greene et al 1642
Called Shawomet until 1648

Potowomut
Purchased 1656

PATIENCE IS.

Purchased 1657

Purchased by Humphrey
Atherton of Connecticut 1659

Quidnesset

HOPE IS.

Purchased 1657

Portsmouth
formerly Pocasset
Settled 1638

Purchased 1637

Purchased by Anne
Hutchinson, Wm.
Coddington et al
1638. Name changed to
Rhode Island, 1644)

Plymouth & Rhode Island
Awarded to Plymouth 1664
Annexed to R.I. 1746

Wickford
Established by Conn. 1664

GOULD IS.
Purchased 1657

Narragansett Country
Disputed territory between
Conn. & Rhode Island

Under Charter of 1662 Connecticut
was allotted the territory easterly
to "Narragansett River."
(Named King's Province
1665–1703)

Pettaquamscut
Purchased 1657

COASTERS IS.
Purchased 1659

GOAT IS.

Newport
Settled 1639

Sokonnet Point

Namkook
(Boston Neck)

DUTCH
Purchased 1658

Purchased by Humphrey
Atherton of Connecticut
1659

Great Swamp

Great Pond

Wood River

Narragansett Bay

Narragansett River

CONANICUT IS.

AQUIDNECK ISLAND

Sakonnet River

CONNECTICUT

Connecticut-Rhode Island boundary as defined in Rhode Island Charter of 1663 according to Rhode Island claim

Ashaway River

PEQUOT COUNTRY

Boundary determined by King's Commissioners 1703 finally adjusted 1728)

Pawcatuck River

Narragansett River

TWENTY MILE LINE 1659

SEVEN MILE LINE 1660

North Branch

South Branch

Pawtuxet River

Salt River

Pettaquamscut River

A T L A N T I C   O C E A N

RHODE ISLAND
AND
PROVIDENCE
PLANTATIONS
1636–1665

- - - - - Permanent Bounds
———— Temporary Bounds

New Shoreham
(Block Island)
Purchased and occupied 1661
Admitted to Colony 1664

MILES
1   0   5   10

Drawn under the supervision of JOHN H. CADY *and* WILLIAM G. ROELKER

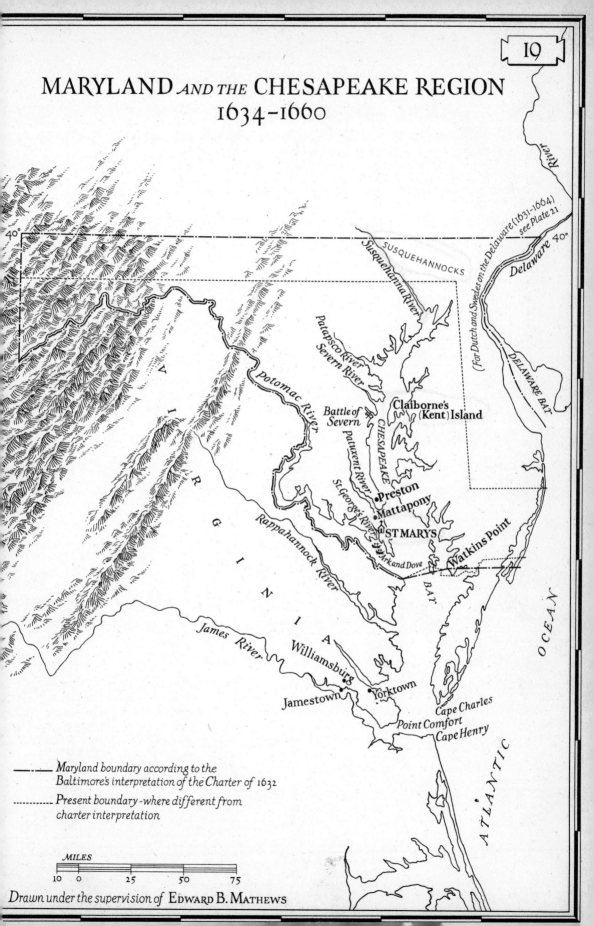

MARYLAND AND THE CHESAPEAKE REGION
1634-1660

SUSQUEHANNOCKS

Susquehanna River

(For Dutch and Swedes on the Delaware (1631-1664) see Plate 21

Delaware River

40°

DELAWARE BAY

Patapsco River
Severn River

Potomac River

V
I
R
G
I
N
I
A

Battle of Severn

Claiborne's (Kent) Island

CHESAPEAKE

Patuxent River

St George's River

Preston
Mattapony

ST MARYS

Ark and Dove

Watkins Point

Rappahannock River

BAY

James River

Williamsburg

Yorktown

Jamestown

Cape Charles

Point Comfort
Cape Henry

OCEAN

ATLANTIC

⎯ ⎯ Maryland boundary according to the
Baltimore's interpretation of the Charter of 1632

· · · · · Present boundary - where different from
charter interpretation

MILES

10   0   25   50   75

Drawn under the supervision of EDWARD B. MATHEWS

PLATE 19

Maryland and the
Chesapeake Region

1634–1660

PLATE 20

New Netherland

1614–1664

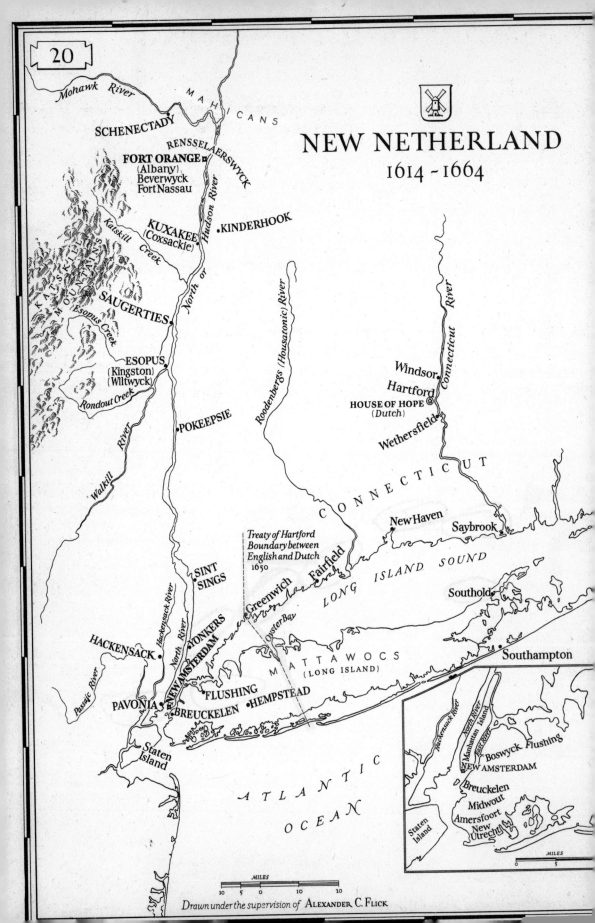

NEW NETHERLAND
1614 - 1664

Mohawk River

MAHICANS

SCHENECTADY

RENSSELAERSWYCK

FORT ORANGE ▪
(Albany)
Beverwyck
Fort Nassau

KUXAKEE
(Coxsackie)

Katskill Creek

• KINDERHOOK

K A T S K I L L   M O U N T A I N S

Esopus Creek

SAUGERTIES •

North or Hudson River

Windsor •

Hartford •

Connecticut River

HOUSE OF HOPE
(Dutch)

ESOPUS
(Kingston)
(Wiltwyck)

Rondout Creek

Roodenbergs (Housatonic) River

Wethersfield •

• **POKEEPSIE**

Walkill River

C O N N E C T I C U T

New Haven •

Saybrook •

*Treaty of Hartford
Boundary between
English and Dutch
1650*

Fairfield

L O N G   I S L A N D   S O U N D

Southold •

**SINT
SINGS** •

Greenwich •

Oyster Bay

Hackensack River

HACKENSACK •

North River

YONKERS
NEW AMSTERDAM

M A T T A W O C S
(LONG ISLAND)

Southampton •

Passaic River

PAVONIA •

BREUCKELEN •

• **FLUSHING**

• **HEMPSTEAD**

*Staten
Island*

A T L A N T I C

O C E A N

Hackensack River

North River

Manhattan Island

East River

Boswyck Flushing

NEW AMSTERDAM

Breuckelen

Midwout

Amersfoort
New
Utrecht

Staten
Island

MILES
0   5

MILES
10 5 0   10   20

Drawn under the supervision of ALEXANDER C. FLICK

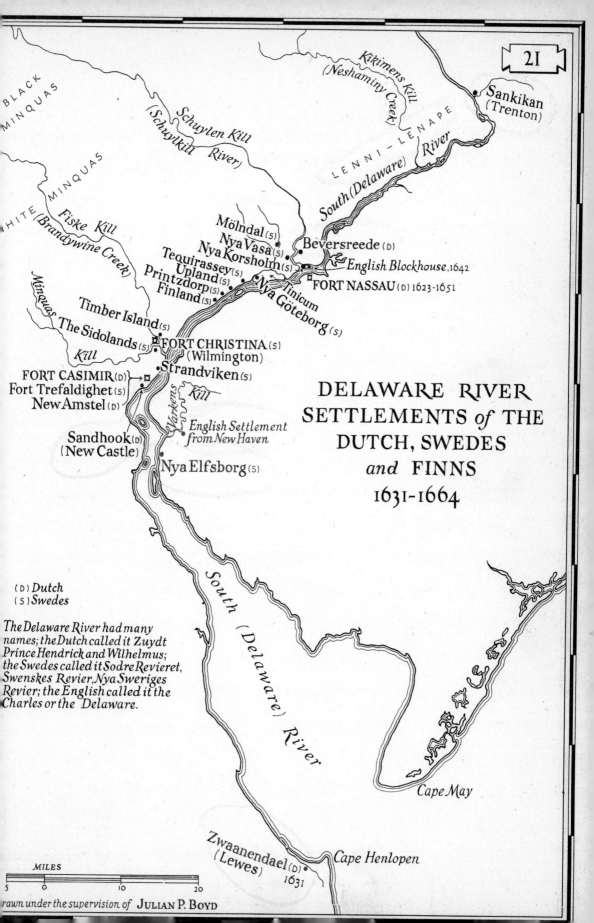

BLACK
MINQUAS

Kikimens Kill
(Neshaminy Creek)

Schuylen Kill

(Schuylkill River)

MINQUAS

Sankikan
(Trenton)

WHITE MINQUAS

LENNI — LENAPE

Fiske Kill

(Brandywine Creek)

South (Delaware) River

Mölndal (s)
Nya Vasa (s)
Nya Korsholm (s)
Tequirassey (s)
Upland (s)
Printzdorp (s)
Finland (s)

Beversreede (D)

English Blockhouse, 1642

Tinicum

Nya Göteborg (s)

FORT NASSAU (D) 1623-1651

Minquas

Timber Island (s)

The Sidolands (s)

Kill

FORT CHRISTINA (s)
(Wilmington)

FORT CASIMIR (D)
Fort Trefaldighet (s)
New Amstel (D)

Strandviken (s)

Varkens Kill

English Settlement
from New Haven

Sandhook (D)
(New Castle)

Nya Elfsborg (s)

DELAWARE RIVER
SETTLEMENTS *of* THE
DUTCH, SWEDES
and FINNS
1631-1664

(D) *Dutch*
(S) *Swedes*

The Delaware River had many
names; the Dutch called it Zuydt
Prince Hendrick and Wilhelmus;
the Swedes called it Sodre Revieret,
Swenskes Revier, Nya Sweriges
Revier; the English called it the
Charles or the Delaware.

South (Delaware) River

Cape May

MILES

5   0   10   20

Zwaanendael (D)
(Lewes)
1631

Cape Henlopen

rawn under the supervision of JULIAN P. BOYD

PLATE 21

Delaware River Settlements
of the
Dutch, Swedes and Finns

1631–1664

PLATE 22

Duke of York's
Proprietary

1664

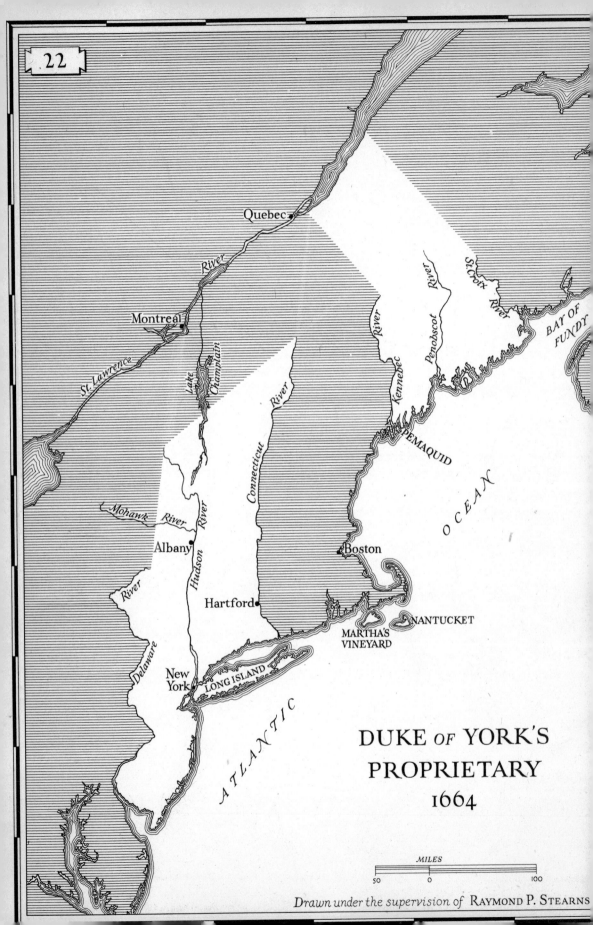

Quebec

Montreal

St. Lawrence River

River

Lake Champlain

Mohawk River

Albany

Hudson River

Connecticut River

Kennebec River

Penobscot River

St. Croix River

BAY OF FUNDY

PEMAQUID

OCEAN

River

Delaware River

New York

LONG ISLAND

Hartford

Boston

MARTHA'S VINEYARD

NANTUCKET

ATLANTIC

DUKE OF YORK'S
PROPRIETARY
1664

MILES

50   0   100

Drawn under the supervision of RAYMOND P. STEARNS

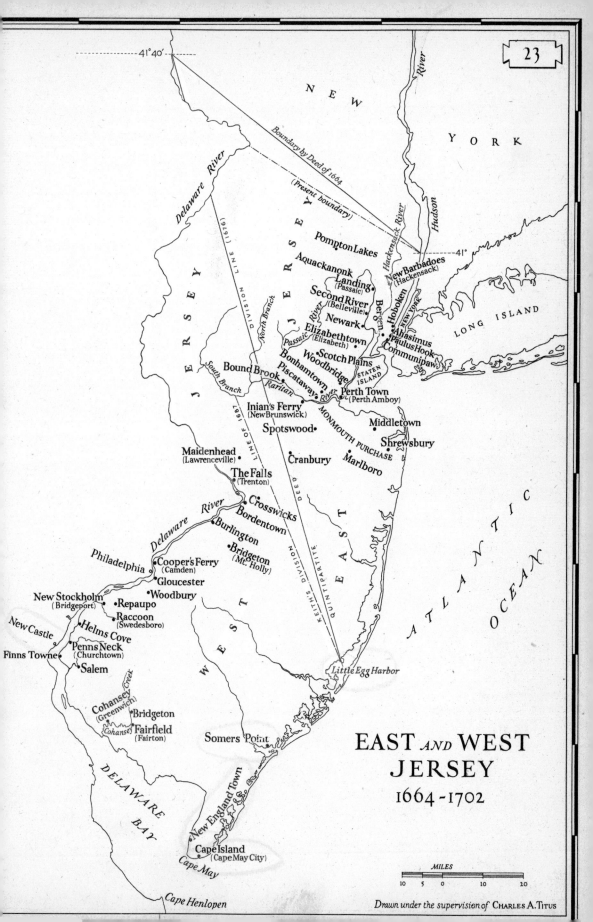

---41°40'---

NEW

YORK

Boundary by Deed of 1664

River

Hudson

(Present boundary)

---41°---

LONG ISLAND

Pompton Lakes

Aquackanonk

Hackensack River

New Barbadoes
(Hackensack)

Delaware River

Landing
(Passaic)

Second River
(Belleville)

River

Bergen

Hoboken

New York

Newark

Ahasimus
Paulus Hook
Communipaw

DIVISION LINE (1676)

Elizabethtown
(Elizabeth)

Passaic

Scotch Plains

River

North Branch

J E R S E Y

Bonhamtown

Woodbridge

Piscataway

STATEN
ISLAND

Bound Brook

South Branch

Raritan

River

Perth Town
(Perth Amboy)

LINE OF 1687

Inian's Ferry
(New Brunswick)

MONMOUTH PURCHASE

Middletown

Spotswood

Shrewsbury

Maidenhead
(Lawrenceville)

Cranbury

Marlboro

The Falls
(Trenton)

DEED

Crosswicks

Bordentown

Delaware River

Burlington

Bridgeton
(Mt. Holly)

Philadelphia

Cooper's Ferry
(Camden)

E A S T

A T L A N T I C

O C E A N

Gloucester

KEITH'S DIVISION

QUINTIPARTITE

New Stockholm
(Bridgeport)

Woodbury

Repaupo

New Castle

Raccoon
(Swedesboro)

W E S T

Helms Cove

Finns Towne

Penns Neck
(Churchtown)

Salem

Little Egg Harbor

Creek

Cohansey
(Greenwich)

Bridgeton

(Cohansey)

Fairfield
(Fairton)

Somers Point

D E L A W A R E

New England Town

B A Y

EAST AND WEST JERSEY
1664-1702

Cape Island
(Cape May City)

Cape May

MILES

10 5 0   10   20

Cape Henlopen

Drawn under the supervision of CHARLES A. TITUS

PLATE 23

East and West
Jersey

1664–1702

PLATE 24

Carolinas
and Virginia

1663–1729

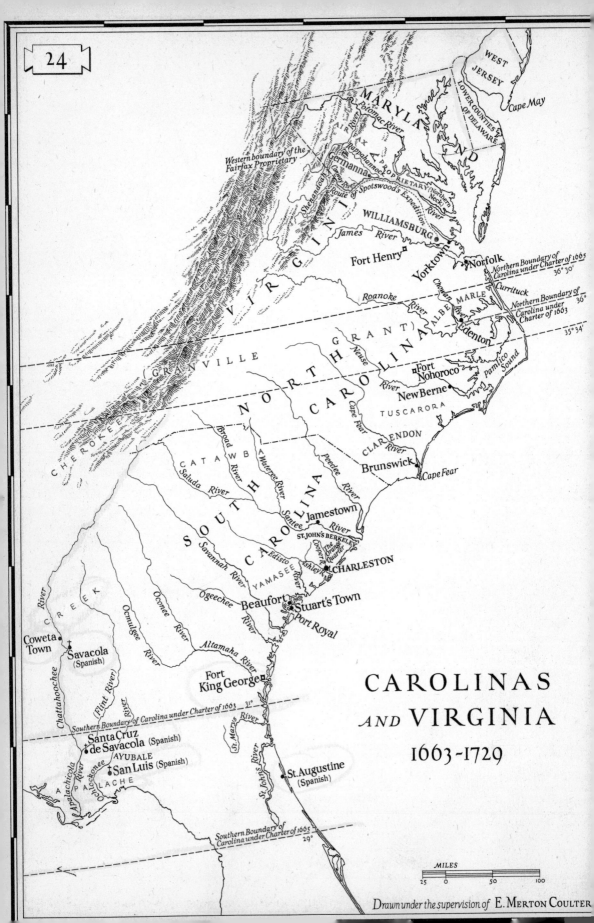

WEST
JERSEY

Cape May

LOWER COUNTIES OF DELAWARE

MARYLA ND

Potomac River

Western boundary of the
Fairfax Proprietary

FAIRFAX PROPRIETARY (Northern Neck)

Rappahannock River

Germanna

Conway River

Route of Spotswood's Expedition

Shenandoah River

WILLIAMSBURG

James River

Fort Henry

Yorktown

Norfolk

Northern Boundary of
Carolina under Charter of 1665   36° 30'

Roanoke

Roanoke River

Currituck

ALBE MARLE

Northern Boundary of
Carolina under
Charter of 1663   36°

35° 34'

Edenton

V I R G I N I A

GRANVILLE

G R A N T)

CHEROKEE

N O R T H

Neuse River

Fort
Nohoroco

C A R O L I N A

New Berne

Pamlico Sound

TUSCARORA

Cape Fear River

CLAR ENDON

Brunswick

Cape Fear

C A T A W B A

Broad River

A Wateree River

Peedee River

Saluda River

S O U T H

C A R O L I N A

Santee River

Jamestown

ST. JOHN'S BERKELEY

The Orange Quarter

CHARLESTON

Savannah River

Edisto River

Cooper River

Ashley River

YAMASEE

Ogeechee River

Beaufort

Stuart's Town

Port Royal

C R E E K

River

Oconee River

Ocmulgee River

Altamaha River

Coweta
Town

Savacola
(Spanish)

Chattahoochee River

(Flint River)

Fort
King George

St. Marys River

Southern Boundary of Carolina under Charter of 1663   31°

Santa Cruz
de Savacola   (Spanish)

AYUBALE

San Luis   (Spanish)

Apalachicola River

Ochlockonee River

A P A L A C H E

St. Johns River

St. Augustine
(Spanish)

CAROLINAS
AND VIRGINIA
1663-1729

Southern Boundary of
Carolina under Charter of 1665   29°

MILES
25   0   50   100

Drawn under the supervision of E. Merton Coulter

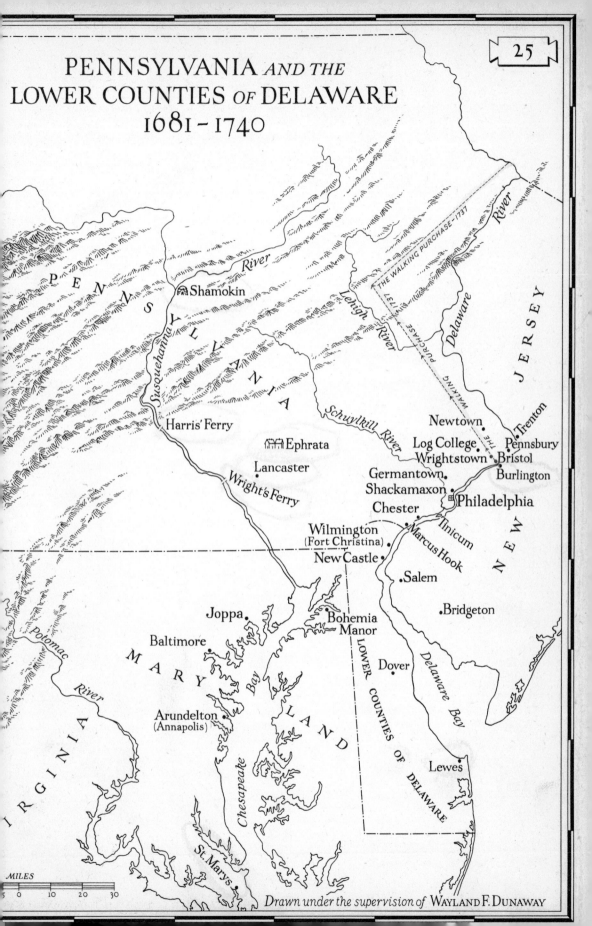

PENNSYLVANIA *AND THE*
LOWER COUNTIES *OF* DELAWARE
1681 - 1740

25

PENNSYLVANIA

Shamokin

River

Susquehanna

Lehigh River

Harris' Ferry

Ephrata

Lancaster

Wright's Ferry

Schuylkill River

THE WALKING PURCHASE - 1737

THE WALKING PURCHASE 1737

Delaware River

NEW JERSEY

Newtown

Trenton

Log College

Pennsbury

Wrightstown

Bristol

Germantown

Burlington

Shackamaxon

Chester

Philadelphia

Tinicum

Wilmington
(Fort Christina)

Marcus Hook

New Castle

NEW

Salem

Bridgeton

Joppa

Bohemia
Manor

Baltimore

MARYLAND

Dover

Delaware Bay

Potomac

River

VIRGINIA

Arundelton
(Annapolis)

Chesapeake Bay

LOWER COUNTIES OF DELAWARE

Lewes

St. Marys

MILES

5 0   10   20   30

Drawn under the supervision of WAYLAND F. DUNAWAY

PLATE 25

Pennsylvania and the Lower Counties of Delaware

1681–1740

PLATE 26

New England

1675

NEW ENGLAND
1675

26

St. Anne Fort (French)

Lake Champlain

Lake St. Sacrement

ABENAKI

(Claimed by both New Hampshire and New York)

MAINE (Joined to Massachusetts)

Androscoggin River

Kennebec River

Damariscotta

St. GEORGE

Pejepscot Falls

PEMAQUID

Casco

Casco Bay

SAGADAHOC

Saco

Saco River

Winter Harbor

Scaticook

NEW HAMPSHIRE

Merrimac River

Wells

Dover

Kittery

York

Portsmouth

Albany

Exeter

Hampton

Salisbury

Newburyport

Haverhill

Bradford

Rowley

Ipswich

Windham

Cape Ann

Hudson River

NEW YORK

Northfield

Chelmsford

Lowell

Andover

Woburn

Gloucester

Deerfield

Groton

Mt. Wachusett

Concord

Cambridge

Charlestown

Salem

Lynn

MASSACHUSETTS

Lancaster

Sudbury

Medford

Hadley

Northampton

Marlborough

Watertown

Roxbury

Boston

Hull

Cohasset

Scituate

Westfield

Springfield

Brookfield

Dedham

Dorchester

Braintree

Weymouth

Hingham

Duxbury

Cape Cod

CONNECTICUT

Connecticut River

Pawtucket Falls

Bridgewater

Taunton

Plymouth

PLYMOUTH

Windsor

Providence

Seekonk River

Middleboro

Assowomset Pond

Sandwich

Eastham

Hartford

Warwick

Swansea

Mount Hope

Yarmouth

Barnstable

Farmington

Quinebaug

RHODE ISLAND

Portsmouth

Wethersfield

Norwich

Dartmouth

Middletown (Mattabesec)

New London

NARRA

KINGS PROVINCE

Newport

Conanicut Island

New Haven

Derby (Paugasset)

Guilford

Saybrook

Stonington

Stratford

Branford

Fishers Island

Block Island

Edgartown

Madeket

Nantucket

Greenwich

Norwalk

Fairfield

LONG ISLAND SOUND

Gardiners Island

Martha's Vineyard

New York

Oyster Bay

Huntington

Setauket

Southold

Easthampton

LONG ISLAND

Southampton

ATLANTIC OCEAN

NOTE.— *Present-day Vermont was, in 1675, claimed by both New York and New Hampshire. All colonial boundaries were in dispute and must be looked upon as approximations only.*

MILES
10   0   25   50

Drawn under the supervision of RAYMOND P. STEARNS

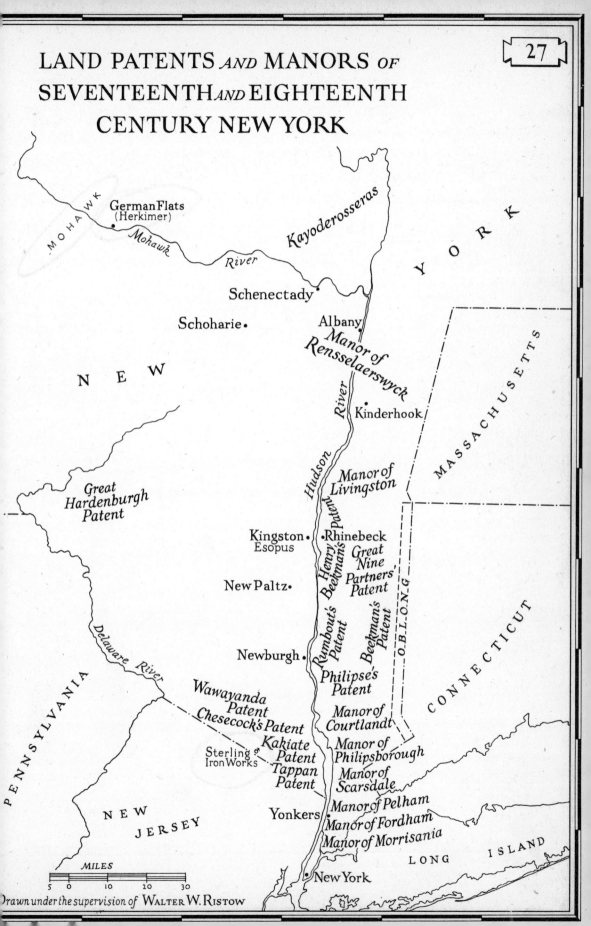

LAND PATENTS AND MANORS OF SEVENTEENTH AND EIGHTEENTH CENTURY NEW YORK

MOHAWK

German Flats
(Herkimer)

Mohawk River

Kayoderosseras

Y O R K

Schenectady

Schoharie

Albany

Manor of
Rensselaerswyck

N E W

Kinderhook

MASSACHUSETTS

Hudson River

Manor of
Livingston

Great
Hardenburgh
Patent

Kingston
Esopus

Rhinebeck

Henry Beekman's Patent

Great
Nine
Partners'
Patent

New Paltz

OBLONG

Delaware River

Rumbout's Patent

Newburgh

Beekman's Patent

CONNECTICUT

Philipse's
Patent

Wawayanda
Patent

Chesecock's Patent

Manor of
Courtlandt

PENNSYLVANIA

Kakiate
Patent

Sterling
Iron Works

Manor of
Philipsborough

Tappan
Patent

Manor of
Scarsdale

N E W

Yonkers

Manor of Pelham

J E R S E Y

Manor of Fordham

Manor of Morrisania

LONG   ISLAND

MILES

5 0 10   20   30

New York

Drawn under the supervision of WALTER W. RISTOW

PLATE 27

Land Patents and Manors of Seventeenth and Eighteenth Century New York

PLATE 28
New France
to 1673

NEW FRANCE
TO 1673

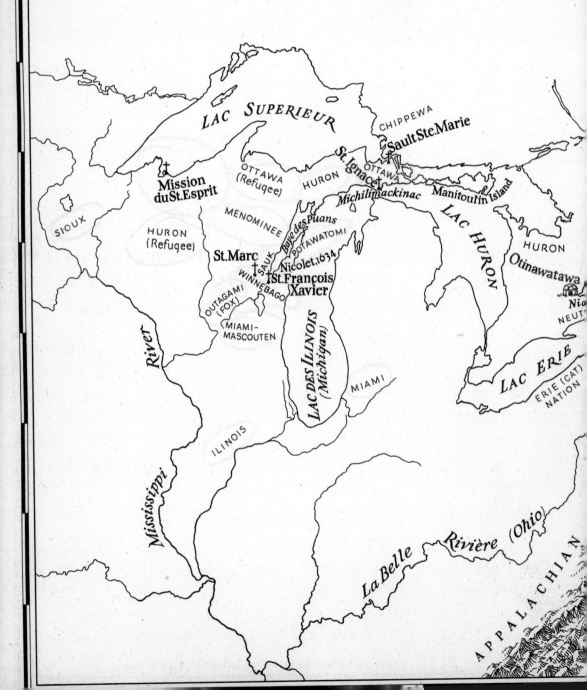

LAC SUPERIEUR

CHIPPEWA

Sault Ste. Marie

OTTAWA
(Refugee)

HURON

St. Ignace

OTTAWA

Michilimackinac

Manitoulin Island

Mission
du St. Esprit

MENOMINEE

baye des Puans

POTAWATOMI

LAC HURON

HURON

SIOUX

HURON
(Refugee)

St. Marc

SAUK

Nicolet, 1634

Otinawatawa

St. François
Xavier

WINNEBAGO

Nia

OUTAGAMI
(FOX)

NEUT

MIAMI-
MASCOUTEN

LAC DES ILINOIS
(Michigan)

MIAMI

LAC ERIE

ERIE (CAT)
NATION

Mississippi River

ILINOIS

La Belle Rivière (Ohio)

APPALACHIAN

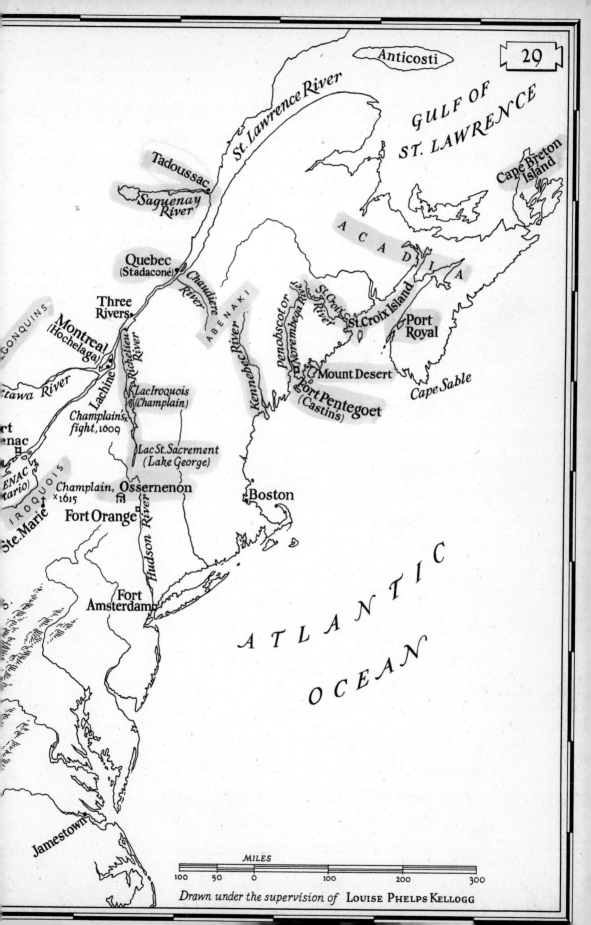

Anticosti

St. Lawrence River

GULF OF
ST. LAWRENCE

Cape Breton
Island

Tadoussac

*Saguenay
River*

A C A D I A

Quebec
(Stadaconé)

*Chaudiere
River*

Three
Rivers

A B E N A K I

St.Croix
River

St.Croix Island

Port
Royal

ALGONQUINS

Montreal
[Hochelaga]

Richelieu River

Lachine

Penobscot or
Norembega River

Mount Desert

Ottawa River

Kennebec River

Lac Iroquois
(Champlain)

*Champlain's
fight, 1609*

Fort Pentegoet
(Castins)

Cape Sable

*Lac St. Sacrement
(Lake George)*

rt
ENAC

Champlain, Ossernenon
×1615

Boston

ENAC
tario)

Fort Orange

IROQUOIS

Ste.Marie

Hudson River

Fort
Amsterdam

A T L A N T I C

O C E A N

Jamestown

MILES

100   50   0   100   200   300

Drawn under the supervision of LOUISE PHELPS KELLOGG

PLATE 29

New France

to 1673

PLATE 30

Michilimackinac

1668–1706

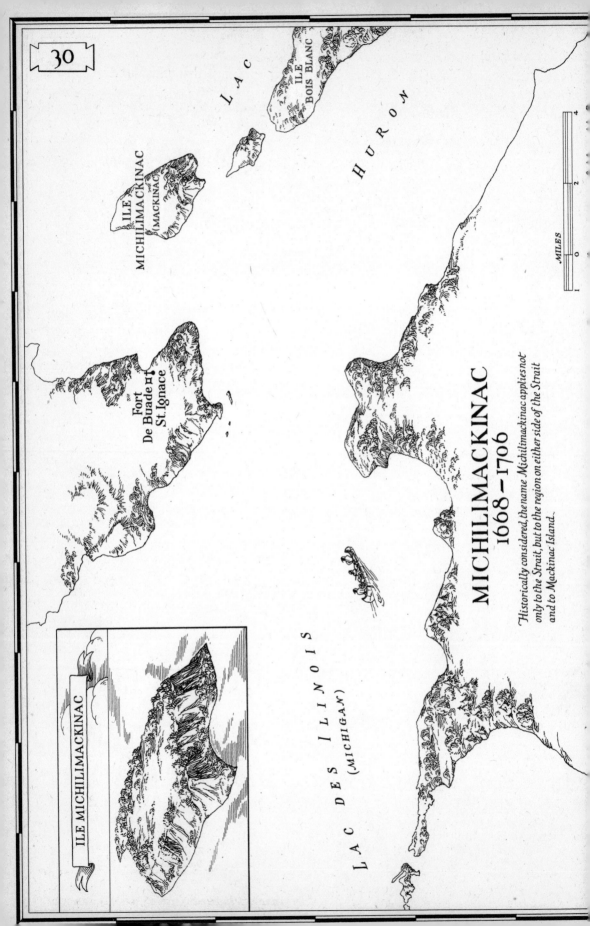

ILE BOIS BLANC

LAC HURON

ILE MICHILIMACKINAC (MACKINAC)

Fort De Buade at St. Ignace

ILE MICHILIMACKINAC

LAC DES ILINOIS (MICHIGAN)

MICHILIMACKINAC
1668–1706

Historically considered, the name Michilimackinac applies not
only to the Strait, but to the region on either side of the Strait
and to Mackinac Island.

MILES

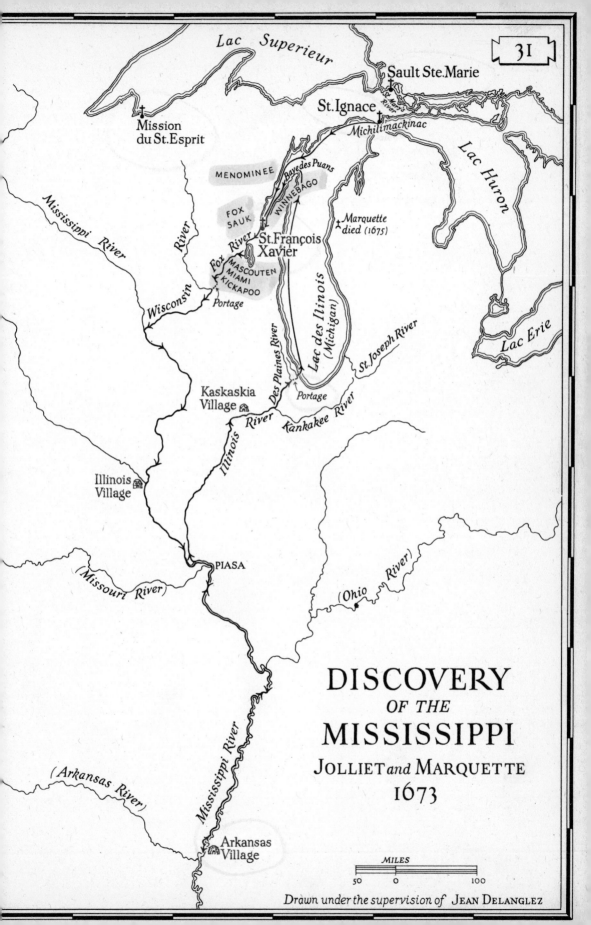

Lac Superieur

Sault Ste. Marie

St. Ignace

Mission du St. Esprit

Michilimackinac

Lac Huron

MENOMINEE

Bayedes Puans

WINNEBAGO

Marquette died (1675)

FOX SAUK

St. François Xavier

Fox River

MASCOUTEN MIAMI KICKAPOO

River

Mississippi River

Wisconsin

Portage

Des Plaines River

Lac des Ilinois (Michigan)

St. Joseph River

Lac Erie

Kaskaskia Village

Portage

Illinois River

Kankakee River

Illinois Village

PIASA

(Missouri River)

(Ohio River)

(Arkansas River)

Mississippi River

Arkansas Village

DISCOVERY
OF THE
MISSISSIPPI
JOLLIET and MARQUETTE
1673

MILES

50   0   100

Drawn under the supervision of JEAN DELANGLEZ

PLATE 31

Discovery of the
Mississippi –
Jolliet and Marquette

1673

PLATE 32

Chicago and Miamis
Portages

1673–1680

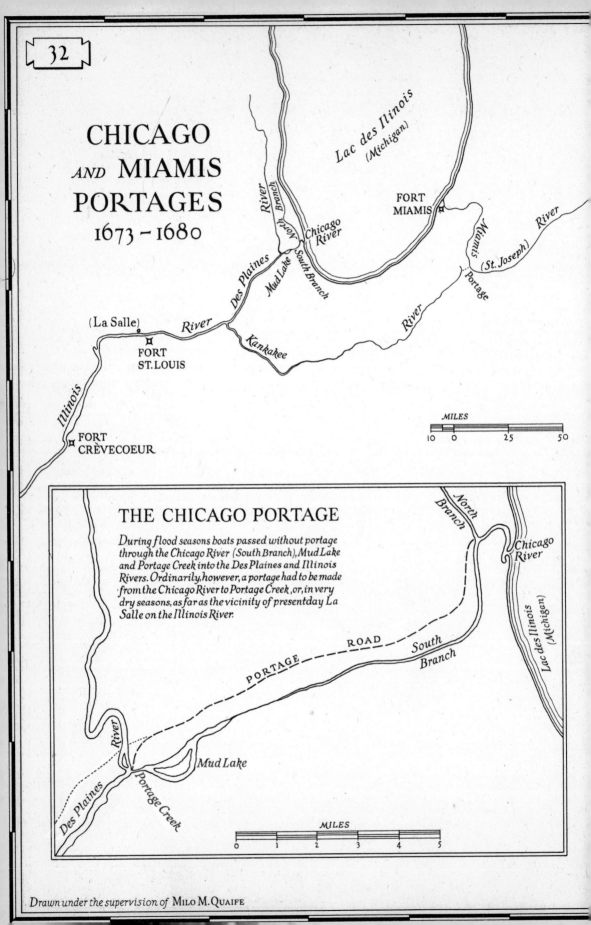

CHICAGO AND MIAMIS PORTAGES
1673 – 1680

Lac des Ilinois (Michigan)

River

North Branch

Chicago River

FORT MIAMIS

Miamis (St. Joseph) River

Des Plaines

Mud Lake

South Branch

Portage

River

(La Salle)

River

FORT ST. LOUIS

Kankakee

River

Ilinois

FORT CRÈVECOEUR

MILES
10   0   25   50

THE CHICAGO PORTAGE

During flood seasons boats passed without portage through the Chicago River (South Branch), Mud Lake and Portage Creek into the Des Plaines and Illinois Rivers. Ordinarily, however, a portage had to be made from the Chicago River to Portage Creek, or, in very dry seasons, as far as the vicinity of present day La Salle on the Illinois River.

North Branch

Chicago River

Lac des Ilinois (Michigan)

PORTAGE   ROAD

South Branch

River

Des Plaines

Portage Creek

Mud Lake

MILES
0   1   2   3   4   5

Drawn under the supervision of MILO M. QUAIFE

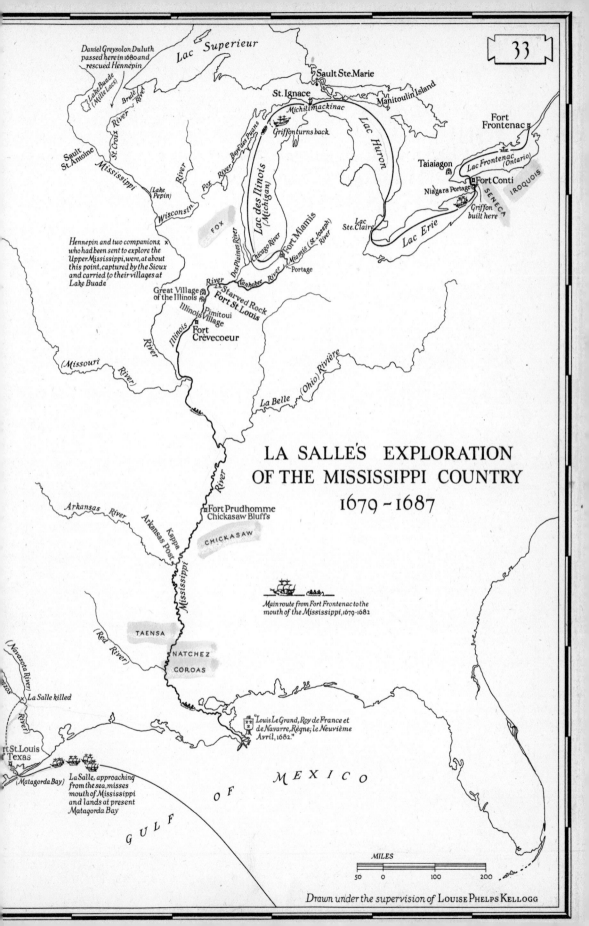

Daniel Greysolon Duluth passed here in 1680 and rescued Hennepin

Lac Superieur

Sault Ste. Marie

St. Ignace

Manitoulin Island

Lake Buade (Mille Lacs)

Brule River

Sault St. Antoine

St. Croix River

Mississippi

Wisconsin River

(Lake Pepin)

Fox River

Bay des Puans

Michillimackinac

Griffon turns back

Lac Huron

Fort Frontenac

Taiaiagon

Lac Frontenac (Ontario)

Fort Conti

Niagara Portage

Griffon built here

SENECA

IROQUOIS

FOX

Fox River

Lac des Illinois (Michigan)

Chicago River

Fort Miamis

Miamis (St. Joseph) River

Portage

Lac Ste. Claire

Lac Erie

Hennepin and two companions, who had been sent to explore the Upper Mississippi, were, at about this point, captured by the Sioux and carried to their villages at Lake Buade

Des Plaines River

Kankakee River

Great Village of the Illinois

Starved Rock

Fort St. Louis

Pimitoui

Illinois Village

Fort Crevecoeur

Illinois River

(Missouri River)

River

La Belle (Ohio) Rivière

LA SALLE'S EXPLORATION
OF THE MISSISSIPPI COUNTRY
1679 ~ 1687

Arkansas River

Arkansas Post

Kappa

Fort Prudhomme
Chickasaw Bluffs

CHICKASAW

Mississippi

Main route from Fort Frontenac to the
mouth of the Mississippi, 1679-1682

(Red River)

TAENSA

NATCHEZ

COROAS

(Navasota River)

La Salle killed

rt St. Louis
of Texas

(Matagorda Bay)

La Salle, approaching
from the sea, misses
mouth of Mississippi
and lands at present
Matagorda Bay

"Louis Le Grand, Roy de France et
de Navarre, Règne; le Neuvième
Avril, 1682."

GULF OF MEXICO

MILES

50   0   100   200

Drawn under the supervision of LOUISE PHELPS KELLOGG

PLATE 33

LaSalle's Exploration
of the Mississippi Country

1679–1687

PLATE 34

Spanish
Florida

1670–1763

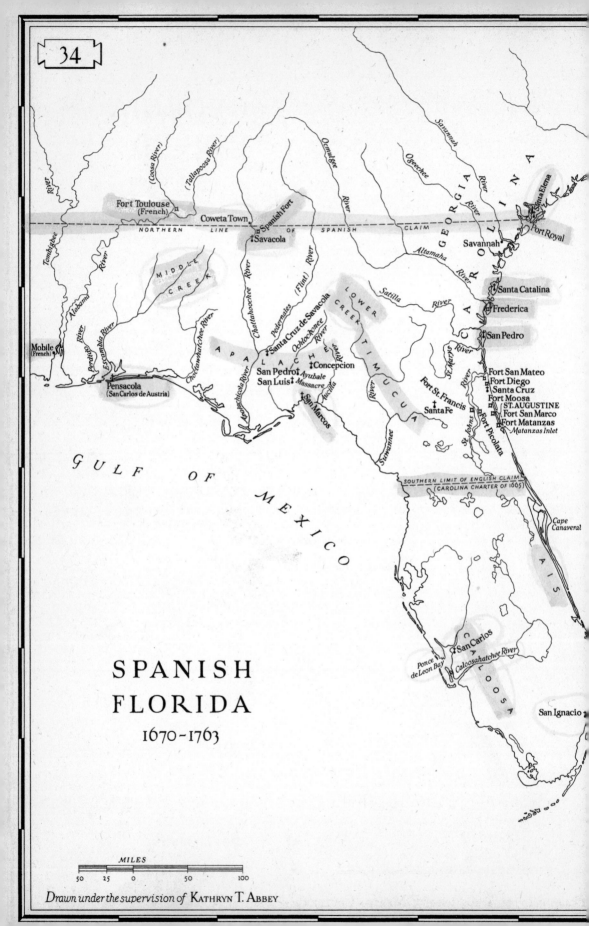

Fort Toulouse
(French)

Coweta Town
NORTHERN   LINE   OF   SPANISH   CLAIM

Spanish Fort
Savacola

MIDDLE

CREEK

APALACHE

Santa Cruz de Savacola
San Pedro
San Luis
Concepcion
Ayubale
Massacre
Auilla
San Marcos

LOWER

CREEK

TIMUCUA

Santa Fe

Fort St. Francis

Mobile
(French)

Pensacola
(San Carlos de Austria)

Tombeebee River

Alabama River

Perdigo River

Escambia River

Choctawhatchee River

Apalachicola River

Chattahoochee River

Pedernales River

Oketockonee River

(Flint) River

Suwannee River

Satilla River

St. Marys River

Santa Catalina

Frederica

San Pedro

Fort San Mateo
Fort Diego
Santa Cruz
Fort Moosa
ST. AUGUSTINE
Fort San Marco
Fort Matanzas
Matanzas Inlet

Fort Picolata

St. Johns River

Santa Elena
Port Royal

GEORGIA

CAROLINA

Savannah

Savannah River

Ogeechee River

Oconee River

Ocmulgee River

Coosa River

Tallapoosa River

Altamaha River

GULF   OF

MEXICO

SOUTHERN LIMIT OF ENGLISH CLAIM
(CAROLINA CHARTER OF 1665)

Cape
Canaveral

AIS

San Carlos

Ponce
de Leon Bay

Caloosahatchee River

CALOOSA

San Ignacio

SPANISH
FLORIDA
1670–1763

MILES

50   25   0   50   100

Drawn under the supervision of KATHRYN T. ABBEY

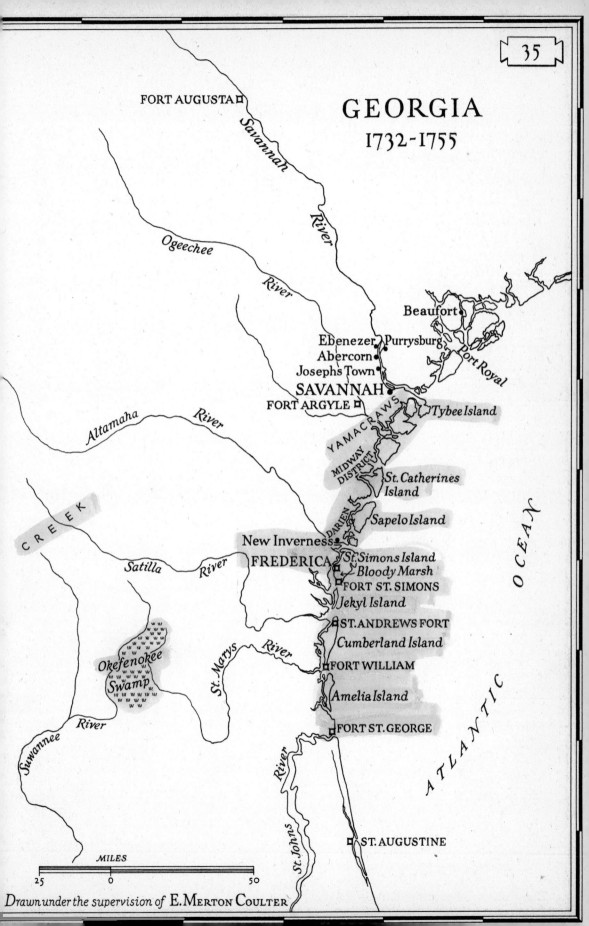

GEORGIA
1732-1755

FORT AUGUSTA ▫

Savannah

River

Ogeechee

River

Beaufort

Ebenezer • Purrysburg
Abercorn •
Josephs Town •
SAVANNAH •
FORT ARGYLE ▫

Altamaha *River*

YAMACRAWS

Tybee Island

MIDWAY DISTRICT

St. Catherines Island

CREEK

Sapelo Island

DARIEN

New Inverness •
FREDERICA ▫ St. Simons Island
Bloody Marsh
▫ FORT ST. SIMONS

Satilla *River*

Jekyl Island

▫ ST. ANDREWS FORT

Cumberland Island

Okefenokee
Swamp

St. Marys *River*

▫ FORT WILLIAM

Amelia Island

O C E A N

▫ FORT ST. GEORGE

Suwannee *River*

A T L A N T I C

St. Johns *River*

Port Royal

▫ ST. AUGUSTINE

MILES
25   0   50

Drawn under the supervision of E. MERTON COULTER

PLATE 35

Georgia

1732–1755

PLATE 36

Trans-Mississippi
French and Spanish

1600–1750

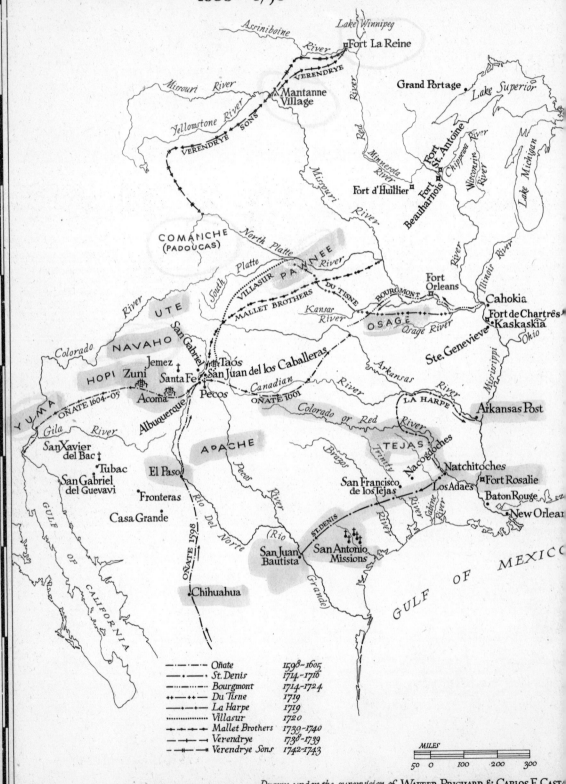

TRANS-MISSISSIPPI - FRENCH & SPANISH
1600 — 1750

36

Assiniboine River

Lake Winnipeg

Fort La Reine

VERENDRYE

Grand Portage

Lake Superior

Missouri River

Mantanne Village

VERENDRYE SONS

Yellowstone River

Red River

Minnesota River

Fort St. Antoine

Chippewa River

Wisconsin River

Fort Beauharnois

Fort d'Huillier

Lake Michigan

Missouri River

COMANCHE (PADOUCAS)

North Platte River

VILLASUR PAWNEE

DU TISNE

BOURGMONT

Fort Orleans

Illinois River

South Platte River

MALLET BROTHERS

Kansas River

OSAGE

Orage River

Cahokia

Fort de Chartres
Kaskaskia

Ohio

Colorado River

UTE

NAVAHO

San Gabriel

Taos

San Juan del los Caballeras

Arkansas River

Ste. Genevieve

Mississippi River

HOPI

Zuni

Jemez

Santa Fe

Acoma

Pecos

Canadian

ONATE 1601

Arkansas River

LA HARPE

Arkansas Post

YUMA

ONATE 1604-05

Albuquerque

Colorado or Red River

Gila River

APACHE

El Paso

Pecos River

TEJAS

Nacogdoches

Natchitoches

San Xavier del Bac

Tubac

San Gabriel del Guevavi

Fronteras

Rio Del Norte

Brazos River

San Francisco de los Tejas

Trinity River

Los Adaes

Fort Rosalie

Baton Rouge

New Orleans

Casa Grande

ONATE 1598

GULF OF CALIFORNIA

(Rio

ST. DENIS

San Juan Bautista

San Antonio Missions

Sabine River

GULF OF MEXICO

Chihuahua

Grande)

—·—·—	Oñate	1598-1605
—··—··—	St. Denis	1714-1716
— — —	Bourgmont	1714-1724
—+—+—	Du Tisne	1719
—◆—◆—	La Harpe	1719
··········	Villasur	1720
— — —	Mallet Brothers	1739-1740
—+—+—	Verendrye	1738-1739
—++—++—	Verendrye Sons	1742-1743

MILES

50 0 100 200 300

Drawn under the supervision of WALTER PRICHARD & CARLOS E. CASTA
The Verendrye routes drawn under the supervision of O. G. LIBBY

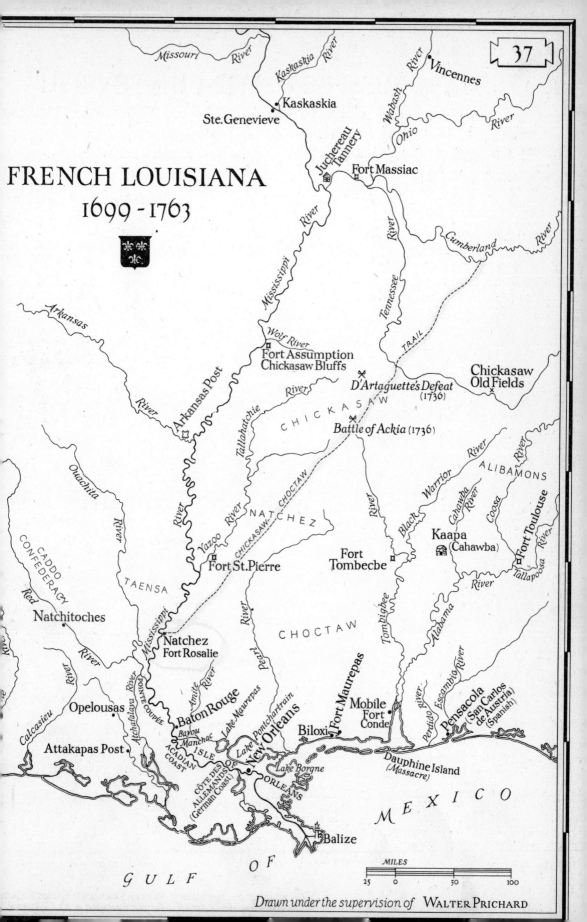

FRENCH LOUISIANA
1699 - 1763

37

Missouri River
Kaskaskia River
• Vincennes
• Kaskaskia
Ste. Genevieve
Ohio
Wabash River
River
Juchereau Tannery
Fort Massiac
Mississippi River
Cumberland River
River
Arkansas
River
Arkansas Post
Wolf River
Fort Assumption
Chickasaw Bluffs
Tennessee River
TRAIL
D'Artaguette's Defeat (1736)
Chickasaw Old Fields
Tallahatchie River
CHICKASAW
River
Battle of Ackia (1736)
ALIBAMONS
Warrior River
Cahawba River
Coosa
Fort Toulouse
CHICKASAW-CHOCTAW
NATCHEZ
Yazoo River
Fort St. Pierre
Fort Tombecbe
Kaapa (Cahawba)
Tallapoosa River
Black River
River
CADDO CONFEDERACY
Ouachita River
TAENSA
CHICKASAW-NATCHEZ
River
CHOCTAW
Tombigbee
River
Natchitoches
Natchez
Fort Rosalie
Pearl River
Alabama River
Red River
Mississippi River
Amite River
Baton Rouge
Perdido River
Pensacola
(San Carlos de Austria)
(Spanish)
Escambia River
Opelousas
Calcasieu River
POINTE COUPÉE
Bayou Manchac
ISLE
Lake Maurepas
Fort Maurepas
Mobile
Fort Condé
Atchafalaya River
Attakapas Post
ACADIAN COAST
CÔTE DES ALLEMANDS (German Coast)
Lake Pontchartrain
New Orleans
Biloxi
Dauphine Island
(Massacre)
OF ORLEANS
Lake Borgne
Balize
GULF OF MEXICO

MILES
25 0   50   100

Drawn under the supervision of WALTER PRICHARD

PLATE 37

French Louisiana

1699–1763

PLATE 38

New England-New York-
New France Frontier

1690–1753

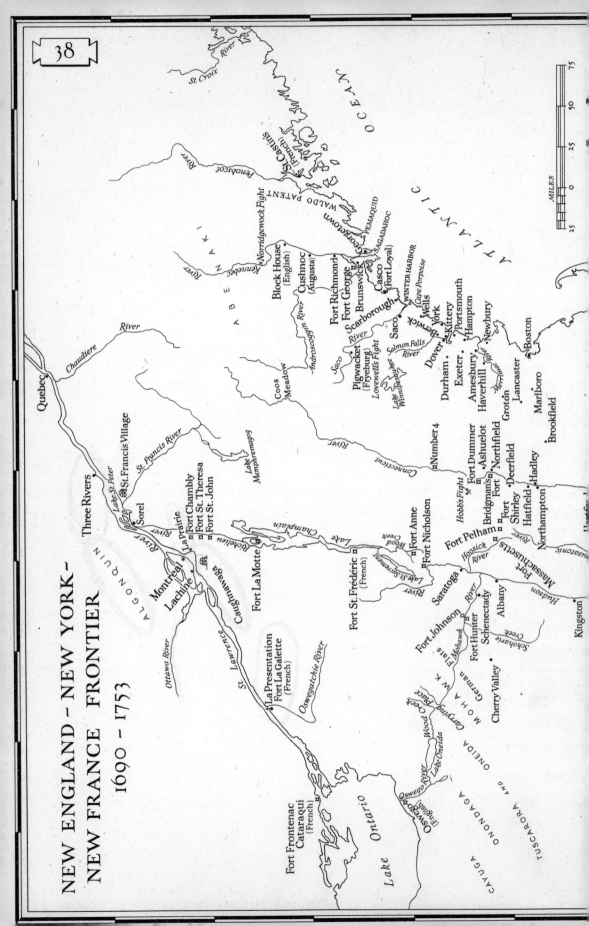

NEW ENGLAND ~ NEW YORK ~ NEW FRANCE FRONTIER
1690 ~ 1753

MILES

25 0 25 50 75

Rivers and Bodies of Water:
St. Croix River
Penobscot River
St. Georges River (Thomaston)
Kennebec River
Androscoggin River
Saco River
Chaudiere River
Connecticut River
St. Lawrence River
Ottawa River
Richelieu River
St. Francis River
Salmon Falls River
Merrimack River
Hudson River
Mohawk River
Schoharie Creek
Wood Creek
Hoosick River
Housatonic River
St. Sacrement River
Oswego River (English)
Oswegatchie River
Lake St. Peter
Lake Memphremagog
Lake Champlain
Lake George (Lake St. Sacrement)
Lake Winnipesaukee
Lake Ontario
Lake Oneida

Regions:
ATLANTIC OCEAN
ABENAKI
ALGONQUIN
WALDO PATENT
MASSACHUSETTS
MOHAWK
ONONDAGA AND ONEIDA
CAYUGA
TUSCARORA

Places:
Quebec
Three Rivers
Sorel
Montreal
Lachine
La Prairie
Caughnawaga
St. Francis Village
Fort Chambly
Fort St. Theresa
Fort St. John
Fort La Motte
La Presentation Fort La Galette (French)
Fort Frontenac Cataraqui (French)
Fort St. Frédéric (French)
Fort Anne
Fort Nicholson
Fort Pelham
Fort Massachusetts
Saratoga
Fort Johnson
Fort Hunter
German Flats
Schenectady
Albany
Cherry Valley
Kingston
Camping Place
Oswego
Hobbs Fight
Bridgman's
Fort
Ashuelot
Northfield
Deerfield
Hatfield
Hadley
Fort Shirley
Fort Dummer
Number 4
Northampton
Coos Meadow
Norridgewock Fight
Block House (English)
Cushnoc (Augusta)
Fort Richmond
Fort George
Brunswick
Scarborough
Georgetown
PEMAQUID
SAGADAHOC
Casco (Fort Loyal)
WINTER HARBOR
Cape Porpoise
Wells
Saco
Berwick
Dover
York
Kittery
Portsmouth
Durham
Exeter
Hampton
Newbury
Amesbury
Haverhill
Groton
Lancaster
Marlboro
Brookfield
Boston
Pigwacket (Fryeburg)
Lovewell's Fight

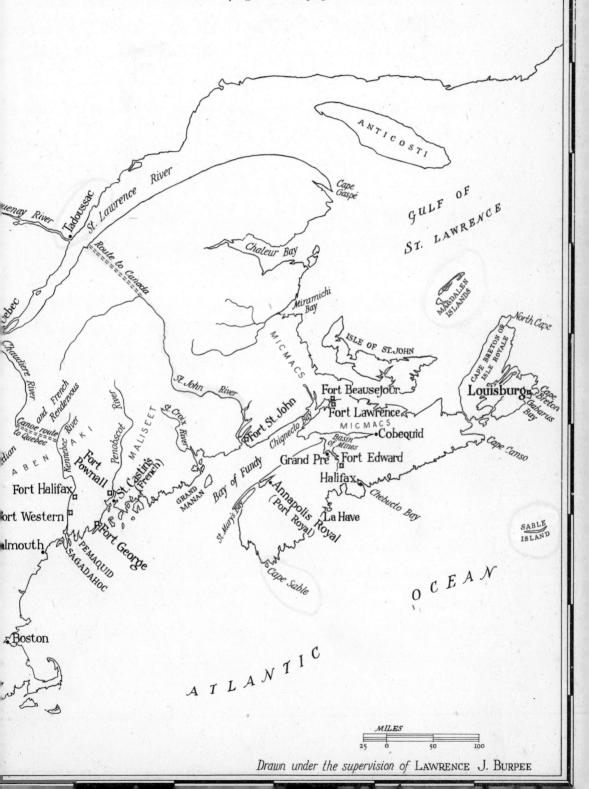

ACADIA AND LOUISBURG
1740 ~ 1755

ANTICOSTI

GULF OF
ST. LAWRENCE

Cape
Gaspé

Chaleur Bay

MAGDALEN
ISLANDS

Miramichi
Bay

ISLE OF ST.JOHN

North Cape

Saguenay River

Tadoussac

St. Lawrence River

Route to Canada

Quebec

Chaudiere River

MICMACS

CAPE BRETON OR
ISLE ROYALE

Louisburg

Cape
Breton

Gabarus
Bay

and French Rendezvous

St. John   River

Canoe route
to Quebec

Kennebec River

A B E N A K I

Penobscot River

St. Croix River

Fort St. John

Chignecto Bay

Fort Beausejour

Fort Lawrence

MICMACS
Cobequid

Basin
of Mines

Fort Edward

Cape Canso

Fort
Pownall

St. Castin's
(French)

M A L I S E E T

GRAND MANAN

Bay of Fundy

Grand Pre

Halifax

Fort Halifax

Chebucto Bay

Indian

Fort Western

almouth

Fort George

PEMAQUID

SAGADAHOC

St. Mary's Bay

Annapolis Royal
(Port Royal)

La Have

SABLE
ISLAND

O C E A N

Cape Sable

Boston

A T L A N T I C

MILES

25   0   50   100

Drawn under the supervision of LAWRENCE J. BURPEE

PLATE 39

Acadia and Louisburg

1740–1755

PLATE 40

Lake Region

1688–1753

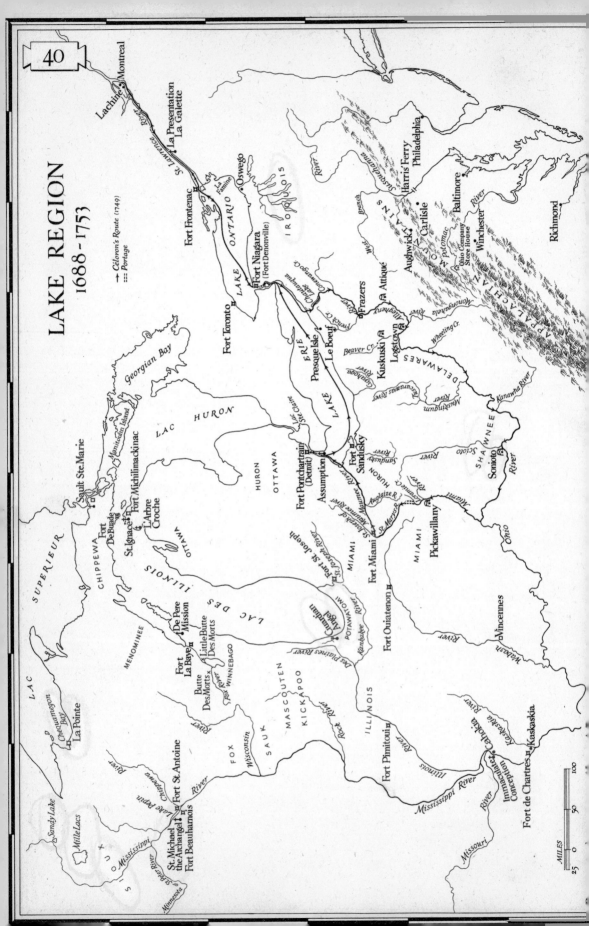

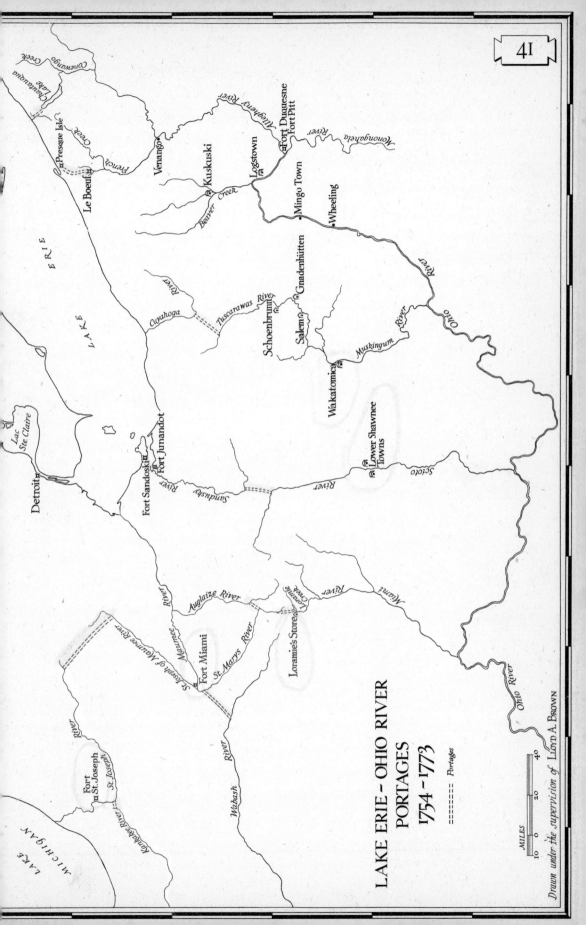

LAKE ERIE ~ OHIO RIVER
PORTAGES
1754 ~ 1773

- - - - - - - Portages

MILES
10   0   20   40

Drawn under the supervision of LLOYD A. BROWN

PLATE 41

Lake Erie-Ohio River
Portages

1754-1773

PLATE 42

Niagara

1754–1764

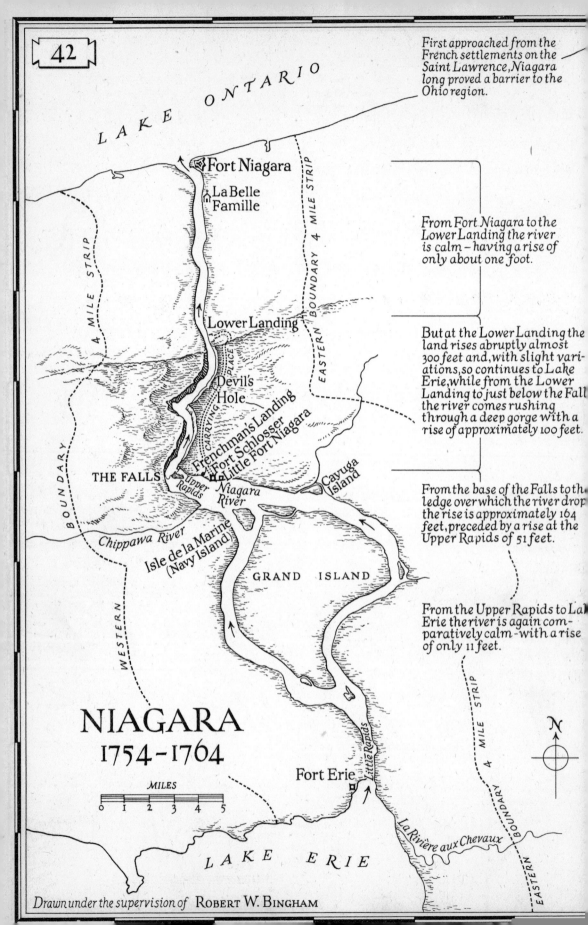

LAKE ONTARIO

First approached from the
French settlements on the
Saint Lawrence, Niagara
long proved a barrier to the
Ohio region.

Fort Niagara

La Belle
Famille

From Fort Niagara to the
Lower Landing the river
is calm – having a rise of
only about one foot.

Lower Landing

EASTERN BOUNDARY 4 MILE STRIP

4 MILE STRIP

Devil's
Hole

But at the Lower Landing the
land rises abruptly almost
300 feet and, with slight variations, so continues to Lake
Erie, while from the Lower
Landing to just below the Fall
the river comes rushing
through a deep gorge with a
rise of approximately 100 feet.

CARRYING PLACE

Frenchman's Landing
Fort Schlosser
Little Fort Niagara

BOUNDARY

THE FALLS

Upper
Rapids

Niagara
River

Cayuga
Island

From the base of the Falls to the
ledge over which the river drop
the rise is approximately 164
feet, preceded by a rise at the
Upper Rapids of 51 feet.

Chippawa River

Isle de la Marine
(Navy Island)

GRAND ISLAND

From the Upper Rapids to La
Erie the river is again com-
paratively calm - with a rise
of only 11 feet.

WESTERN BOUNDARY

4 MILE STRIP

NIAGARA
1754–1764

MILES

0 1 2 3 4 5

Fort Erie

Little Rapids

N

LAKE ERIE

La Rivière aux Chevaux

EASTERN BOUNDARY

Drawn under the supervision of ROBERT W. BINGHAM

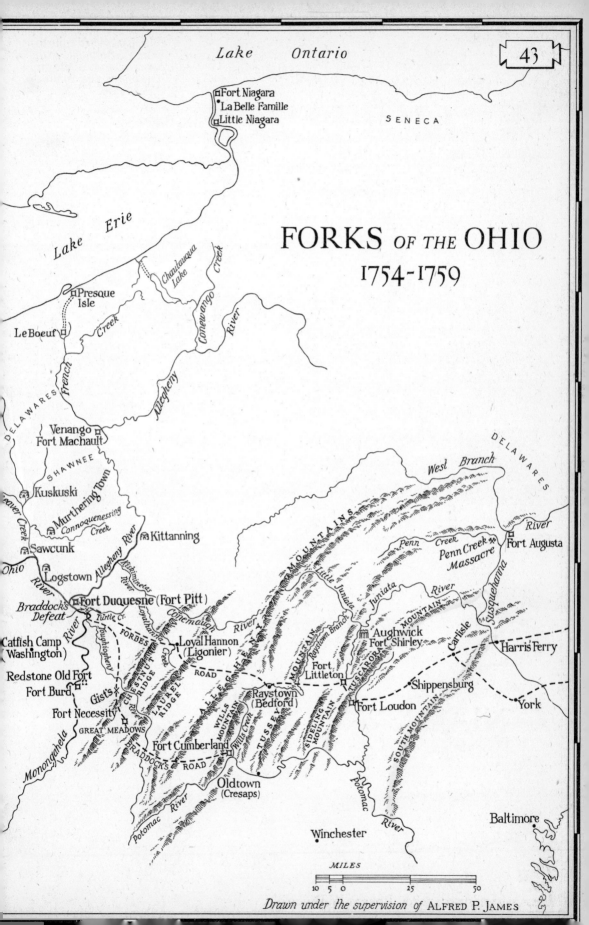

Lake Ontario

□Fort Niagara
•La Belle Famille
□Little Niagara

SENECA

Lake Erie

FORKS OF THE OHIO
1754-1759

Chautauqua Lake

□Presque Isle

Le Boeuf □

French Creek

Conewango Creek

Allegheny River

DELAWARES

Venango
Fort Machault

DELAWARES

West Branch

SHAWNEE

Kuskuski

Murthering Town

Connoquenessing Creek

Beaver Creek

Sawcunk

Kittanning

Penn Creek

Penn Creek Massacre

River

☒Fort Augusta

Ohio

Logstown

Allegheny River

Kiskiminetas River

MOUNTAINS

Little Juniata River

Juniata River

Susquehanna

Braddock's Defeat

Fort Duquesne (Fort Pitt)

Turtle Cr.

Loyalhanna Creek

Conemaugh River

MOUNTAIN

Raystown branch

MOUNTAIN

Aughwick
Fort Shirley

Carlisle

Harris Ferry

Catfish Camp
(Washington)

FORBES

Youghiogheny River

CHESTNUT RIDGE

•Loyal Hannon
(Ligonier)

ROAD

ALLEGHENY

Fort Littleton

TUSCARORA

Redstone Old Fort
Fort Burd

Gist's

LAUREL RIDGE

Fort Loudon

•Shippensburg

York

Fort Necessity

Cheat River

Raystown
(Bedford)

WILLS MOUNTAIN

TUSSEY MOUNTAIN

SIDELING MOUNTAIN

GREAT MEADOWS

BRADDOCK'S ROAD

Fort Cumberland □

Wills Creek

Monongahela

Oldtown
(Cresaps)

SOUTH MOUNTAIN

Potomac River

Potomac River

Winchester

Baltimore

MILES

10 5 0   25   50

Drawn under the supervision of ALFRED P. JAMES

PLATE 43

Forks of the Ohio

1754–1759

PLATE 44

French and Indian War

Northern Area

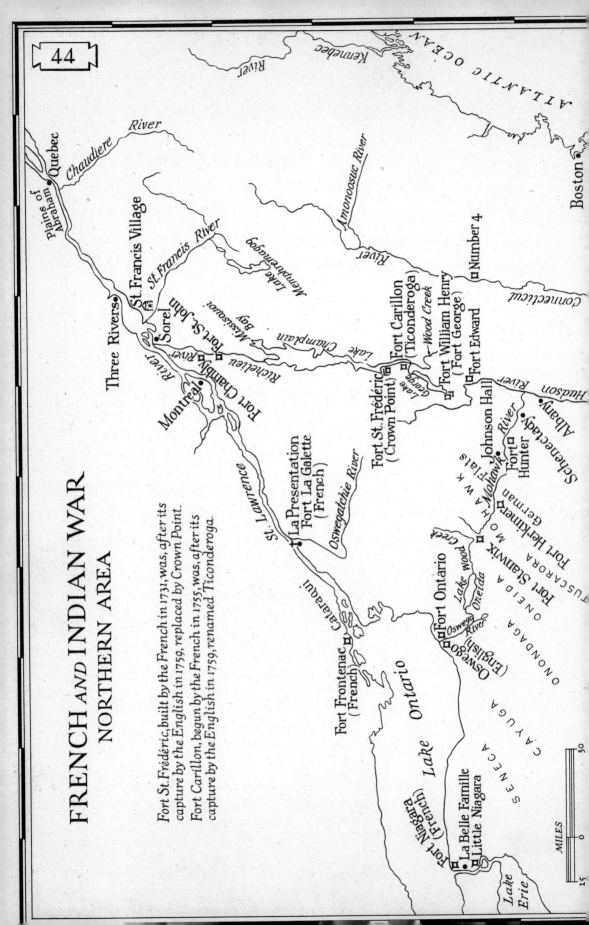

FRENCH AND INDIAN WAR
NORTHERN AREA

Fort St. Frédéric, built by the French in 1731, was, after its capture by the English in 1759, replaced by Crown Point. Fort Carillon, begun by the French in 1755, was, after its capture by the English in 1759, renamed Ticonderoga.

44

MILES

0 | 25 | 50

Quebec
Plains of Abraham
Chaudiere River
St. Francis Village
St. Francis River
Three Rivers
Sorel
Fort St. John
Montreal
Fort Chambly
River
Richelieu River
Missisquoi Bay
Lake Memphramagog
Lake Champlain
Kennebec River
Amonoosuc River
River
Connecticut
Boston
Number 4
Fort Carillon (Ticonderoga)
Wood Creek
Fort William Henry (Fort George)
Fort Edward
Lake George
Fort St. Frédéric (Crown Point)
Hudson River
Albany
Schenectady
Fort Hunter
Johnson Hall
Mohawk River
MOHAWK
Fort Herkimer
German Flats
TUSCARORA
ONEIDA
Fort Stanwix
Oneida Lake
Wood Creek
Oswego River
ONONDAGA
Fort Ontario
Oswego (English)
CAYUGA
SENECA
St. Lawrence River
La Presentation Fort La Galette (French)
Oswegatchie River
Cataraqui
Fort Frontenac (French)
Lake Ontario
Fort Niagara (French)
La Belle Famille
Little Niagara
Lake Erie

ATLANTIC OCEAN

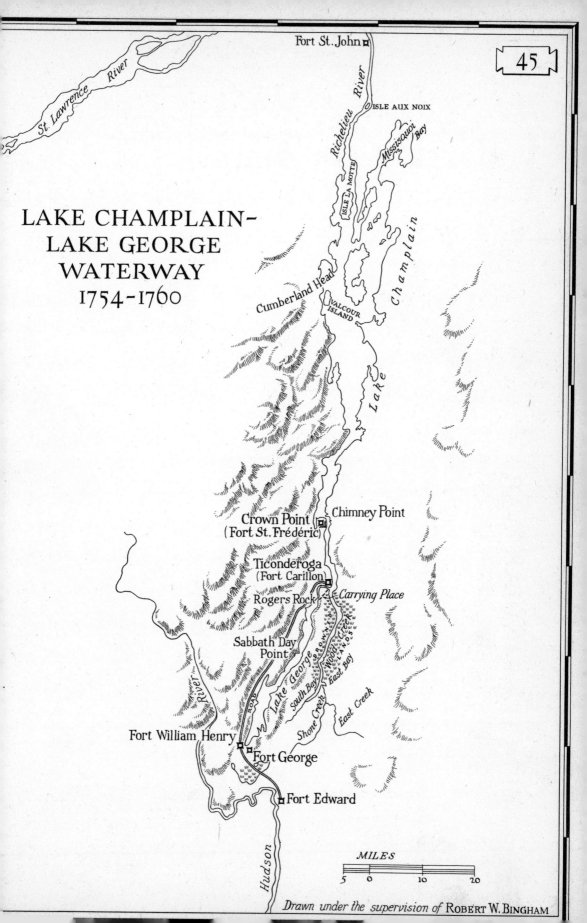

LAKE CHAMPLAIN-
LAKE GEORGE
WATERWAY
1754-1760

Fort St. John

Richelieu River

ISLE AUX NOIX

Missisquoi Bay

ISLE LA MOTTE

Lake Champlain

Cumberland Head

VALCOUR ISLAND

Crown Point
(Fort St. Frédéric)   Chimney Point

Ticonderoga
(Fort Carillon)

Rogers Rock   Carrying Place

Sabbath Day
Point

Lake George

WOOD CREEK

South Bay   East Bay

Shone Creek   East Creek

River

ROAD

Fort William Henry

Fort George

Fort Edward

Hudson

St. Lawrence River

MILES

5 0   10   20

Drawn under the supervision of ROBERT W. BINGHAM

PLATE 45

Lake Champlain-Lake Georg
Waterway

1754–1760

PLATE 46

Detroit

1763–1764

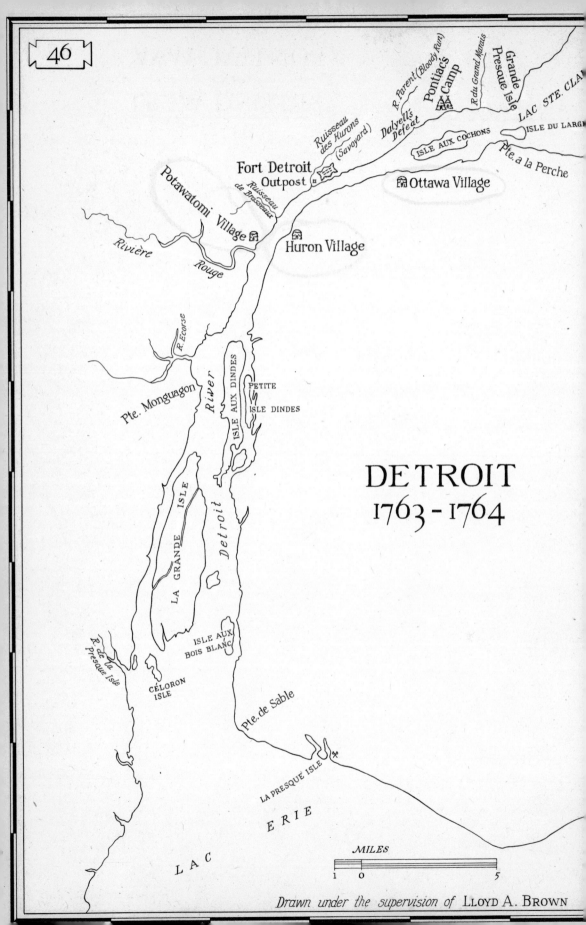

Grande
Presque Isle
R. du Grand Marais
Pontiac's Camp
R. Parent (Bloody Run)
Dalyell's Defeat
LAC STE. CLA
ISLE DU LARG
Ruisseau
des Hurons
(Savoyard)
ISLE AUX COCHONS
Pte. a la Perche
Fort Detroit
Outpost
Ottawa Village
Ruisseau
de Brosseaux
Potawatomi Village
Huron Village
Rivière
Rouge
R. Ecorse
Pte. Monguagon
ISLE AUX DINDES
PETITE
ISLE DINDES
River
DETROIT
1763 - 1764
LA GRANDE ISLE
Detroit
ISLE AUX
BOIS BLANC
R. de la
Presque Isle
CÉLORON
ISLE
Pte. de Sable
LA PRESQUE ISLE
E R I E
L A C
MILES
1   0   5

Drawn under the supervision of LLOYD A. BROWN

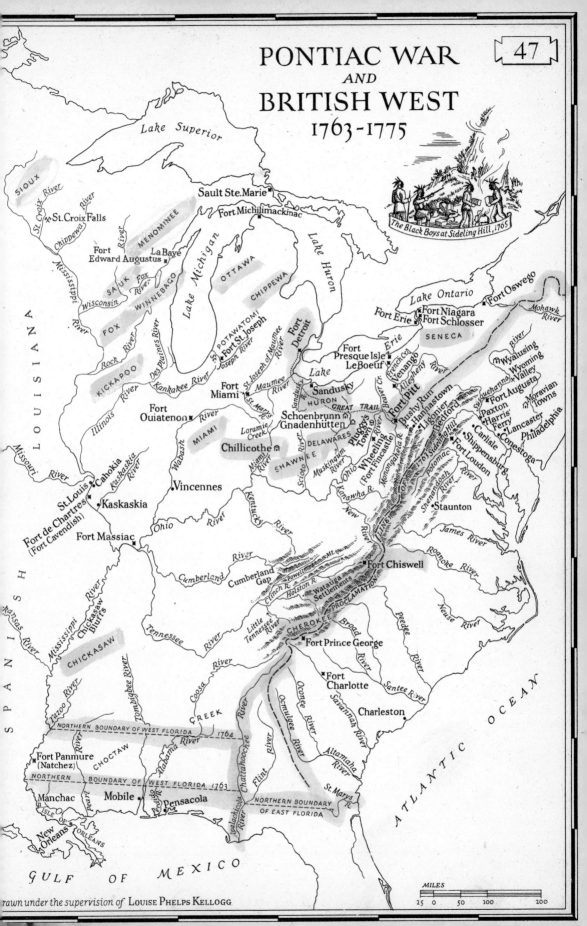

PONTIAC WAR
AND
BRITISH WEST
1763–1775

47

The Black Boys at Sideling Hill, 1765

Lake Superior

SIOUX

St. Croix Falls

Menominee

Sault Ste. Marie

Fort Michilimackinac

Fort Edward Augustus

La Baye

SAUK

WINNEBAGO

OTTAWA

CHIPPEWA

Lake Michigan

Lake Huron

FOX

KICKAPOO

POTAWATOMI

Fort St. Joseph

Fort Detroit

Fort Erie   Fort Niagara

Lake Ontario   Fort Oswego

Fort Schlosser

Mohawk River

SENECA

Fort Presque Isle
LeBoeuf

Erie

Venango

Allegheny River

Wyalusing

Wyoming Valley

Fort Augusta

Moravian Towns

Fort Miami

Lake HURON

Sandusky

GREAT TRAIL

Fort Pitt

Bushy Run

Hannastown

Ligonier

Bedford

Paxton

Harris Ferry

Lancaster

Conestoga

Philadelphia

Fort Ouiatenon

MIAMI

Loramie Creek

Schoenbrunn
Gnadenhütten

DELAWARES

Pluggy's Town

Wheeling

Fort Fincastle

Carlisle

Shippensburg

Fort Loudon

Chillicothe

SHAWNEE

Scioto River

Muskingum River

Ohio River

Monongahela R.

Fort Bedford

1767 Sideling Hill

Potomac River

Shenandoah River

Cahokia

St. Louis

Kaskaskia

Fort de Chartres
(Fort Cavendish)

Vincennes

Kaskaskia River

Wabash River

Kentucky River

New River

Kanawha River

Staunton

James River

Fort Massiac

Ohio River

Cumberland River

Cumberland Gap

Powell River

Clinch R.

Holston River

Watauga Settlements

PROCLAMATION

Fort Chiswell

Roanoke River

Neuse River

Tennessee River

Little Tennessee River

CHEROKEE

Fort Prince George

Broad River

Peedee River

CHICKASAW

Chickasaw Bluffs

Coosa River

CREEK

Fort Charlotte

Santee River

Charleston

Savannah River

NORTHERN BOUNDARY OF WEST FLORIDA 1764

Alabama River

Tombigbee River

Ocmulgee River

Oconee River

Savannah River

Fort Panmure
(Natchez)

CHOCTAW

NORTHERN   BOUNDARY OF WEST FLORIDA 1763

Pearl River

Chattahoochee River

Flint River

Altamaha River

St. Marys R.

Manchac

Mobile

Pensacola

NORTHERN BOUNDARY
OF EAST FLORIDA

ATLANTIC OCEAN

New Orleans

ISLE OF ORLEANS

GULF   OF   MEXICO

LOUISIANA

SPANISH

Mississippi River

Missouri River

Arkansas River

Yazoo River

ISLE OF

MILES

25 0   50   100   200

rawn under the supervision of LOUISE PHELPS KELLOGG

PLATE 47

Pontiac War
and
British West
1763–1775

PLATE 48

Illinois Country

1700–1763

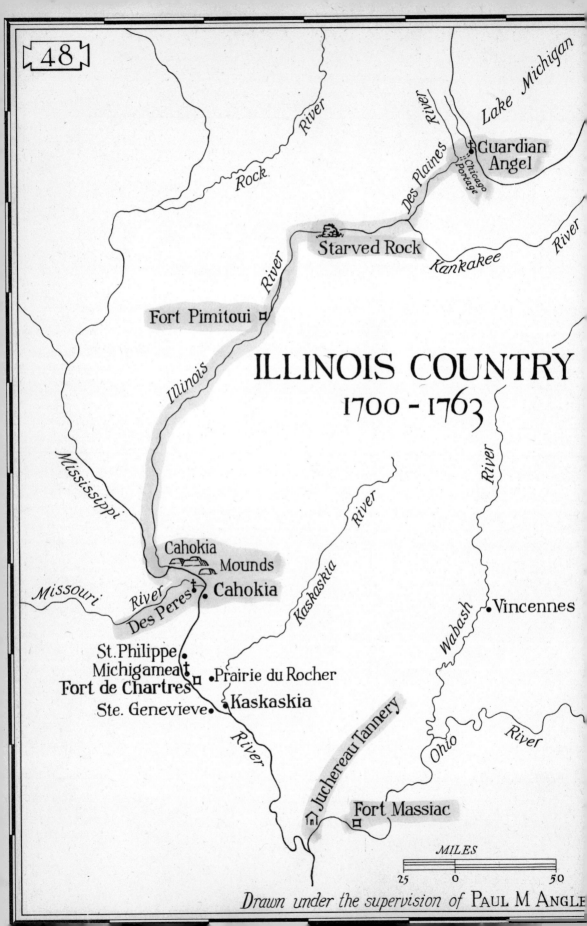

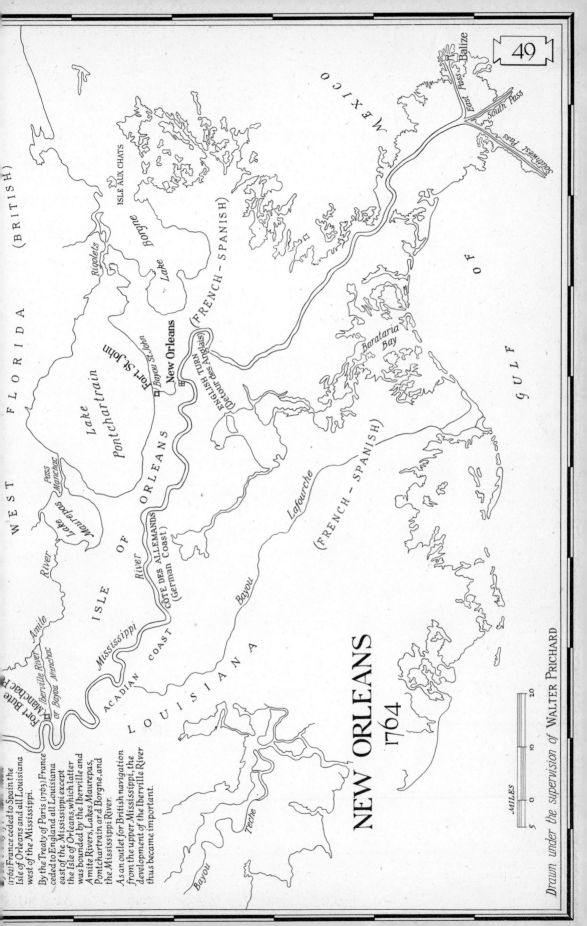

NEW ORLEANS
1764

(1762) France ceded to Spain the
Isle of Orleans and all Louisiana
west of the Mississippi.

By the Treaty of Paris (1763) France
ceded to England all Louisiana
east of the Mississippi except
the Isle of Orleans, which latter
was bounded by the Iberville and
Amite Rivers, Lakes Maurepas,
Pontchartrain and Borgne, and
the Mississippi River.

As an outlet for British navigation
from the upper Mississippi, the
development of the Iberville River
thus became important.

MILES

5   0   10   20

Drawn under the supervision of WALTER PRICHARD

GULF OF MEXICO

Balize

East Pass

South Pass

Southwest Pass

ISLE AUX CHATS

Lake Borgne

Rigolets

(FRENCH – SPANISH)

Barataria
Bay

(FRENCH – SPANISH)

Lafourche

Bayou

ENGLISH TURN
(Détour des Anglais)

New Orleans

Bayou St. John

Fort St. John

Lake Pontchartrain

WEST FLORIDA (BRITISH)

Pass Manchac

Lake
Maurepas

Amite River

Iberville River
or Bayou Manchac

Fort Bute

Fort Manchac

ISLE OF ORLEANS

Mississippi River

CÔTE DES ALLEMANDS
(German Coast)

ACADIAN COAST

LOUISIANA

Teche

Bayou

PLATE 49

New Orleans

1764

PLATE 50

British Florida

1763–1783

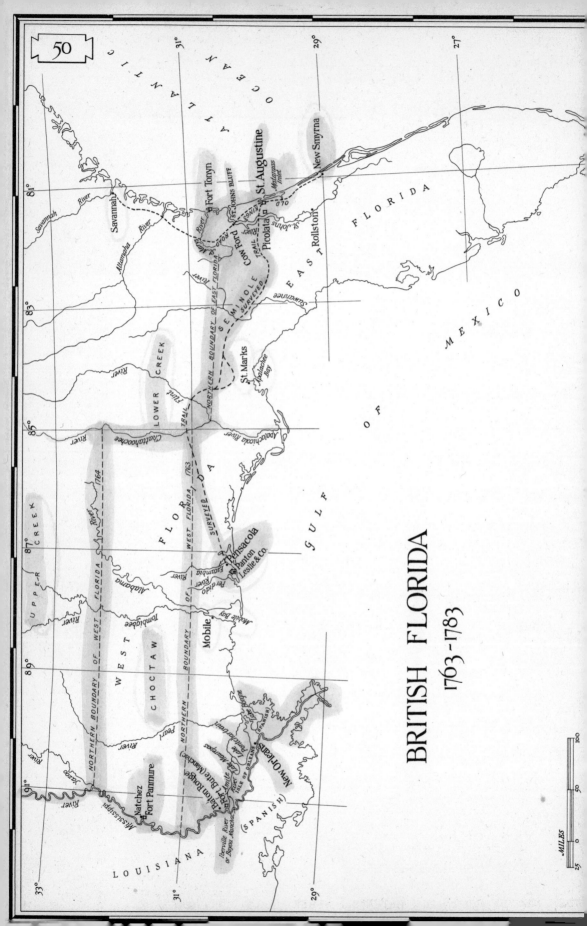

BRITISH FLORIDA
1763-1783

MILES

ATLANTIC OCEAN

GULF OF MEXICO

EAST FLORIDA

WEST FLORIDA

FLORIDA

LOUISIANA (SPANISH)

UPPER CREEK

LOWER CREEK

CHOCTAW

SEMINOLE

Savannah River
Altamaha River
Ocmulgee River
Chattahoochee River
Flint Trail
Apalachicola River
Alabama River
Tombigbee River
Pearl River
Mississippi River
Yazoo River
Perdido River
Escambia River
Suwannee River
St. Johns River
St. Marys River

Savannah
Fort Tonyn
St. Augustine
New Smyrna
Matanzas Inlet
St. Johns Bluff
Picolata
Rollston
St. Johns
Cow Ford
KINGS ROAD
SEMINOLE TRAIL SURVEYED
NORTHERN BOUNDARY OF EAST FLORIDA
St. Marks
Apalache Bay
SURVEYED WEST FLORIDA, 1763
Pensacola
Panton Leslie & Co.
Mobile
Mobile Bay
NORTHERN BOUNDARY OF WEST FLORIDA
1764
Natchez
Fort Panmure
Baton Rouge
Fort Bute (Manchac)
New Orleans
Lake Pontchartrain
Lake Maurepas
Iberville River or Bayou Manchac
Amite River
Bayou Lafourche

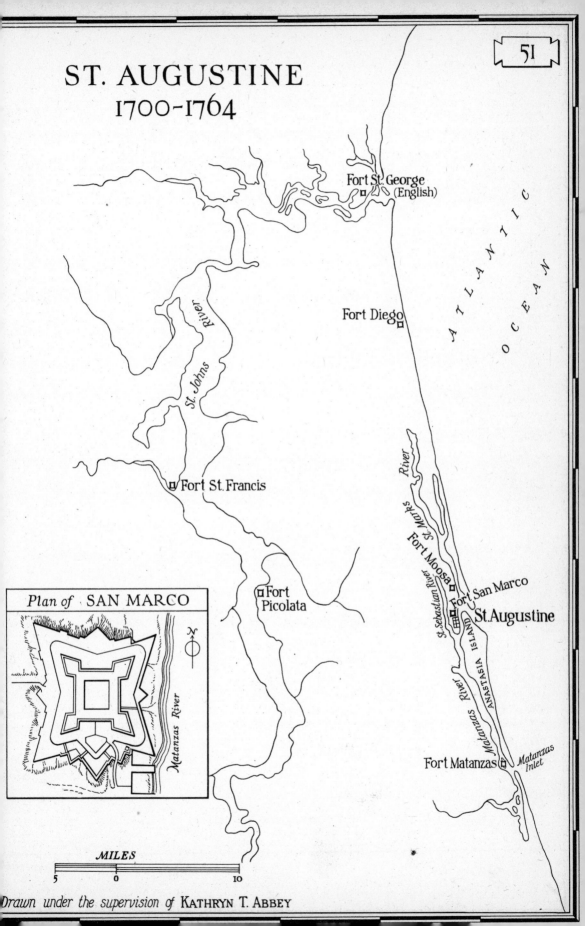

ST. AUGUSTINE
1700-1764

Fort St. George
(English)

ATLANTIC OCEAN

Fort Diego

St. Johns River

Fort St. Francis

Fort Picolata

St. Marks River

Fort Moosa

St. Sebastian River

Fort San Marco

St. Augustine

ANASTASIA ISLAND

Matanzas River

Fort Matanzas

Matanzas Inlet

Plan of SAN MARCO

Matanzas River

MILES

5   0   10

Drawn under the supervision of KATHRYN T. ABBEY

PLATE 51

St. Augustine

1700–1764

PLATE 52

California, New Mexico,
Texas and Louisiana

1763–1802

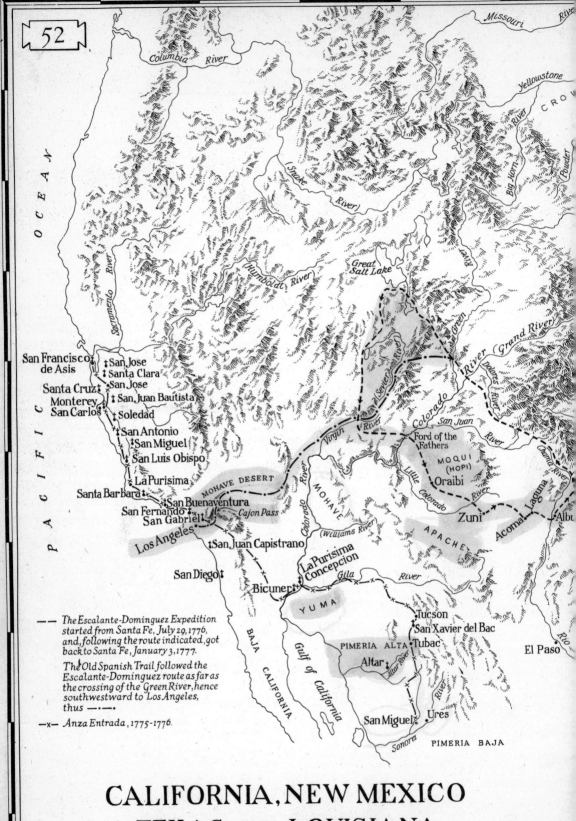

OCEAN

Missouri River

Columbia River

Yellowstone River

CROW

Snake River

(Humboldt River)

Great Salt Lake

Green River (Grand River)

Sacramento River

San Francisco de Asis

‡San Jose
‡Santa Clara
‡San Jose
Santa Cruz
Monterey
San Carlos
‡San Juan Bautista
‡Soledad

‡San Antonio
‡San Miguel
‡San Luis Obispo

‡La Purisima

Santa Barbara‡

‡San Buenaventura
San Fernando‡
San Gabriel‡
Los Angeles

MOHAVE DESERT

Cajon Pass

Colorado River

MOHAVE

Virgin River

Colorado River

Ford of the Fathers

San Juan River

Dolores River

MOQUI (HOPI)

Oraibi

Chama River

PACIFIC

(Williams River)

Little Colorado River

Zuni

Acoma Laguna

Albu-

‡San Juan Capistrano

La Purisima Concepcion

APACHE

San Diego‡

Bicuner‡

Gila River

YUMA

Tucson
San Xavier del Bac
Tubac

El Paso

BAJA CALIFORNIA

Gulf of California

PIMERIA ALTA

Altar‡

Altar River

Rio

San Miguel‡ Ures

Sonora River

PIMERIA BAJA

−− The Escalante-Dominguez Expedition started from Santa Fe, July 29, 1776, and, following the route indicated, got back to Santa Fe, January 3, 1777.

The Old Spanish Trail followed the Escalante-Dominguez route as far as the crossing of the Green River, hence southwestward to Los Angeles, thus —·—

−x− Anza Entrada, 1775-1776.

CALIFORNIA, NEW MEXICO
TEXAS AND LOUISIANA
1763–1802

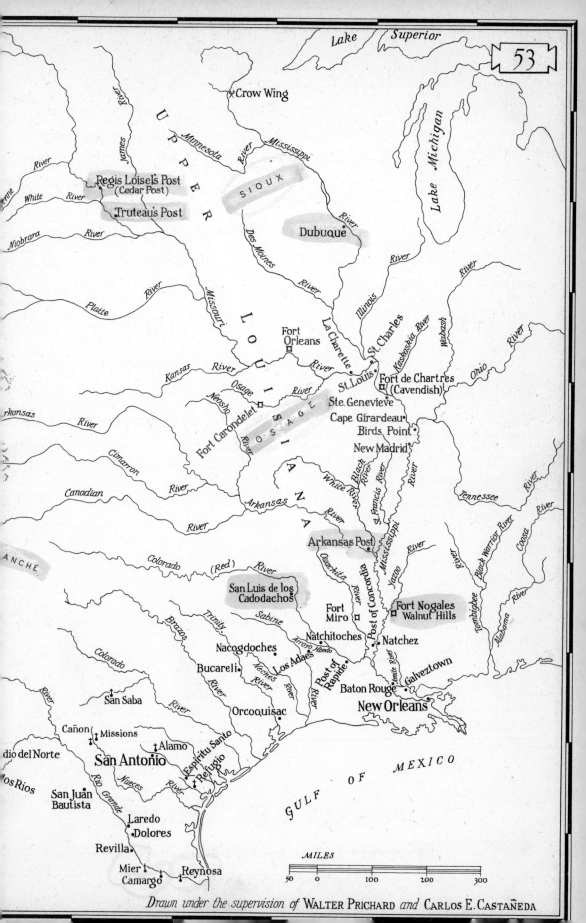

Drawn under the supervision of WALTER PRICHARD and CARLOS E. CASTAÑEDA

PLATE 53

California, New Mexico,
Texas and Louisiana

1763–1802

PLATE 54

Triangular Trade

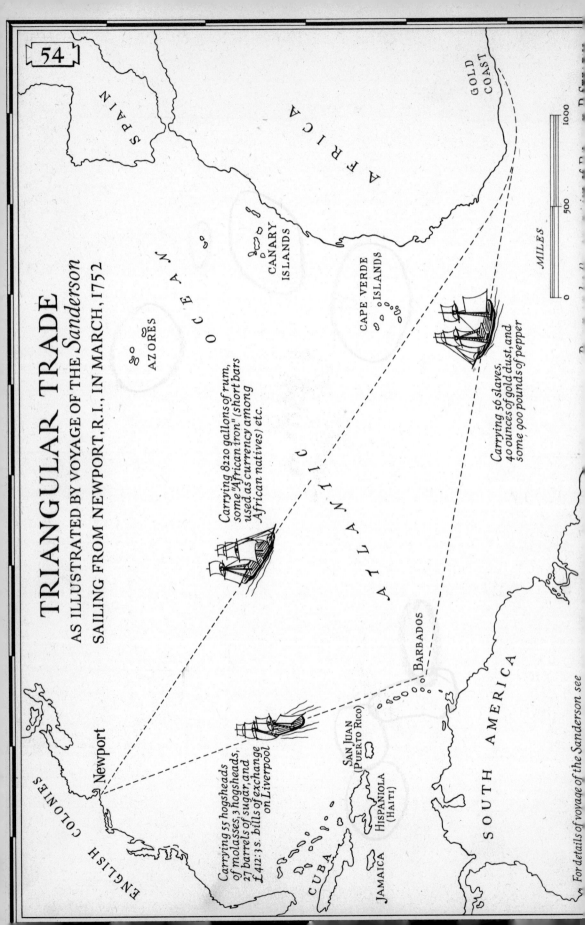

TRIANGULAR TRADE

AS ILLUSTRATED BY VOYAGE OF THE *Sanderson*
SAILING FROM NEWPORT, R.I., IN MARCH, 1752

54

SPAIN

AFRICA

GOLD COAST

OCEAN

AZORES

CANARY ISLANDS

CAPE VERDE ISLANDS

ATLANTIC

Carrying 8220 gallons of rum, some "African iron" (short bars used as currency among African natives) etc.

Carrying 56 slaves, 40 ounces of gold dust, and some 900 pounds of pepper

MILES

0   500   1000

ENGLISH COLONIES

Newport

Carrying 55 hogsheads of molasses, 3 hogsheads, 27 barrels of sugar, and £412:3s. bills of exchange on Liverpool

CUBA

JAMAICA

HISPANIOLA (HAITI)

SAN JUAN (PUERTO RICO)

BARBADOS

SOUTH AMERICA

For details of voyage of the Sanderson see

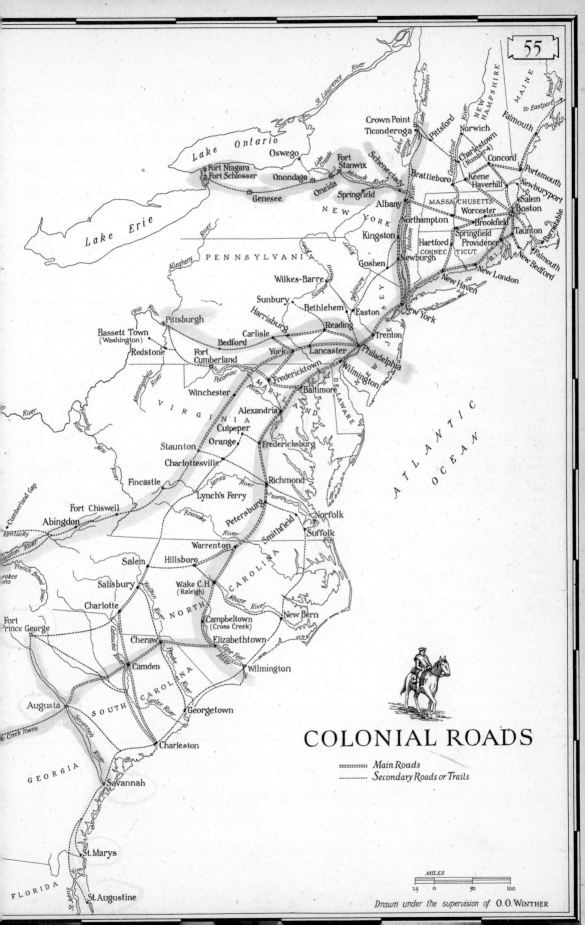

COLONIAL ROADS

========= Main Roads
--------- Secondary Roads or Trails

Drawn under the supervision of O. O. WINTHER

MILES
25   0   50   100

PLATE 55

Colonial Roads

PLATE 56

Appalachia

1690–1756

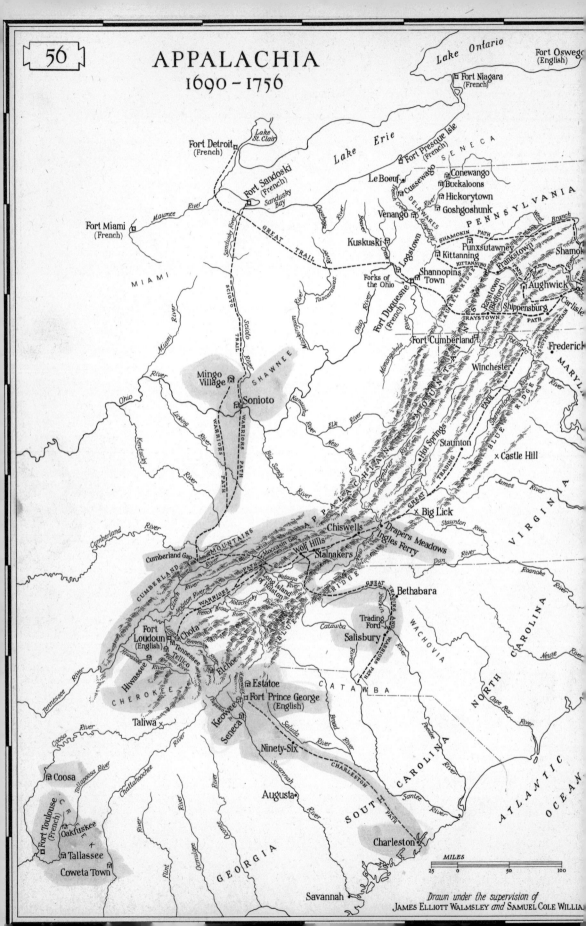

APPALACHIA
1690–1756

Lake Ontario

Fort Oswego
(English)

Fort Niagara
(French)

Lake Erie

SENECA

Fort Presque Isle
(French)

Lake
St. Clair

Fort Detroit
(French)

Fort Sandoski
(French)

Sandusky Bay

Le Boeuf

Conewango
Cussewago
Buckaloons
Hickorytown
Goshgoshunk

DELAWARES

Venango

PENNSYLVANIA

Maumee River

Fort Miami
(French)

MIAMI

Sandusky River

GREAT TRAIL

Kuskuski

Logstown

SHAMOKIN PATH

Punxsutawney
Kittanning
Frankstown
Shamok

LAUREL RIDGE 1762

KITTANNING

Beaver River

Cuyahoga River

Shannopins
Town

Aughwick

Scioto River

Forks of
the Ohio

RAYSTOWN (Bedford)

Raystown
Shippensburg

Carlisle

SCIOTO TRAIL

Tuscarawas

Muskingum River

Ohio River

Fort Duquesne
(French)

Monongahela River

RAYSTOWN PATH

Fort Cumberland

Frederick

MARYL

Mingo
Village

SHAWNEE

Soninto

WARRIORS PATH

Kanawha River

Winchester

Potomac River

Shenandoah River

Staunton

BLUE RIDGE

Hot Springs

TRADING

× Castle Hill

Ohio River

Licking River

Big Sandy

Elk River

New River

Greenbrier

James River

VIRGINIA

Kentucky River

APPALACHIAN MOUNTAINS

Cumberland River

Chiswells

Drapers Meadows
Ingles Ferry

Big Lick ×

Staunton River

Cumberland Gap

MOUNTAINS

Moccasin Gap
Wolf Hills

CUMBERLAND

Clinch River

PATH

Stalnakers

New River

Dan River

Roanoke River

WARRIORS PATH

Powell River

Holston River

Watauga River

Long Island
of Holston

BLUE RIDGE

GREAT WAGON ROAD

Bethabara

Jackson River

French Broad River

Nolachucky River

Chota

Tennessee River

Fort
Loudoun
(English)

Tellico

Elchoe

Catawba River

Trading
Ford

Salisbury

WACHOVIA

WARRIORS PATH

NORTH
CAROLINA

Neuse River

Cape Fear River

Hiwassee

Estatoe

CHEROKEE

Taliwa

Keowee

Fort Prince George
(English)

Seneca

C A T A W B A

Tennessee River

Ninety-Six

Saluda River

Broad River

Pee Dee River

SOUTH
CAROLINA

ATLANTIC OCEAN

Coosa

Fort Toulouse
(French)

Oakfuskee

Tallapoosa River

CREEK

Tallassee

Coweta Town

GEORGIA

Chattahoochee River

Flint River

Ocmulgee River

Savannah River

Augusta

CHARLESTON PATH

Santee River

Charleston

Savannah

MILES
25 0   50   100

Drawn under the supervision of
JAMES ELLIOTT WALMSLEY *and* SAMUEL COLE WILLIA

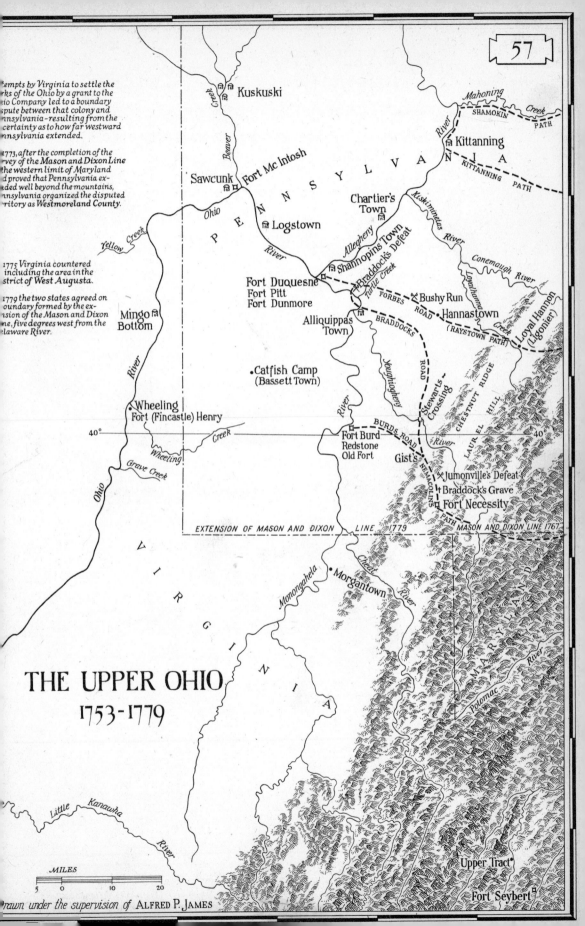

Kuskuski

Mahoning

SHAMOKIN

Creek PATH

Kittanning

KITTANNING PATH

Fort McIntosh

Sawcunk

Beaver Creek

PENNSYLVANIA

Chartier's Town

Ohio River

Logstown

Keskiminetas River

Conemaugh River

Shannopins Town

Braddock's Defeat

Fort Duquesne
Fort Pitt
Fort Dunmore

Allegheny

Turtle Creek

Bushy Run

FORBES ROAD

Hannastown

Loyalhanna Creek

Loyal Hannon (Ligonier)

Yellow Creek

Mingo Bottom

Alliquippas Town

BRADDOCKS

(RAYSTOWN PATH)

Catfish Camp
(Bassett Town)

Youghiogheny River

BRADDOCKS ROAD

Stewarts Crossing

CHESTNUT RIDGE

River LAUREL HILL

Wheeling
Fort (Fincastle) Henry

40°   40°

Wheeling Creek

BURDS ROAD

Fort Burd
Redstone
Old Fort

Gist's

Grave Creek

Ohio River

NEMACOLINS

Jumonville's Defeat
Braddock's Grave
Fort Necessity

EXTENSION OF MASON AND DIXON   LINE   1779

PATH   MASON AND DIXON LINE 1767

V I R G I N I A

Monongahela

Cheat River

Morgantown

M A R Y L A N D

Potomac River

THE UPPER OHIO

1753-1779

Little Kanawha River

Upper Tract

Fort Seybert

MILES

5   0   10   20

Drawn under the supervision of ALFRED P. JAMES

Attempts by Virginia to settle the
forks of the Ohio by a grant to the
Ohio Company led to a boundary
dispute between that colony and
Pennsylvania - resulting from the
uncertainty as to how far westward
Pennsylvania extended.

In 1773, after the completion of the
survey of the Mason and Dixon Line
to the western limit of Maryland
had proved that Pennsylvania extended well beyond the mountains,
Pennsylvania organized the disputed
territory as Westmoreland County.

In 1775 Virginia countered
by including the area in the
District of West Augusta.

In 1779 the two states agreed on
a boundary formed by the extension of the Mason and Dixon
Line, five degrees west from the
Delaware River.

PLATE 57

The Upper Ohio

1753–1779

PLATE 58

Shenandoah Valley

1716–1780

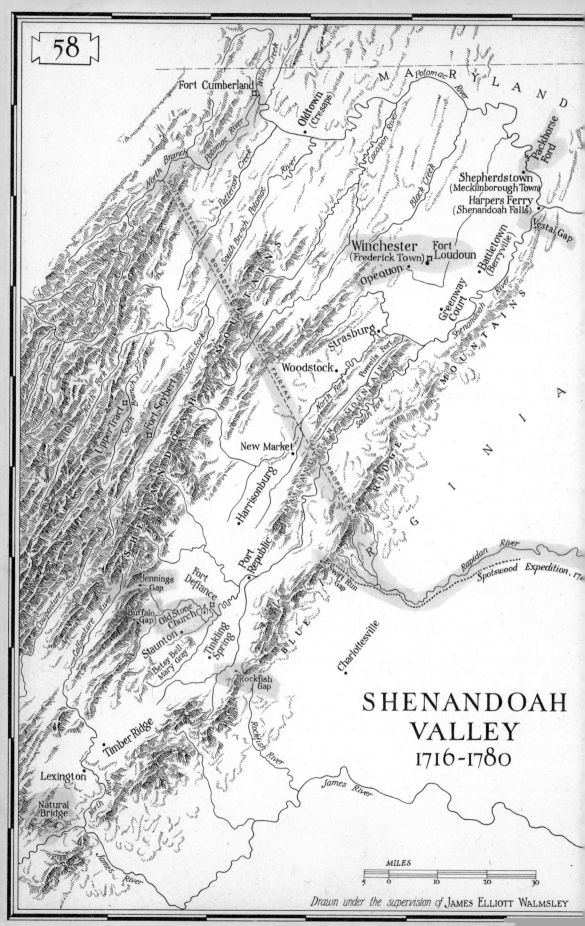

58

MARYLAND

Fort Cumberland

Oldtown
(Cresaps)

Potomac River

Wills Creek

North Branch

South Western Potomac River

Patterson Creek

Cacapon River

Black Creek

Packhorse Ford

Shepherdstown
(Mecklinborough Town)

Harpers Ferry
(Shenandoah Falls)

Vestal Gap

BOUNDARY MOUNTAINS

Winchester
(Frederick Town)

Fort Loudoun

Battletown
(Berryville)

Opequon

South Branch Potomac River

Greenway Court

Shenandoah River

Strasburg

Fort Fairfax

Woodstock

Powells Fort

North Fork

FORT SEYBERT MOUNTAINS

Fort Seybert

Upper Tract

North Fork

South Branch

South Fork

South Fork South Fork

New Market

MASSANUTTEN MOUNTAINS

South Fork

BLUE RIDGE MOUNTAINS

VIRGINIA

Harrisonburg

PROPRIETARY

SHENANDOAH RIVER

Port
Republic

Swift Run
Gap

Rapidan River

Spotswood Expedition, 17

Jennings
Gap

Fort
Defiance

Cowpasture River

Calfpasture River

Buffalo
Gap

Old Stone
Church

BLUE

Staunton

Betsy Bell
Mary Gray

Tinkling
Spring

Charlottesville

Rockfish
Gap

RIDGE

Timber Ridge

Rockfish River

SHENANDOAH
VALLEY
1716-1780

Lexington

North River

Natural
Bridge

James River

James River

MILES

5 0 10 20 30

Drawn under the supervision of JAMES ELLIOTT WALMSLEY

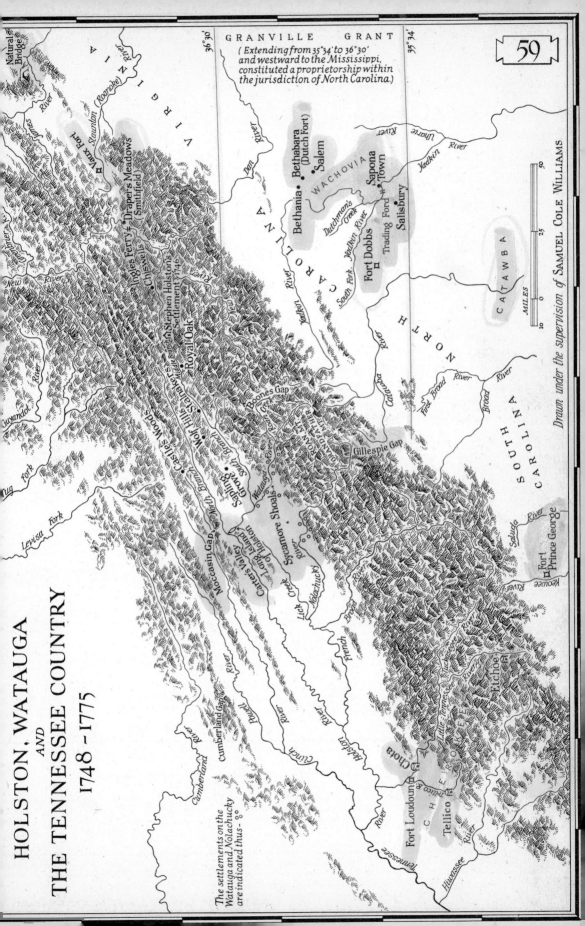

HOLSTON, WATAUGA
AND
THE TENNESSEE COUNTRY
1748–1775

The settlements on the
Watauga and Nolachucky
are indicated thus - °°

GRANVILLE GRANT
(Extending from 35°34' to 36°30'
and westward to the Mississippi,
constituted a proprietorship within
the jurisdiction of North Carolina.)

36°30'   35°34'

Drawn under the supervision of SAMUEL COLE WILLIAMS

Natural Bridge

VIRGINIA

Vaux Fort
Ingles Ferry = Drapers Meadows (Smithfield)
Chiswells
Royal Oak
Stephen Holston's Settlement 1746

Dan River

Bethabara (Dutch Fort)
Salem
Bethania

WACHOVIA

Sapona Town
Trading Ford
Salisbury

Fort Dobbs

NORTH CAROLINA

CATAWBA

Yadkin River
Uharie River

South Fork Yadkin River
Dutchman's Creek

First Broad River
Broad River

SOUTH CAROLINA

Boones Gap
Gillespie Gap

Castle's Wood
Wolf Hills
Sapling Grove
Gunow's Branch
Moccasin Gap
Carters Valley
Long Island of Holston
Sycamore Shoals

New River
Clinch River
Powell River
Cumberland Gap
Cumberland River
Levisa Fork
Rug Fork
Cuyandot River

Lick Creek
Nolachucky
Watauga River
French Broad River
Holston River

Fort Prince George
Keowee River
Saluda River

Chota
Fort Loudoun
Tellico R.
CHEROKEE
Little Tennessee River
Tuckasegee River
Etchoe

Tennessee River
Hiwassee River

MILES
0   10   25   50

PLATE 59

Holston, Watauga
and
the Tennessee Country

1748-1775

PLATE 60

Proclamation Line of 1763,
Indian Cessions
and the Land Companies

PROCLAMATION LINE OF 1763
INDIAN CESSIONS
AND THE LAND COMPANIES

— — — — The Proclamation of 1763 forbade the purchase or settlement of Indian lands westerly of a line running through the heads of the rivers which fell into the Atlantic from the west or northwest.

—x—x— Tryon's Line, 1767, (by agreement with the Cherokee) directed that no white settlement should be made westerly of a line running from a point where Reedy River was intersected by the then North Carolina-South Carolina boundary, to Tryon's Mountain and thence to Fort Chiswell.

—+—+— The Treaty of Fort Stanwix, 1768, (with the Iroquois) extinguished Iroquois claims to the lands southeasterly of a line running from Fort Stanwix to Fort Pitt, and thence along the southern bank of the Ohio to the mouth of the Tennessee (Cherokee) River.

—o—o— The Treaty of Hard Labor, 1768, (with the Cherokee) confirmed Tryon's Line
—x—x— of 1767 and extended it from Fort Chiswell to the mouth of the Kanawha River.

—•—•— The Treaty of Lochaber, 1770, (with the Cherokee) moved the northern part of the line established at the Treaty of Hard Labor westerly to run from six miles east of Long Island of Holston directly to the mouth of the Kanawha River. Lochaber was the name of the plantation of Alexander Cameron, Assistant Commissioner of Indian Affairs for the Southern Provinces.

—••—••— Donelson's Line. When Col. Donelson acting for Virginia, and Chief Attakullakulla and Alex. Cameron, acting for the Cherokee, came to run the Lochaber Line, some agreement was entered into by which it was turned westward and made to run with the Kentucky (Louisa) River.

The Treaty of Sycamore Shoals, 1775, negotiated between the Transylvania Company and the Cherokee, consumated the sale, by the Cherokee, of TRANSYLVANIA, comprising the land lying between the Kentucky River and the south watershed of the Cumberland River plus a path from the white settlements to the newly acquired lands.

•••••••••• VANDALIA originated in the grant, by the Iroquois at the Treaty of Fort Stanwix, of a tract, between Pennsylvania and the Little Kanawha, known as "Indiana."

Settlements on the Watauga and Nolachucky are indicated thus - ‰

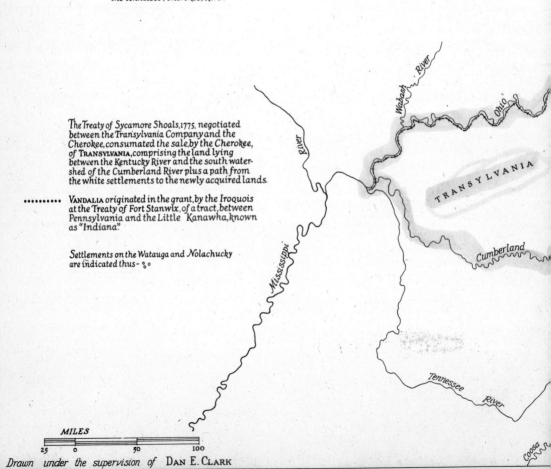

MILES
25   0   50   100

Drawn under the supervision of DAN E. CLARK

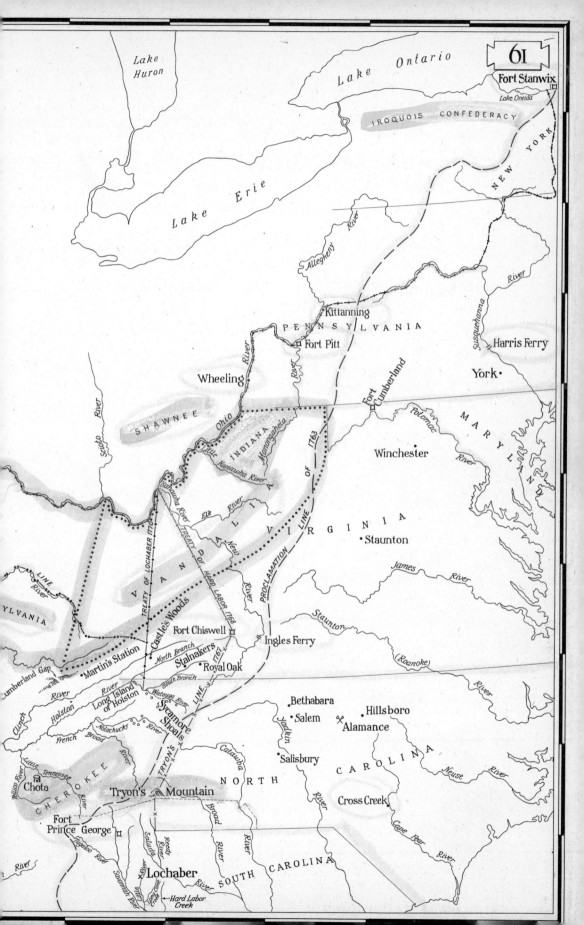

Lake Huron

Lake Ontario

Lake Oneida

IROQUOIS CONFEDERACY

Lake Erie

NEW YORK

Allegheny *River*

River

Susquehanna *River*

Kittanning

PENNSYLVANIA

Harris Ferry

Fort Pitt

York •

Wheeling

SHAWNEE

Ohio *River*

River

Fort Cumberland

MARYLAND

INDIANA

Monongahela

Little Kanawha River

Elk *River*

LINE OF 1763

Potomac *River*

Winchester

Kanawha River

TREATY OF LOCHABER 1770

New *River*

V A N D A L I A

VIRGINIA

• Staunton

Scioto River

PROCLAMATION

James *River*

River

River

LINE

TREATY OF HARD LABOR 1768

River

Staunton *River*

Castle's Woods

Fort Chiswell

Ingles Ferry

(Roanoke) *River*

YLVANIA

North Branch

Stalnakers
1767

• Royal Oak

Cumberland Gap

Martin's Station

River

Clinch *River*

Holston *River*

Long Island of Holston

South Branch

Watauga River

LINE

Bethabara •

River

• Salem

Hillsboro •

Yadkin

⚔ Alamance

Sycamore Shoals

French *Broad*

Nolachucky

TRYON'S

• Salisbury

Catawba *River*

N O R T H

C A R O L I N A

Neuse *River*

CHEROKEE

Tennessee River

River

Little *River*

Chota

Pigeon River

LINE

Broad *River*

Yadkin *River*

Cross Creek •

Tryon's ⤬ Mountain

Reedy *River*

River

Cape Fear *River*

Fort Prince George

Tugaloo *River*

Saluda *River*

SOUTH CAROLINA

⤬ Lochaber

Savannah River

Little River

Long Cane Creek

← Hard Labor Creek

River

PLATE 61

Proclamation Line of 1763,
Indian Cessions
and the Land Companies

PLATE 62

Wilderness Road
and Kentucky

1774–1785

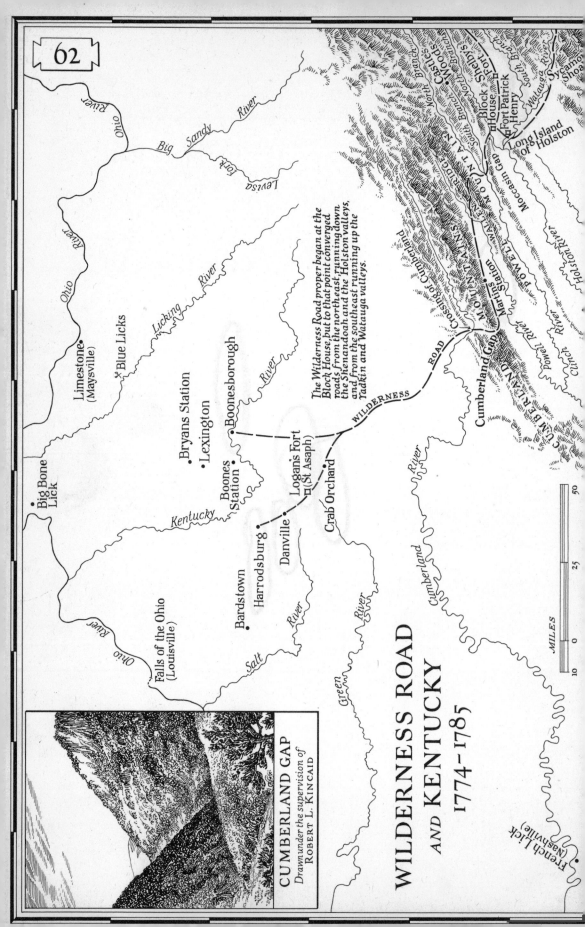

Ohio River

Big Sandy River

Levisa Fork

Ohio River

Licking River

Limestone (Maysville)

✕ Blue Licks

Big Bone Lick

Bryans Station

Lexington

Boonesborough

Kentucky River

Boones Station

Logan's Fort (St Asaph)

Crab Orchard

Harrodsburg

Danville

Bardstown

Falls of the Ohio (Louisville)

Ohio River

Kentucky River

Salt River

Green River

Cumberland River

The Wilderness Road proper began at the Block House, but to that point converged roads: from the northeast, running down the Shenandoah and the Holston valleys, and from the southeast running up the Yadkin and Watauga valleys.

WILDERNESS ROAD

CROSSING OF CUMBERLAND

Cumberland Gap

Martins Station

POWELL MOUNTAIN

CUMBERLAND MOUNTAIN

BLUE RIDGE MOUNTAINS

North Branch

South Branch

Castles Woods

Block House

Fort Patrick Henry

Long Island of Holston

Watauga River

Sycamore Shoals

Moccasin Gap

Clinch River

Holston River

Powell River

French Lick (Nashville)

WILDERNESS ROAD
AND KENTUCKY
1774–1785

MILES

50

25

0

10

CUMBERLAND GAP
Drawn under the supervision of
ROBERT L. KINCAID

DUNMORE'S WAR
1774

—·—· Lord Dunmore, starting from Winchester, augmented
his army at Pittsburgh and Wheeling from which latter
place he marched for the Shawnee towns, ordering
Col. Lewis to meet him on the Ohio.

—×—× On Dunmore's order Col. Andrew Lewis assembled,
at the Levels of the Greenbrier, the militia from
Augusta, Botetourt and Fincastle counties, and
marched up the Kanawha to meet Dunmore.

Winchester

Bedford

Fort
Cumberland

Staunton

BOTETOURT
Fincastle
(Botetourt C.H.)

Drapers Meadows

Pittsburgh
(Fort Dunmore)

Youghiogheny

Redstone

Camp Union
Levels of Greenbrier
Culbertsons
Bottom

Ingles Ferry
Fort Chiswell

Baker's Cabin
Massacre
April 30

Catfish Camp
(Washington)

Wheeling
Fort Fincastle
Fort Henry

Grave Creek

Royal Oak

Stalnakers

Schoenbrunn

Newcomers Town
Delaware Village

Wakatomica
Shawnee Villages

Fort Gower

Burning Spring

Battle of
Point Pleasant
October 10

Rye Cove
(Blackburns)

John Floyd turned
300 acres of land for
George Mason April 18, 1774

Camp Charlotte

Chillicothe
Shawnee Village

Floyd surveyed
400-500 acres for
Patrick Henry,
May 2, 1774

FINCASTLE COUNTY

Big Sandy

Floyd surveyed
1000 acres
May 4, 1774

Floyd surveyed 1000 acres
May 11, 1774

Floyd surveyed 2000 acres
May 9, 1774

Limestone
(Maysville)

Floyd surveyed 800 acres
for Col. Preston, May 11, 1774

Big Bone Lick

Floyd surveyed 1000 acres
for William Christian,
May 11, 1774

Surveyors warned of
Indian War by messengers
from Pittsburgh, May 26, 1774

Several surveys
made May 13-15, 1774

Surveys made
May 20-June 8, 1774

Floyd and Taylor surveyed
many thousands of acres
here, July, 1774

Harrodsburg
Found destroyed July 14, 1774

Return route of surveyors

Floyd surveyed
several thousand
acres June, 1774

Falls of the Ohio
(Louisville)

Kentucky

Cumberland Gap

MILES
10   25   50

Drawn under the supervision of LOUISE PHELPS KELLOGG

PLATE 63

Dunmore's War

1774

PLATE 64

Concord and Lexington

April 18-19, 1775

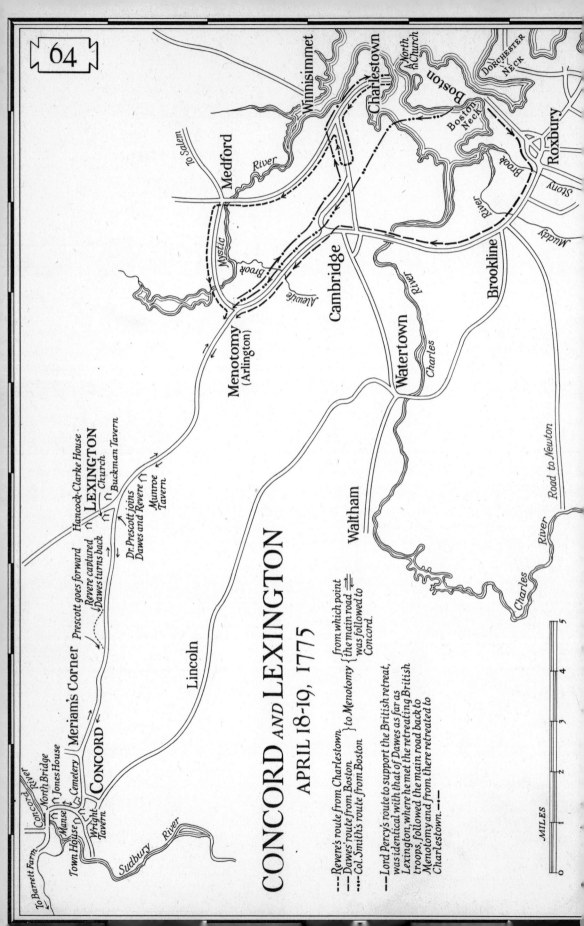

CONCORD AND LEXINGTON
APRIL 18-19, 1775

Boston

North A.Church

Dorchester Neck

Charlestown

Winnisimmet

Roxbury

Boston Neck

Stony

Brook

Muddy

River

Brookline

Medford

To Salem

River

Mystic

Brook

Cambridge

Alewive

Watertown

Charles River

Menotomy
(Arlington)

Waltham

Road to Newton

LEXINGTON
Church

Buckman Tavern

Munroe Tavern

Hancock-Clarke House

Dr. Prescott joins Dawes and Revere

Prescott goes forward

Revere captured
Dawes turns back

Lincoln

Charles River

Sudbury River

Meriam's Corner

CONCORD

Cemetery

Jones House

Manse

North Bridge

Concord River

To Barrett Farm

Town House

Wright Tavern

--- Revere's route from Charlestown.
--- Dawes's route from Boston.
···· Col. Smith's route from Boston.

} to Menotomy { from which point the main road was followed to Concord.

— Lord Percy's route to support the British retreat, was identical with that of Dawes as far as Lexington, where he met the retreating British troops, followed the main road back to Menotomy and from there retreated to Charlestown. ·—·

MILES

0 1 2 3 4 5

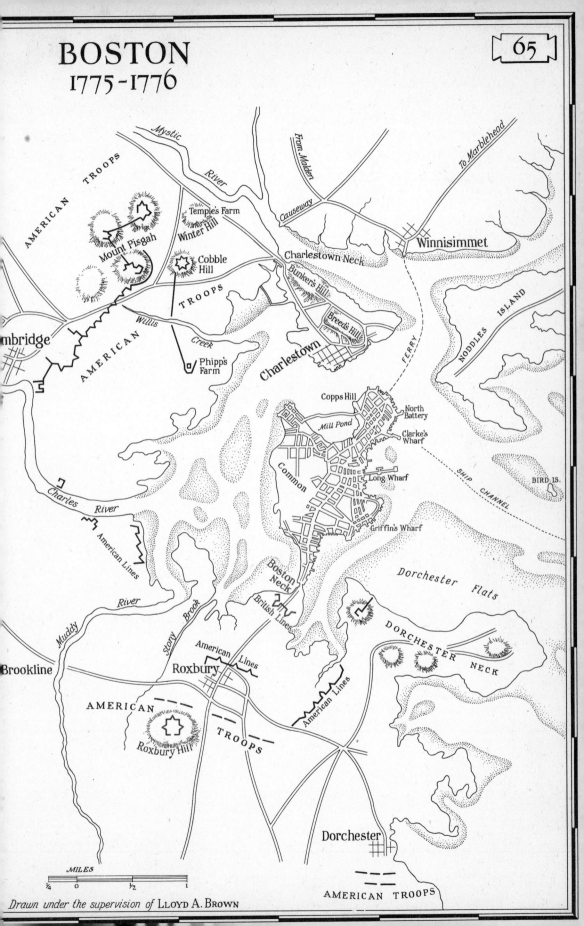

BOSTON
1775-1776

65

MILES

Drawn under the supervision of LLOYD A. BROWN

PLATE 65

Boston

1775–1776

PLATE 66

The
Thirteen Colonies

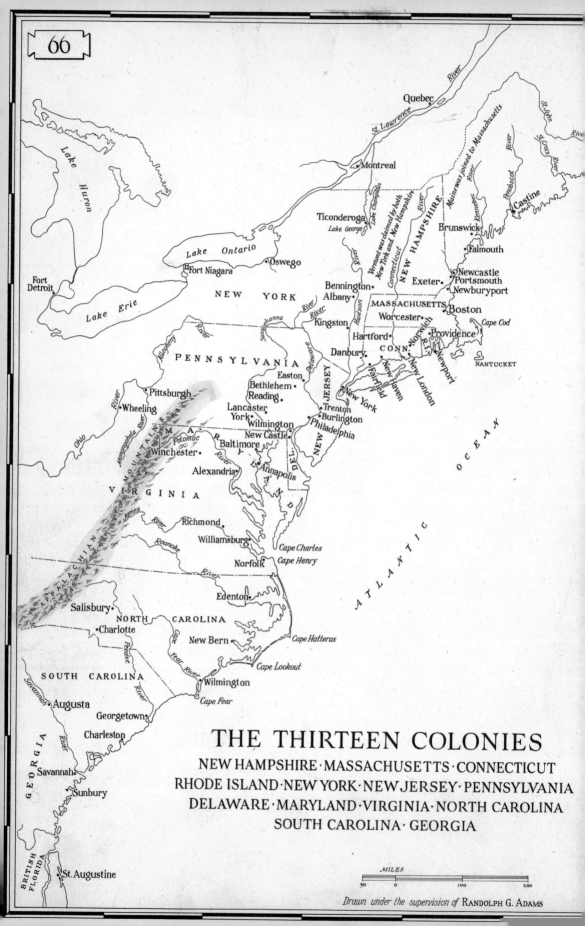

THE THIRTEEN COLONIES

NEW HAMPSHIRE · MASSACHUSETTS · CONNECTICUT
RHODE ISLAND · NEW YORK · NEW JERSEY · PENNSYLVANIA
DELAWARE · MARYLAND · VIRGINIA · NORTH CAROLINA
SOUTH CAROLINA · GEORGIA

MILES

Drawn under the supervision of RANDOLPH G. ADAMS

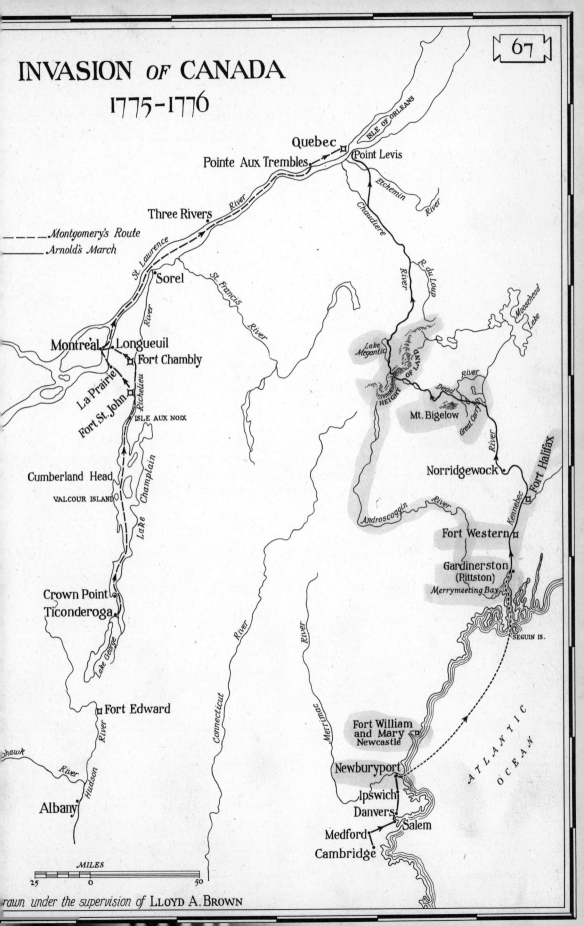

INVASION OF CANADA
1775–1776

Montgomery's Route ------
Arnold's March ———

ISLE OF ORLEANS

Quebec
Point Levis
Pointe Aux Trembles
Etchemin River
Chaudiere River
R. du Loup
St. Lawrence River
Three Rivers
Moosehead Lake
Sorel
St. Francis River
Lake Megantic
HEIGHT OF LAND
Dead River
Great Carry
Richelieu River
Montreal Longueuil
Fort Chambly
La Prairie
Fort St. John
ISLE AUX NOIX
Mt. Bigelow
Androscoggin River
Norridgewock
Fort Halifax
Kennebec River
Fort Western
Cumberland Head
VALCOUR ISLAND
Lake Champlain
Gardinerston
(Pittston)
Merrymeeting Bay
Crown Point
Ticonderoga
SEGUIN IS.
Lake George
Connecticut River
Merrimac River
Fort Edward
Fort William
and Mary
Newcastle
ATLANTIC OCEAN
Mohawk River
Hudson River
Newburyport
Ipswich
Albany
Danvers
Salem
Medford
Cambridge

MILES
25   0   50

Drawn under the supervision of LLOYD A. BROWN

PLATE 67

Invasion of Canada

1775–1776

PLATE 68

Moores Creek Bridge

Feb. 27, 1776

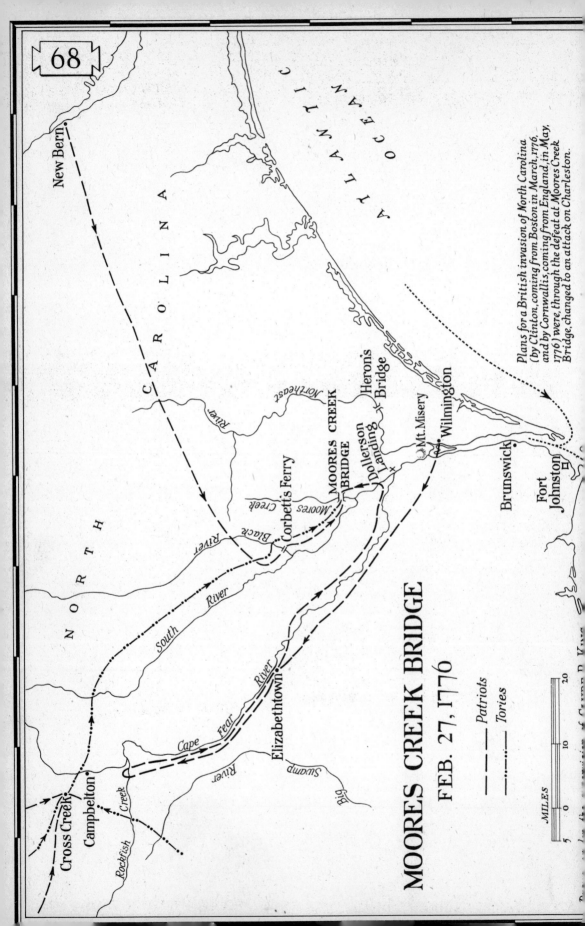

ATLANTIC OCEAN

NORTH CAROLINA

New Bern

Northeast River

Heron's Bridge

Dollerson Landing

MOORES CREEK BRIDGE

Corbetts Ferry

Moores Creek

Black Creek

River

Mt. Misery

Wilmington

Brunswick

Fort Johnston

South River

River

Elizabethtown

Cape Fear River

Swamp

Big River

Campbelton

Cross Creek

Rockfish Creek

Plans for a British invasion of North Carolina (by Clinton, coming from Boston in March, 1776, and by Cornwallis, coming from England in May, 1776) were, through the defeat at Moores Creek Bridge, changed to an attack on Charleston.

MOORES CREEK BRIDGE
FEB. 27, 1776

Patriots — — —
Tories ··—··—

MILES
5   0   10   20

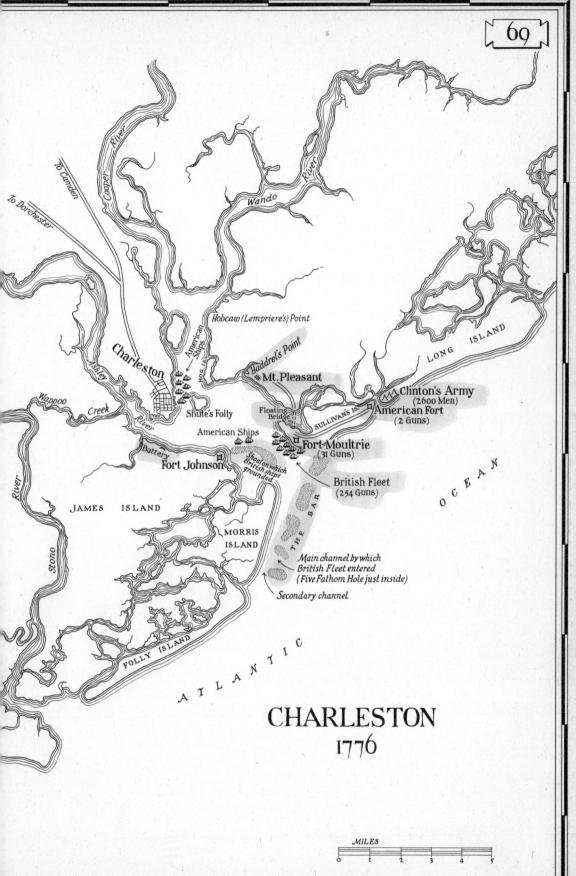

To Camden

To Dorchester

Cooper River

Wando River

Ashley River

Charleston

Hobcaw (Lempriere's) Point

Haddrel's Point

Mt. Pleasant

HOG IS.

American Ships

Shute's Folly

Floating Bridge

SULLIVAN'S IS.

LONG ISLAND

Clinton's Army
(2600 Men)

American Fort
(2 Guns)

American Ships

Fort Moultrie
(31 Guns)

Battery

Fort Johnson

Shoal on which
British ships
grounded

British Fleet
(254 Guns)

OCEAN

Wappoo Creek

JAMES ISLAND

MORRIS
ISLAND

THE BAR

Main channel by which
British Fleet entered
(Five Fathom Hole just inside)

Secondary channel

Stono River

FOLLY ISLAND

A T L A N T I C

CHARLESTON
1776

MILES

0 1 2 3 4 5

Drawn under the supervision of D.D. WALLACE

PLATE 69

Charleston

1776

PLATE 70

New York

1776

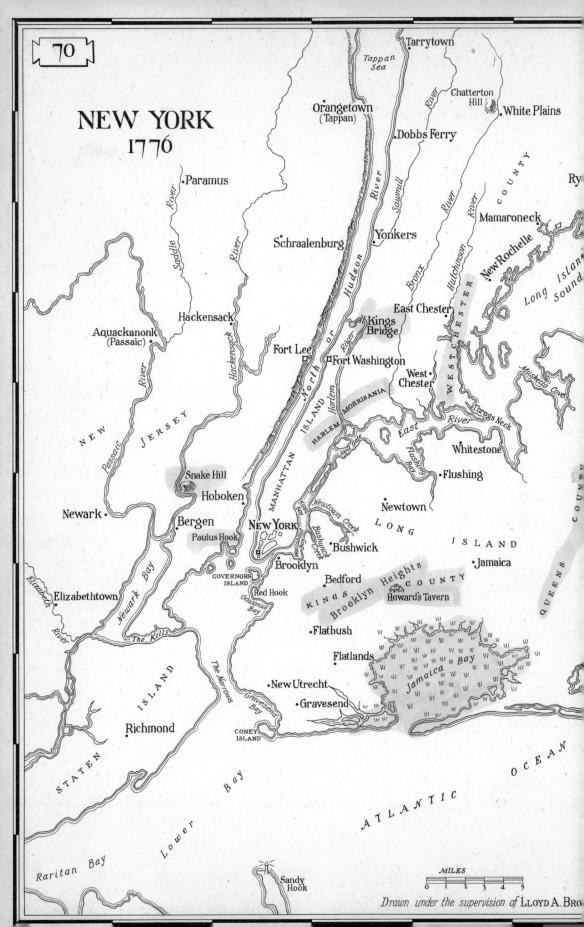

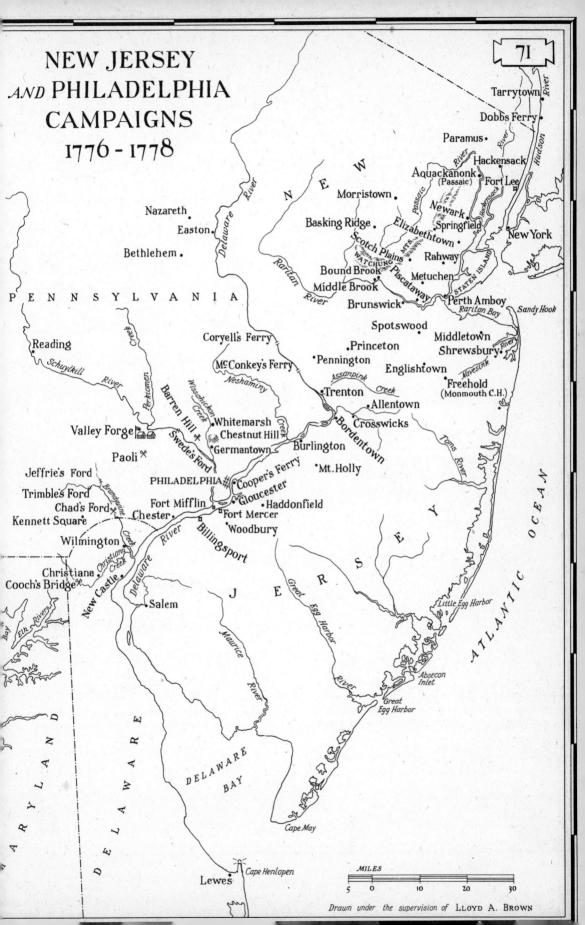

NEW JERSEY AND PHILADELPHIA CAMPAIGNS 1776 - 1778

PENNSYLVANIA

NEW JERSEY

MARYLAND

DELAWARE

ATLANTIC OCEAN

Tarrytown
Dobbs Ferry
Paramus
Hackensack
Aquackanonk (Passaic)
Fort Lee
Morristown
Newark
Basking Ridge
Elizabethtown
Springfield
New York
Scotch Plains
Rahway
Bound Brook
Piscataway
Metuchen
Middle Brook
Staten Island
Brunswick
Perth Amboy
Raritan Bay
Sandy Hook
Spotswood
Middletown
Shrewsbury
Princeton
Pennington
Englishtown
Freehold (Monmouth C.H.)
Trenton
Allentown
Bordentown
Crosswicks
Nazareth
Easton
Bethlehem
Reading
Coryell's Ferry
McConkey's Ferry
Neshaminy
Valley Forge
Whitemarsh
Chestnut Hill
Barren Hill
Swede's Ford
Germantown
Burlington
Mt. Holly
Paoli
PHILADELPHIA
Cooper's Ferry
Jeffrie's Ford
Gloucester
Trimble's Ford
Fort Mifflin
Haddonfield
Chad's Ford
Chester
Fort Mercer
Kennett Square
Billingsport
Woodbury
Wilmington
Christiana
New Castle
Cooch's Bridge
Salem

Delaware River
Raritan River
Passaic River
Hackensack River
Hudson River
Schuylkill River
Perkiomen Creek
Wissahickon Creek
Brandywine Creek
Christiana Creek
Assanpink Creek
Navesink River
Toms River
Maurice River
Great Egg Harbor River
Elk River

Little Egg Harbor
Absecon Inlet
Great Egg Harbor
Cape May
DELAWARE BAY
Cape Henlopen
Lewes

WATCHUNG MTS.

MILES
5   0   10   20   30

Drawn under the supervision of LLOYD A. BROWN

PLATE 71

New Jersey and Philadelphia Campaigns

1776–1778

PLATE 72

Burgoyne's Invasion

1777

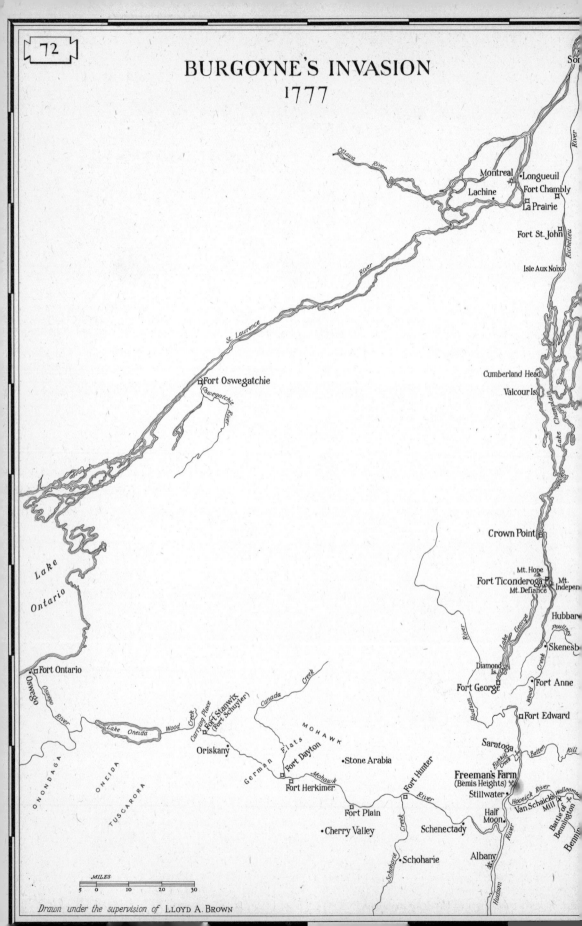

BURGOYNE'S INVASION
1777

Ottawa River

St. Lawrence River

Montreal
Lachine
•Longueuil
Fort Chambly
La Prairie
Fort St. John
Isle Aux Noix
Richelieu

Fort Oswegatchie

Oswegatchie River

Cumberland Head
Valcour Is.

Lake Champlain

Lake Ontario

Crown Point

Mt. Hope
Fort Ticonderoga
Mt. Defiance
Mt. Independen

Hubbar

Lake George

poultn

Skenesb

Diamond Is.

Fort George

Wood Creek

•Fort Anne

Fort Ontario

Oswego River

Carrying Place
Fort Stanwix
(Fort Schuyler)

Canada Creek

Hudson River

Fort Edward

Saratoga

Battet

Kill

Lake Oneida

Wood Creek

MOHAWK

Fishkill Creek

Oriskany

German Flats

Fort Dayton

•Stone Arabia

Fort Hunter

Freeman's Farm
(Bemis Heights)

Hoosick River

Walloomse

ONONDAGA

ONEIDA

Mohawk River

Fort Herkimer

River

Stillwater

Van Schaick's
Mill

Battle of
Bennington

TUSCARORA

Fort Plain

Half
Moon

Schenectady

Bennin

•Cherry Valley

Schoharie Creek

•Schoharie

Albany

Hudson River

MILES
5 0   10   20   30

Drawn under the supervision of LLOYD A. BROWN

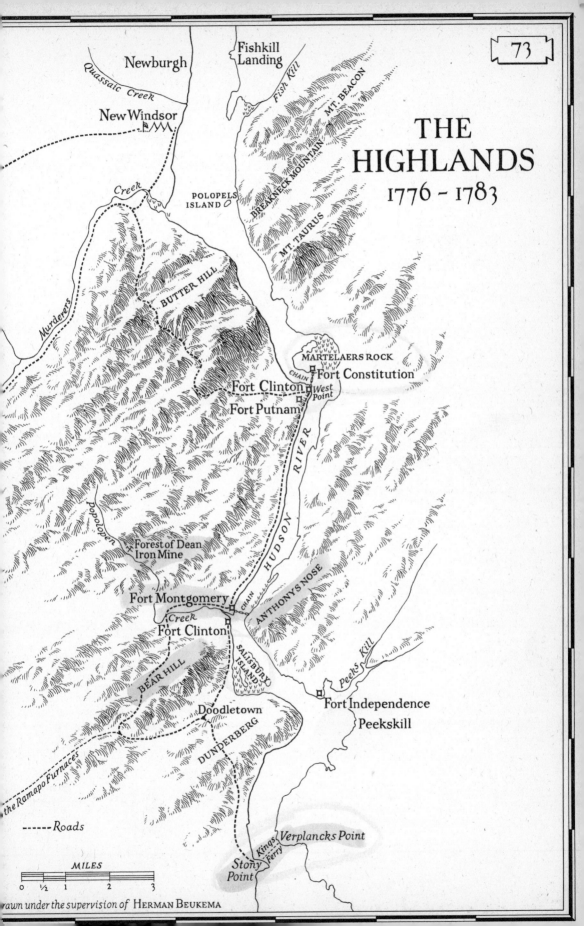

Newburgh

Quassaic Creek

Fishkill Landing

Fish Kill

MT. BEACON

New Windsor

THE
HIGHLANDS
1776 - 1783

Creek

POLOPELS ISLAND

BREAKNECK MOUNTAIN

MT. TAURUS

Murderers

BUTTER HILL

MARTELAERS ROCK

CHAIN

Fort Constitution

Fort Clinton

West Point

Fort Putnam

HUDSON RIVER

Popolopen

Forest of Dean Iron Mine

CHAIN

Fort Montgomery

ANTHONYS NOSE

Creek

Fort Clinton

SALISBURY ISLAND

Peeks Kill

BEAR HILL

Fort Independence

Doodletown

Peekskill

DUNDERBERG

the Ramapo Furnaces

------ Roads

MILES

0   ½   1   2   3

Kings Ferry

Verplancks Point

Stony Point

rawn under the supervision of HERMAN BEUKEMA

PLATE 73

The Highlands

1776-1783

PLATE 74

The Revolutionary War in the South

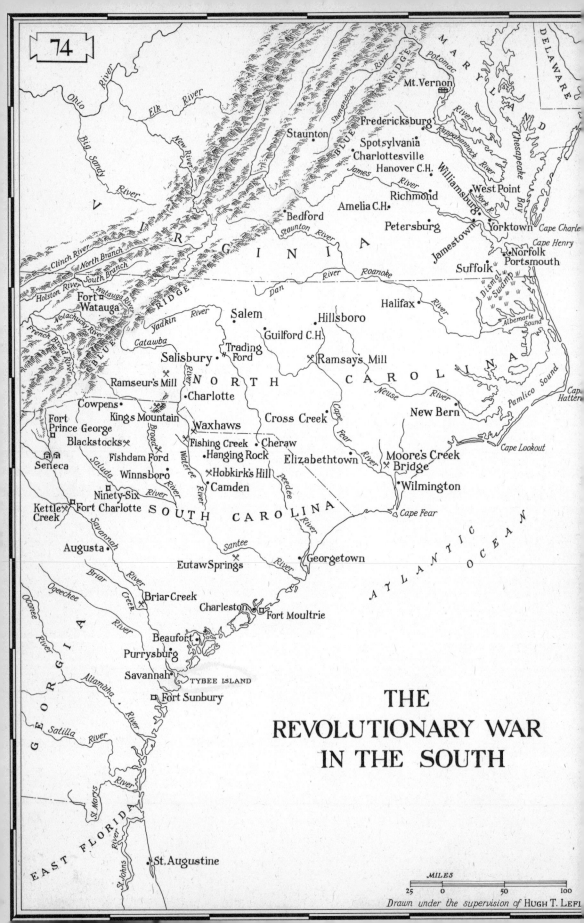

74

THE
REVOLUTIONARY WAR
IN THE SOUTH

MILES

25   0   50   100

Drawn under the supervision of HUGH T. LEFI

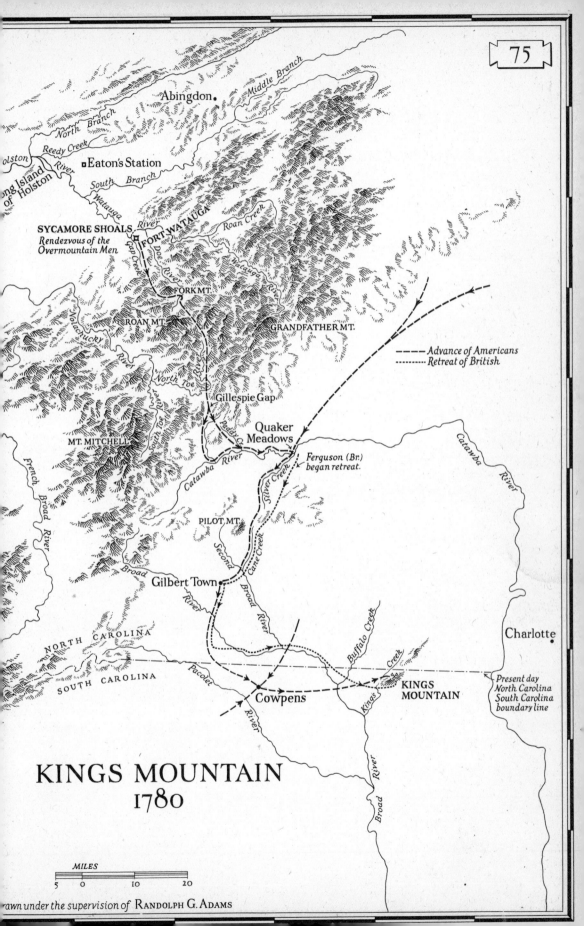

Abingdon.

Middle Branch

North Branch

Reedy Creek

olston

River

Long Island of Holston

□ Eaton's Station

South Branch

Watauga

River

Roan Creek

SYCAMORE SHOALS
Rendezvous of the Overmountain Men

FORT WATAUGA

Gap Creek

Doe River

Watauga River

FORK MT.

ROAN MT.

GRANDFATHER MT.

Nolachucky

River

- - - *Advance of Americans*
········· *Retreat of British*

North Toe

Gillespie Gap

MT. MITCHELL

South Toe River

Paddy Cr.

Quaker Meadows

Ferguson (Br.) began retreat.

Catawba River

Silver Creek

Catawba River

PILOT MT.

French Broad River

Second Broad

Cane Creek

Broad River

Gilbert Town

NORTH CAROLINA

River

Pacolet

SOUTH CAROLINA

Buffalo Creek

Kings Creek

Charlotte

Present day North Carolina South Carolina boundary line

Cowpens

River

KINGS MOUNTAIN

Kings

River

Broad River

KINGS MOUNTAIN
1780

MILES

5 0 10 20

rawn under the supervision of RANDOLPH G. ADAMS

PLATE 75

Kings Mountain

1780

PLATE 76

Cherokee-Creek
Country

1760–1781

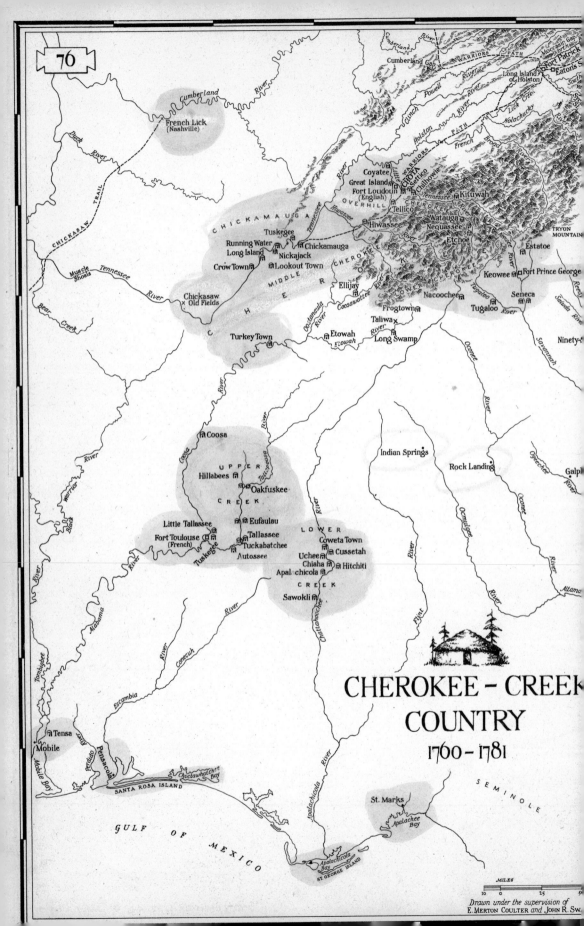

Cumberland Gap

WARRIORS·PATH

Moccasin Gap

Fort Patrick

Eatons S.

Cumberland River

Long Island of Holston

Powell River

Clinch River

South

French Lick (Nashville)

Holston River

French Broad River

Lick Creek

Nolachucky

Duke River

Chickasaw Trail

Coyatee

Great Island

Fort Loudoun (English)

CHOTA

Settico

Chilhowie

OVERHILL

Tellico

Hiwassee

Kituwah

Watauga

Nequassee

Etchoe

TRYON MOUNTAIN

Muscle Shoals

Tennessee River

Bear Creek

Cumberland River

CHICKAMAUGA

Tuskegee

Running Water

Long Island

Nickajack

Chickamauga

Crow Town

Lookout Town

MIDDLE

CHEROKEE

LOWER CHEROKEE

Estatoe

Keowee

Fort Prince George

Seneca

Tugaloo

Sauda River

Reedy

Ellijay

Nacoochee

Chickasaw Old Fields

Oostanaula River

Coosawattee River

Frogtown

Taliwa

Etowah

Etowah River

Long Swamp

Turkey Town

Oconee River

Savannah

Ninety-

Coosa

Indian Springs

Rock Landing

Galp

Ocmulgee River

Oconee River

Ogechee River

UPPER

Hillabees

Oakfuskee

CREEK

Coosa River

Tallapoosa River

Little Tallassee

Eufaulau

Fort Toulouse (French)

Tuskegee

Tallassee

Tuckabatchee

Autossee

LOWER

Coweta Town

Cussetah

Uchee

Chiaha

Hitchiti

Apalachicola

CREEK

Sawokli

Chattahoochee River

Flint River

Altama

River

Warrior River

Black River

Alabama River

Conecuh River

Tensa

Mobile

Tombigbee River

Escambia River

Perdido River

Pensacola

Perdido River

Santa Rosa Island

Choctawhatchee Bay

SEMINOLE

St. Marks

Apalachee Bay

Apalachicola Bay

St. George Island

GULF   OF   MEXICO

CHEROKEE – CREEK
COUNTRY
1760 – 1781

MILES

10   0   25

Drawn under the supervision of
E. MERTON COULTER *and* JOHN R. SW

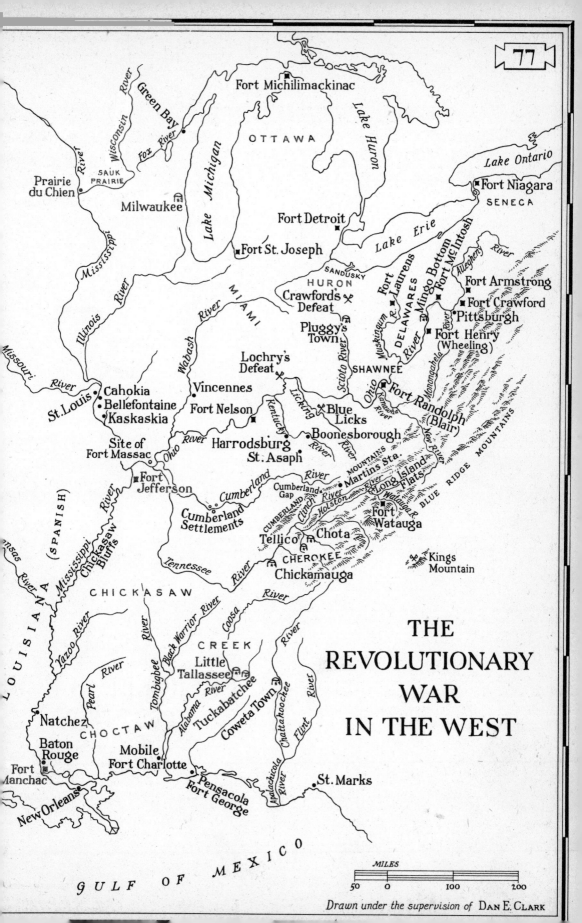

Fort Michilimackinac

Green Bay

Wisconsin River

Fox River

OTTAWA

Lake Huron

Lake Ontario

Fort Niagara

SENECA

SAUK PRAIRIE

Prairie du Chien

Milwaukee

Lake Michigan

Fort Detroit

Fort St. Joseph

Lake Erie

Fort McIntosh

Allegheny River

Fort Armstrong

Fort Crawford

Pittsburgh

Mississippi River

Illinois River

MIAMI River

SANDUSKY

HURON

Crawford's Defeat

Fort Laurens

Mingo Bottom

DELAWARES

Muskingum River

Fort Henry (Wheeling)

Missouri River

Wabash River

Pluggy's Town

Scioto River

SHAWNEE

Monongahela River

River

Lochry's Defeat

Licking River

Ohio

Kanawha River

Fort Randolph (Blair)

Cahokia

Vincennes

Blue Licks

St. Louis

Bellefontaine

Fort Nelson

Kentucky River

Boonesborough

New River

Kaskaskia

River

Harrodsburg

St. Asaph

River

MOUNTAINS

Martins Sta.

BLUE RIDGE MOUNTAINS

Site of Fort Massac

Ohio

Cumberland River

Cumberland Gap

Long Island Flats

Fort Jefferson

Clinch River

Holston River

Watauga R.

LOUISIANA (SPANISH)

Mississippi River

Cumberland Settlements

CUMBERLAND

Tellico

Chota

Fort Watauga

Chickasaw Bluffs

Tennessee River

CHEROKEE

Kings Mountain

Arkansas River

CHICKASAW

Chickamauga

River

River

CREEK

Coosa River

Black Warrior River

Yazoo River

Little Tallassee

River

Pearl River

Tombigbee River

CHOCTAW

Alabama River

Tuckabatchee

Coweta Town

Chattahoochee River

Flint River

THE
REVOLUTIONARY
WAR
IN THE WEST

Natchez

Baton Rouge

Fort Manchac

Mobile

Fort Charlotte

Pensacola
Fort George

Apalachicola River

St. Marks

New Orleans

MILES

50   0   100   200

G U L F   O F   M E X I C O

Drawn under the supervision of DAN E. CLARK

PLATE 77

The Revolutionary
War in the West

PLATE 78

Iroquois Frontier

1768–1780

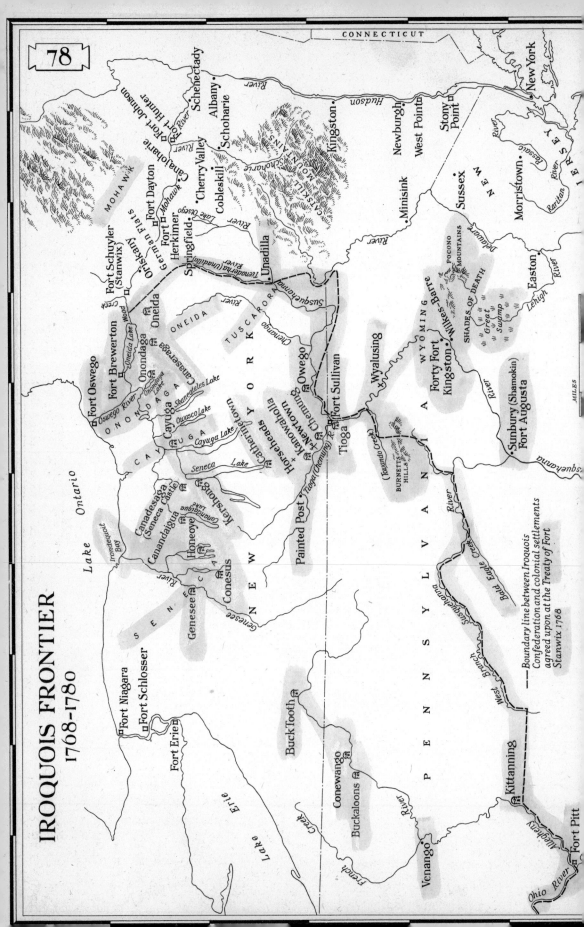

IROQUOIS FRONTIER
1768-1780

CONNECTICUT

New York

Schenectady
Albany
Schoharie
Kingston
Newburgh
West Point
Stony Point
Morristown

Fort Johnson
Fort Hunter
Canajoharie
Cherry Valley
Cobleskill
Springfield
Fort Dayton
Fort Herkimer
German Flats

CATSKILL MOUNTAINS

Hudson River
Schoharie River
Mohawk River

Minisink
Sussex
Raritan River
Passaic River

NEW JERSEY

Fort Schuyler (Stanwix)
Oneida
Fort Brewerton
Fort Oswego
Onondaga
Oneida Lake
Wood Creek
Oriskany

Unadilla
Trenaderaha (Unadilla) River
Susquehanna River

Pocono Mountains
Delaware River
Lehigh River
Easton

ONEIDA
TUSCARORA

ONONDAGA
Onondaga Lake
Oswego River
Cazenovia
Owasco Lake
Skaneateles Lake

Cayuga
Cayuga Lake

Owego
Fort Sullivan
Chenango River

Wyalusing

WYOMING
Forty Fort
Wilkes-Barre
Kingston

SHADES OF DEATH
Great Swamp

CAYUGA

Catharinetown
Newtown
Kanawholia
Chemung
Horseheads
Tioga (Chemung) R.
Painted Post
Tioga

Seneca Lake
Kershong

BURNETTS HILLS
(Towando Creek)

P E N N S Y L V A N I A

Sunbury (Shamokin)
Fort Augusta

Susquehanna River

Canadesaga (Seneca Castle)
Canandaigua Lake
Canandaigua
Honeoye
Conesus

Irondequoit Bay

Genesee River
SENECA

NEW YORK

Lake Ontario

Fort Niagara
Fort Schlosser
Fort Erie

BuckTooth

Conewango
Buckaloons

Venango

Lake Erie

Kittanning

West Branch
Susquehanna
Bald Eagle Creek

Allegheny River
French Creek
Ohio River
Fort Pitt

MILES

–—–— Boundary line between Iroquois
Confederation and colonial settlements
agreed upon at the Treaty of Fort
Stanwix 1768

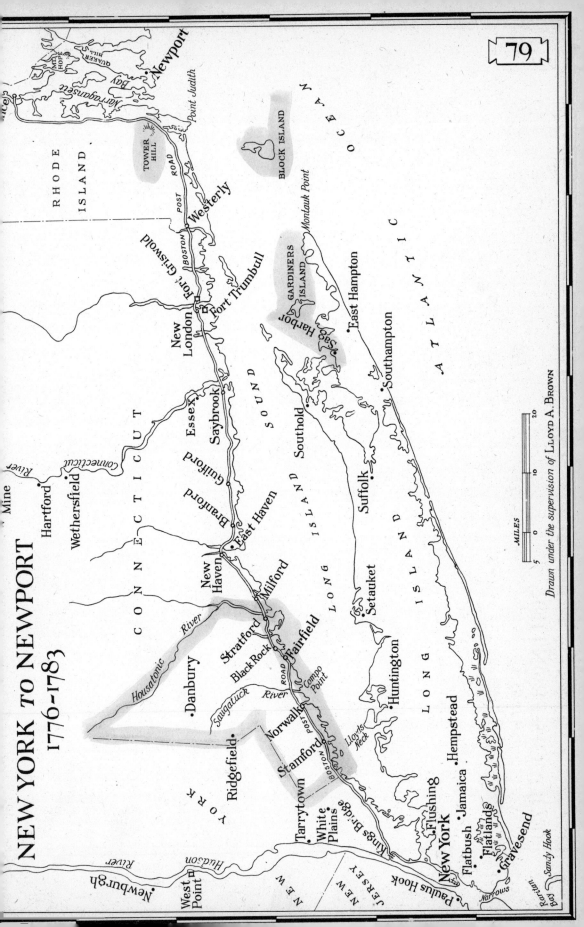

NEW YORK TO NEWPORT
1776-1783

Drawn under the supervision of Lloyd A. Brown

MILES
5 10 20

RHODE ISLAND

Newport

Narragansett Bay

MT. HOPE
QUAKER HILL

Point Judith

TOWER HILL

BLOCK ISLAND

ATLANTIC OCEAN

Westerly

BOSTON POST ROAD

Fort Griswold

Fort Trumbull

New London

Montauk Point

GARDINERS ISLAND

Sag Harbor

East Hampton

Southampton

CONNECTICUT

Essex

Saybrook

Guilford

Branford

East Haven

SOUND

Southold

Suffolk

Setauket

LONG ISLAND

Connecticut River

Hartford

Wethersfield

Mine

River

Housatonic River

New Haven

Milford

Stratford

Black Rock

Fairfield

Compo Point

Saugatuck River

ROAD

Danbury

Norwalk

BOSTON POST ROAD

Stamford

Ridgefield

Huntington

Lloyds Neck

LONG ISLAND

Hempstead

Flushing

Jamaica

Flatbush

Flatlands

Gravesend

NEW YORK

YORK

Tarrytown

White Plains

Kings Bridge

New York

Paulus Hook

NEW JERSEY

West Point

Newburgh

Hudson River

Sandy Hook

Raritan Bay

Narrows

PLATE 79

New York to Newport

1776–1783

PLATE 80

The March to Yorktown and Battle of Chesapeake Capes

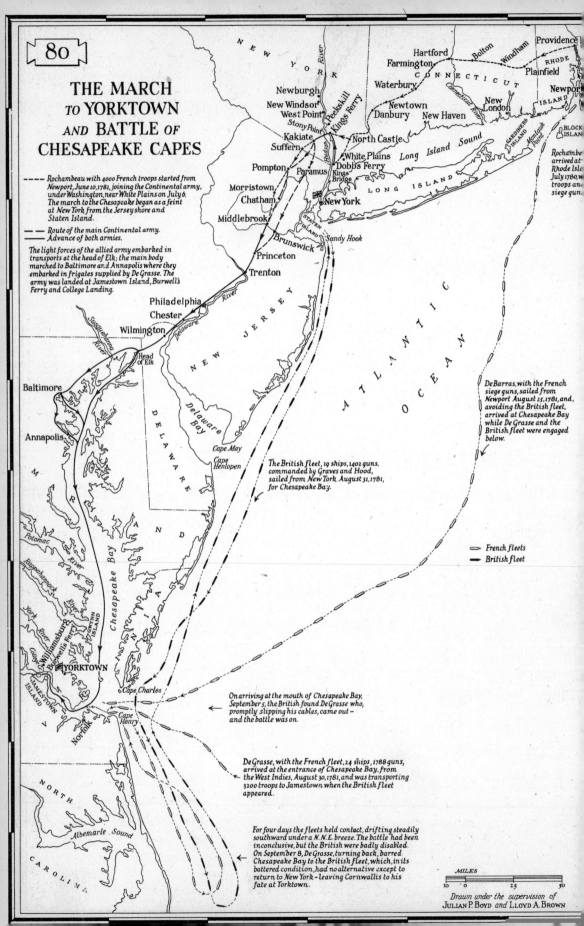

THE MARCH
TO YORKTOWN
AND BATTLE OF
CHESAPEAKE CAPES

- - - - Rochambeau with 4000 French troops started from
 Newport, June 10, 1781, joining the Continental army,
 under Washington, near White Plains on July 6.
 The march to the Chesapeake began as a feint
 at New York from the Jersey shore and
 Staten Island.

———— Route of the main Continental army.
 Advance of both armies.

The light forces of the allied army embarked in
transports at the head of Elk; the main body
marched to Baltimore and Annapolis where they
embarked in frigates supplied by De Grasse. The
army was landed at Jamestown Island, Burwell's
Ferry and College Landing.

Rochambeau
arrived at
Rhode Isle
July 1780, w
troops an
siege gun.

De Barras, with the French
siege guns, sailed from
Newport August 25, 1781, and,
avoiding the British fleet,
arrived at Chesapeake Bay
while De Grasse and the
British fleet were engaged
below.

The British fleet, 19 ships, 1401 guns,
commanded by Graves and Hood,
sailed from New York August 31, 1781,
for Chesapeake Bay.

◁═ French fleets
━━ British fleet

On arriving at the mouth of Chesapeake Bay,
September 5, the British found De Grasse who,
promptly slipping his cables, came out —
and the battle was on.

De Grasse, with the French fleet, 24 ships, 1788 guns,
arrived at the entrance of Chesapeake Bay, from
the West Indies, August 30, 1781, and was transporting
3200 troops to Jamestown when the British fleet
appeared.

For four days the fleets held contact, drifting steadily
southward under a N.N.E. breeze. The battle had been
inconclusive, but the British were badly disabled.
On September 8, De Grasse, turning back, barred
Chesapeake Bay to the British fleet, which, in its
battered condition, had no alternative except to
return to New York — leaving Cornwallis to his
fate at Torktown.

MILES
10 0   25   50

Drawn under the supervision of
JULIAN P. BOYD and LLOYD A. BROWN

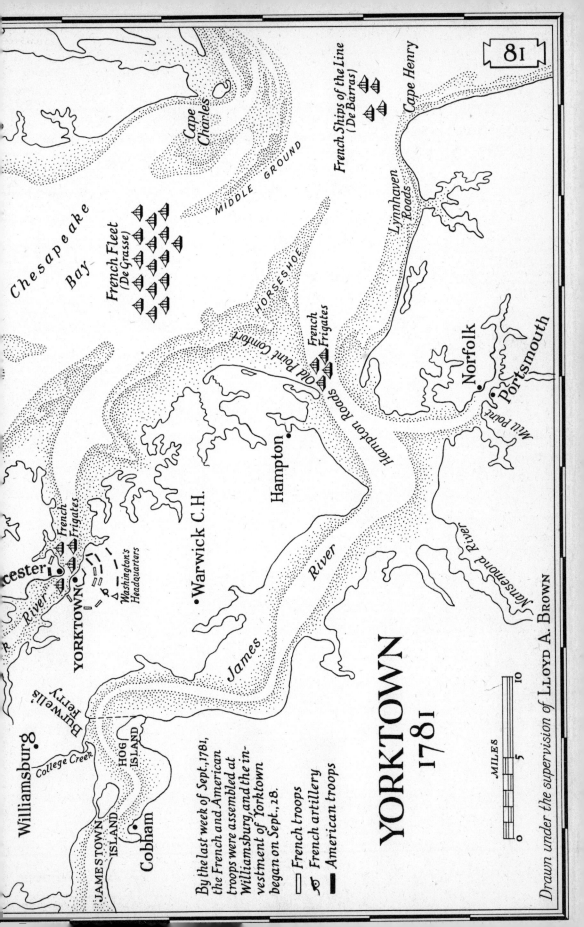

81

French Ships of the Line
(De Barras)

Cape Henry

Cape Charles

MIDDLE GROUND

Lynnhaven Roads

Chesapeake Bay

French Fleet
(De Grasse)

HORSESHOE

French Frigates

Old Point Comfort

Norfolk

Portsmouth

Hampton Roads

Mill Point

Hampton

Warwick C.H.

James River

Nansemond River

French Frigates

Williamsburg

Burwell's Ferry

College Creek

JAMESTOWN ISLAND

HOG ISLAND

Cobham

Gloucester

R. River

YORKTOWN

Washington's Headquarters

By the last week of Sept., 1781,
the French and American
troops were assembled at
Williamsburg, and the in-
vestment of Yorktown
began on Sept., 28.

French troops
French artillery
American troops

YORKTOWN
1781

MILES
0 5 10

Drawn under the supervision of LLOYD A. BROWN

PLATE 81

Yorktown

1781

PLATE 82

The United States

1783–1802

THE UNITED STATES, 1783–1802

Lake of the Woods

INDEFINITE BOUNDARY

Grand Portage

Lake Superior

Fort Michilimackinac

CANADA

St. Lawrence River

INDEFINITE BOUNDARY

St. John

St. Croix River

MAINE
(Joined to Mass.)

Pte. au Fer
Oswegatchie
Fort Haldimand

Montpelier

VT. (Admitted 1791)

Connecticut River

NEW HAMPSHIRE

Portland

Concord

NORTHWEST

INDIANA

Green Bay

Lake Michigan

NORTHWEST TERRITORY

DIVISION LINE OF 1800

Detroit

Fort Miamis

Lake Huron

Lake Erie

Maumee River

River

1787

TERRITORY 1800

Lake Ontario

Fort Ontario
Oswego

Fort Niagara

NEW YORK

Albany

Hudson River

Mohawk River

Boston

MASS.

Providence

Hartford

CONN.

New Haven

Albany

TERRITORY

Fort Recovery

1800

Wabash River

Miami River

Ohio River

PENNSYLVANIA

Pittsburgh

Allegheny River

Monongahela River

Susquehanna River

NEW JERSEY

Trenton

New York

Philadelphia

Wilmington

DEL.

LOUISIANA

Cahokia
Kaskaskia

Vincennes

Cincinnati

Marietta

Kentucky River

Baltimore

MARYLAND

Potomac River

Washington

Annapolis

Ohio River

KENTUCKY
(Admitted 1792)

SOUTH OF THE RIVER OHIO

Cumberland River

VIRGINIA

James River

Richmond

Roanoke River

TERRITORY

Fort San Fernando
(Spanish)

Nashville

TENNESSEE
(Admitted 1796)

Tennessee River

NORTH CAROLINA

Raleigh

Mississippi River

Yazoo River

Fort Nogales
(Spanish)

Tombigbee River

NORTHERN SPANISH CLAIM UNTIL 1795

GEORGIA

Coosa River

River

SOUTH CAROLINA

Columbia

Savannah River

SPANISH

MISSISSIPPI

Natchez
Fort Adams

TERRITORY
(1798)

Alabama River

Chattahoochee River

Flint River

Savannah

St. Marys River

SPANISH

FLORIDA

GULF OF MEXICO

ATLANTIC OCEAN

The Northwest Territory of 1787 was formed from Western
Lands claimed by NEW YORK, through questionable Indi[an]
cessions (ceded to the U.S. in 1782); by VIRGINIA, throu[gh]
the Charter of 1609, giving limits from "sea to sea, west an[d]
northwest," and through conquest (ceded to the U.S. in 178[4],
with the exception of the Virginia Military District, see Pl[ate]
by MASSACHUSETTS, through the Charter of 1629, givin[g]
limits from sea to sea (ceded to the U.S. in 1785); by
CONNECTICUT, through the Charter of 1662, giving lim[its]
from sea to sea (ceded to the U.S. in 1786, with the except[ion]
of the Western Reserve, see Plate 85).

KENTUCKY was a part of Virginia until admitted as a
separate state in 1792 (see Plate 84). West Virginia did not e[xist].

TENNESSEE was a part of North Carolina until admitt[ed]
as a state in 1796 (see Plate 84).

For the Western Land claims of South Carolina
and Georgia, see Plates 88–89.

MILES
50   0   100   200   300

Drawn under the supervision of O. M. DICKERSON and FRANCIS P. WEISENBURGER

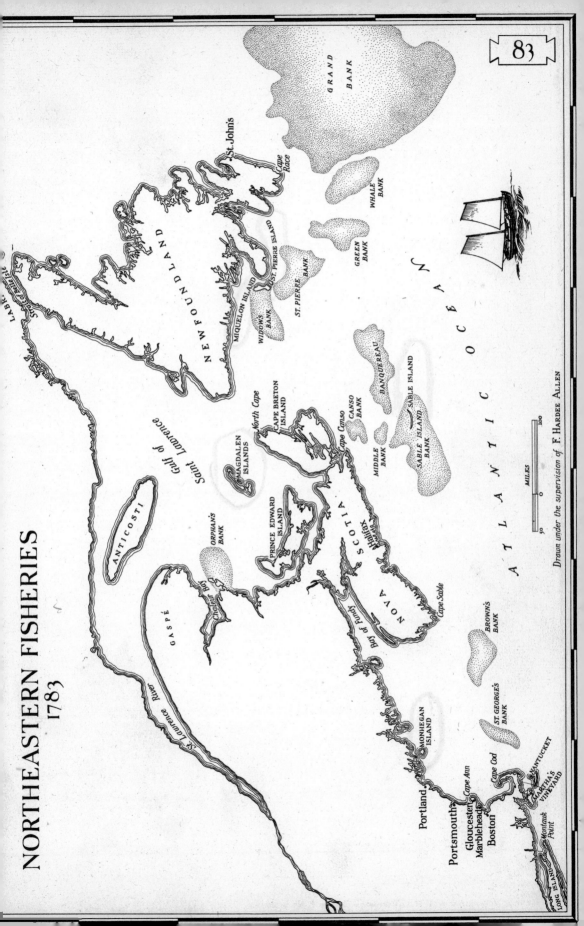

NORTHEASTERN FISHERIES
1783

83

Drawn under the supervision of F. Hardee Allen

GRAND BANK

St. John's

Cape Race

WHALE BANK

GREEN BANK

ST. PIERRE ISLAND

ST. PIERRE BANK

MIQUELON ISLAND

WIDOWS BANK

NEWFOUNDLAND

LABRADOR

Strait of Belle Isle

Gulf of Saint Laurence

ANTICOSTI

North Cape

MAGDALEN ISLANDS

CAPE BRETON ISLAND

Cape Canso

CANSO BANK

BANQUEREAU

SABLE ISLAND

SABLE ISLAND BANK

MIDDLE BANK

PRINCE EDWARD ISLAND

ORPHAN'S BANK

Chaleur Bay

GASPÉ

St. Laurence River

SCOTIA

Halifax

NOVA

Bay of Fundy

Cape Sable

BROWN'S BANK

MONHEGAN ISLAND

Portland

Cape Ann

Portsmouth

Gloucester

Marblehead

Boston

Cape Cod

ST. GEORGE'S BANK

NANTUCKET

MARTHA'S VINEYARD

Montauk Point

LONG ISLAND

ATLANTIC OCEAN

MILES
50 0 100

PLATE 83

Northeastern Fisheries

1783

PLATE 84

State of Franklin
and
Cumberland Settlements

1779–1796

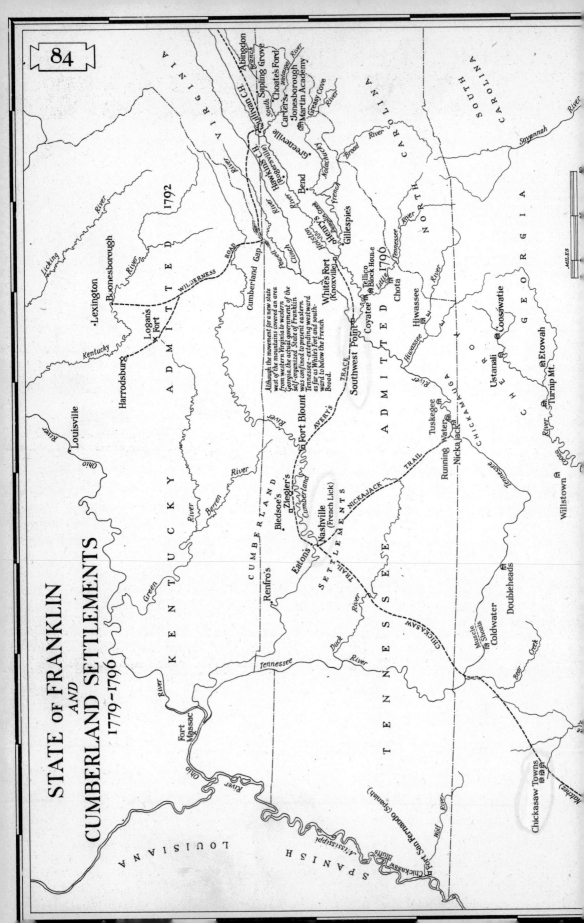

STATE OF FRANKLIN
AND
CUMBERLAND SETTLEMENTS
1779–1796

84

Although the movement for a new state west of the mountains covered an area from western Virginia to western Georgia, the actual government of the self-organized State of Franklin was confined to present eastern Tennessee—extending westward as far as White's Fort and southward to below the French Broad.

VIRGINIA

NORTH CAROLINA

SOUTH CAROLINA

GEORGIA

KENTUCKY

TENNESSEE

LOUISIANA

SPANISH

CHEROKEE

ADMITTED 1792

ADMITTED 1796

Abingdon
Sapling Grove
Sullivan C.H.
Choate's Ford
South
Carter's
Holston River
Jonesborough
Martin Academy
Greeneville
Grassy Cove
Greasy Cove
Hawkins C.H.
Bend
Nolachucky River
Watauga River
French Broad
Gillespies
White's Fort (Knoxville)
Little 1790
Tellico
Block House
Coyatee
Chota
Hiwassee
Coosawatie
Ustanali
Turnip Mt.
Etowah
Willstown
Doubleheads
Coldwater
Muscle Shoals
Running Water
Nickajack
Tuskegee
NICKAJACK
Southwest Point
Fort Blount
AVERY'S
TRACE
Ziegler's
Bledsoe's
Nashville (French Lick)
Eaton's
Renfros
CUMBERLAND
CHICKAMAUGA
CHICKASAW TRAIL
TRAIL
Lexington
Boonesborough
Logan's Fort
Harrodsburg
Louisville
Fort Massac
Licking River
Kentucky River
Green River
Barren River
Cumberland Gap
WILDERNESS ROAD
Powell's River
Clinch River
Holston River
Broad
Nolachucky
French Broad
Tennessee River
Little Tennessee River
Hiwassee River
Coosa River
Savannah River
Chattooga
Tennessee
Duck River
Beaver Creek
CUMBERLAND SETTLEMENTS
Ohio River
Mississippi River
Wolf River
Chickasaw Bluffs
Fort San Fernando (Spanish)
Chickasaw Towns
Natchez
Savannah

MILES

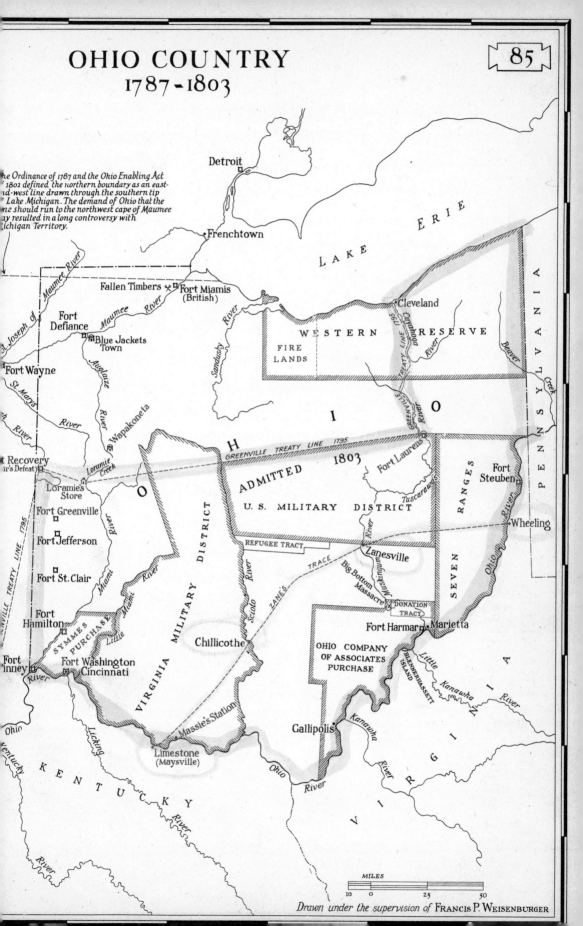

OHIO COUNTRY
1787-1803

The Ordinance of 1787 and the Ohio Enabling Act
of 1802 defined the northern boundary as an east-
and-west line drawn through the southern tip
of Lake Michigan. The demand of Ohio that the
line should run to the northwest cape of Maumee
Bay resulted in a long controversy with
Michigan Territory.

Detroit

Frenchtown

LAKE ERIE

Maumee River

Fallen Timbers ✕ ⊡ Fort Miamis
(British)

Fort
Defiance

⊡ Blue Jackets
Town

St. Joseph of the Maumee River

Maumee River

Sandusky River

Cleveland

WESTERN   RESERVE

FIRE
LANDS

Cuyahoga River

Greenville Treaty Line 1795

Beaver Creek

PENNSYLVANIA

Fort Wayne

St. Marys River

Auglaize River

⊡ Wapakoneta

O   H   I   O

Greenville Treaty Line 1795

ADMITTED   1803

Fort Laurens

Fort
Steuben

St. Marys River

Loramie Creek

Ft. Recovery
St. Clair's Defeat

Loramie's
Store

Fort Greenville

Fort Jefferson

Fort St. Clair

U. S. MILITARY DISTRICT

REFUGEE TRACT

ZANE'S   TRACE

Tuscarawas River

SEVEN   RANGES

Ohio River

Wheeling

GREENVILLE TREATY LINE 1795

O   H   I   O

VIRGINIA   MILITARY   DISTRICT

Miami River

Scioto River

Big Bottom
Massacre

Muskingum River

Zanesville

DONATION
TRACT

Fort
Hamilton

SYMMES
PURCHASE

Little Miami River

Chillicothe

Fort Washington
Cincinnati

Fort Finney

Ohio River

Kentucky River

KENTUCKY

Licking River

Massie's Station

Limestone
(Maysville)

Ohio River

OHIO COMPANY
OF ASSOCIATES
PURCHASE

Fort Harmar ● Marietta

BLENNERHASSETT ISLAND

Little Kanawha River

Gallipolis ●

Kanawha River

V   I   R   G   I   N   I   A

MILES
10   0   25   50

Drawn under the supervision of FRANCIS P. WEISENBURGER

PLATE 85

Ohio Country

1787–1803

GEOGRAPHER'S LINE
AND
THE SEVEN RANGES

Based on survey begun in 1785 by Thomas Hutchins, Geographer to the United States. Physical features follow presentday surveys.

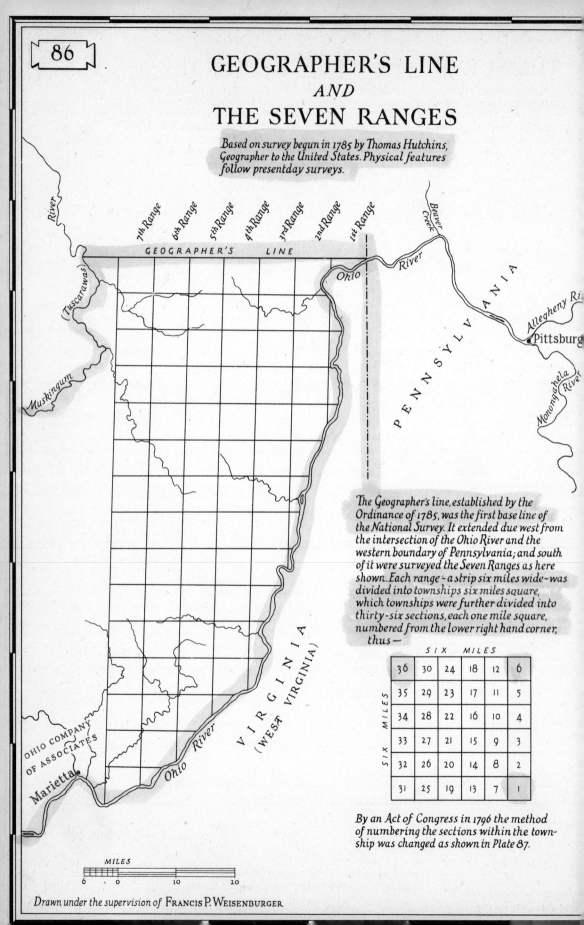

7th Range   6th Range   5th Range   4th Range   3rd Range   2nd Range   1st Range

GEOGRAPHER'S LINE

Beaver Creek

Ohio   River

(Tuscarawas)

River

Muskingum

P E N N S Y L V A N I A

Allegheny Ri—

Pittsburg

Monongahela River

The Geographer's line, established by the Ordinance of 1785, was the first base line of the National Survey. It extended due west from the intersection of the Ohio River and the western boundary of Pennsylvania; and south of it were surveyed the Seven Ranges as here shown. Each range ~ a strip six miles wide~was divided into townships six miles square, which townships were further divided into thirty-six sections, each one mile square, numbered from the lower right hand corner, thus—

V I R G I N I A
(WEST VIRGINIA)

OHIO COMPANY OF ASSOCIATES

Marietta

Ohio River

SIX		MILES			
36	30	24	18	12	6
35	29	23	17	11	5
34	28	22	16	10	4
33	27	21	15	9	3
32	26	20	14	8	2
31	25	19	13	7	1

SIX MILES

By an Act of Congress in 1796 the method of numbering the sections within the township was changed as shown in Plate 87.

MILES

6   0   10   20

Drawn under the supervision of FRANCIS P. WEISENBURGER

THE SURVEY OF THE PUBLIC DOMAIN

is based upon the Ordinance of 1785. Beginning with the Seven Ranges (see Plate 86),
this survey was continued across the country, although there still remains, in the mountain-
ous sections of the Far West, over one hundred million acres of unsurveyed land. However,
with a few local exceptions, the survey applies in every state in the Union, except in the
Thirteen Colonies and in Maine, Vermont, Kentucky, Tennessee, West Virginia, and Texas.
From arbitrarily selected east-and-west Base Lines and north-and-south Meridians,
the land is surveyed into Ranges of Townships, lying north and south of the Base Lines,
and east and west of the Meridians. The Ranges are numbered east and west from the
Meridians. The Townships, each six miles square, are numbered north and south from
the Base Lines. The diagrams below illustrate the actual survey east of the Sixth
Principal Meridian and south of a Base Line located on 40° north latitude.

**TOWNSHIP 2, South, Range 13 East
of the Sixth Principal Meridian.**

In 1796 Congress directed that the
method of numbering the sections
should be as here shown, thus dis-
carding the method followed in the
Seven Ranges, (see Plate 86).
This method of numbering has pre-
vailed in all surveys subsequent
to that date.

**SECTION 25, Township 2,
South, Range 13 East of the
Sixth Principal Meridian.**

A Section contains 640 acres

**NORTHEAST ONE-FOURTH of Section 25,
Township 2, South, Range 13 East of
the Sixth Principal Meridian,**

A Quarter Section contains 160 acres

which, by this description, can be instantly located
as lying in an exact place in northeastern Kansas.

drawn under the supervision of
PAUL WALLACE GATES

PLATE 87

The Survey of the
Public Domain

PLATE 88

Georgia's Western Lands,
Mississippi Territory
and
East and West Florida

1783–1819

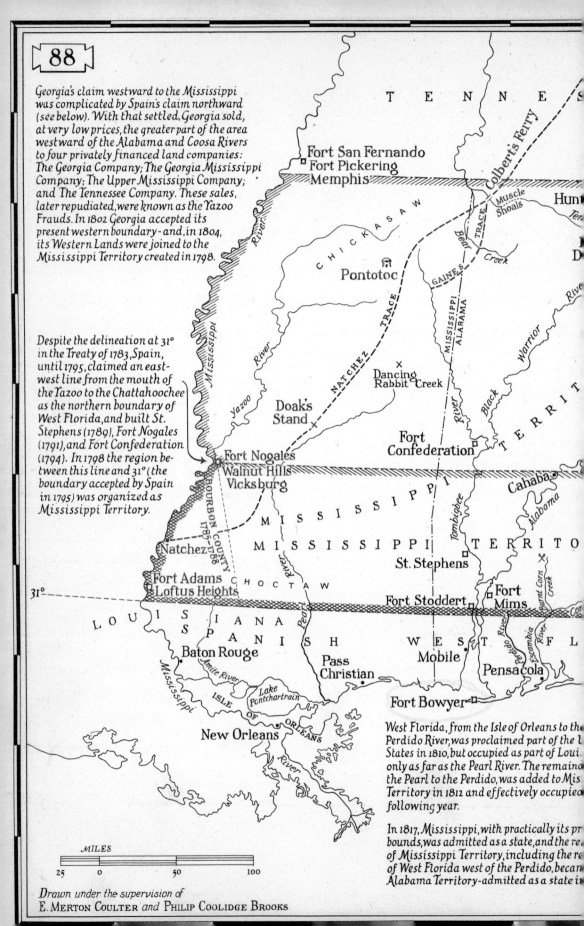

Georgia's claim westward to the Mississippi
was complicated by Spain's claim northward
(see below). With that settled, Georgia sold,
at very low prices, the greater part of the area
westward of the Alabama and Coosa Rivers
to four privately financed land companies:
The Georgia Company; The Georgia Mississippi
Company; The Upper Mississippi Company;
and The Tennessee Company. These sales,
later repudiated, were known as the Yazoo
Frauds. In 1802 Georgia accepted its
present western boundary - and, in 1804,
its Western Lands were joined to the
Mississippi Territory created in 1798.

Despite the delineation at 31°
in the Treaty of 1783, Spain,
until 1795, claimed an east-
west line from the mouth of
the Yazoo to the Chattahoochee
as the northern boundary of
West Florida, and built St.
Stephens (1789), Fort Nogales
(1791), and Fort Confederation
(1794). In 1798 the region between this line and 31° (the
boundary accepted by Spain
in 1795) was organized as
Mississippi Territory.

TENNES...

Fort San Fernando
Fort Pickering
Memphis

Colbert's Ferry

Muscle Shoals

Hunt...

D...

CHICKASAW

Pontotoc

NATCHEZ TRACE

GAINES TRACE

Bear Creek

MISSISSIPPI
ALABAMA

Warrior

River

Black

TERRIT...

Dancing
Rabbit Creek ×

Doak's
Stand

Fort
Confederation

Cahaba

Alabama

Fort Nogales
Walnut Hills
Vicksburg

BOURBON COUNTY
1785-1788

Natchez

MISSISSIPPI

MISSISSIPPI

TERRITO...

St. Stephens

Tombigbee River

Fort Adams
Loftus Heights

CHOCTAW

Pearl River

31° - - -

Fort Stoddert

Fort
Mims

Burnt Corn Creek ×

Co...

LOUISIANA

SPANISH

WEST

FL...

Baton Rouge

Amite River

Pass
Christian

Mobile

Pensacola

Perdido River

Escambia River

Mississippi

ISLE

Lake
Pontchartrain

OF

ORLEANS

Fort Bowyer

New Orleans

River

West Florida, from the Isle of Orleans to the
Perdido River, was proclaimed part of the U...
States in 1810, but occupied as part of Loui...
only as far as the Pearl River. The remain...
the Pearl to the Perdido, was added to Mis...
Territory in 1812 and effectively occupie...
following year.

In 1817, Mississippi, with practically its pr...
bounds, was admitted as a state, and the re...
of Mississippi Territory, including the re...
of West Florida west of the Perdido, becam...
Alabama Territory - admitted as a state i...

MILES

25   0   50   100

Drawn under the supervision of
E. MERTON COULTER and PHILIP COOLIDGE BROOKS

GEORGIA'S WESTERN LANDS
MISSISSIPPI TERRITORY
AND
EAST *AND* WEST
FLORIDA
1783~1819

OVERHILL
CHEREKEE

Little Tennessee River

NORTH CAROLINA

Hiwassee

CHEROKEE River

MIDDLE

Running
Water

Ustanali

(New
Echota) River

Dahlonega

Etowah

LOWER CHEROKEE

Chatooga River

*In the belief that the
Chatooga did not reach
the No. Car. line, So. Car.
in 1787, ceded to the U.S.,
a 12-mile wide strip of
Georgia's
Western Lands.*

Tugaloo River

Petersburg

Broad River

SOUTH CAROLINA

allasahatchee

ether

Horseshoe Bend
(Tohopeka)

Indian
Springs

Fort
Wilkinson

Oconee River

Augusta

Savannah

Louisville

Ogeechee

River

River

uckabatchee

Coweta
Town

LOWER CREEK

allabee Creek

River

Fort
Hawkins

Ocmulgee River

G E O R G I A

River

River

Altamaha River

Savannah

A T L A N T I C   O C E A N

Chattahoochee River

Flint

Fort Scott

Fowltown

SEMINOLE

St. Mary's River

Fernandina
AMELIA ISLAND

SPANISH   EAST   FLORIDA

Apalachicola River

Fort Gadsden
(Negro Fort)

St. Marks

Apalachee
Bay

Bowlegs
Town

Suwannee River

St. Johns River

St. Augustine

*East Florida was ceded to the
United States by the Adams-Onís
Treaty of 1819, which also ended
disputes over West Florida. All the
territory east of the Perdido became
the Territory of Florida in 1822, and
was admitted as a state in 1845.*

MAUGA

key
wn

a
Emuctau Ck
River

ssee
n

A

PLATE 89

Georgia's Western Lands,
Mississippi Territory
and
East and West Florida

1783–1819

PLATE 90

Indian Land Cessions

1784-1798

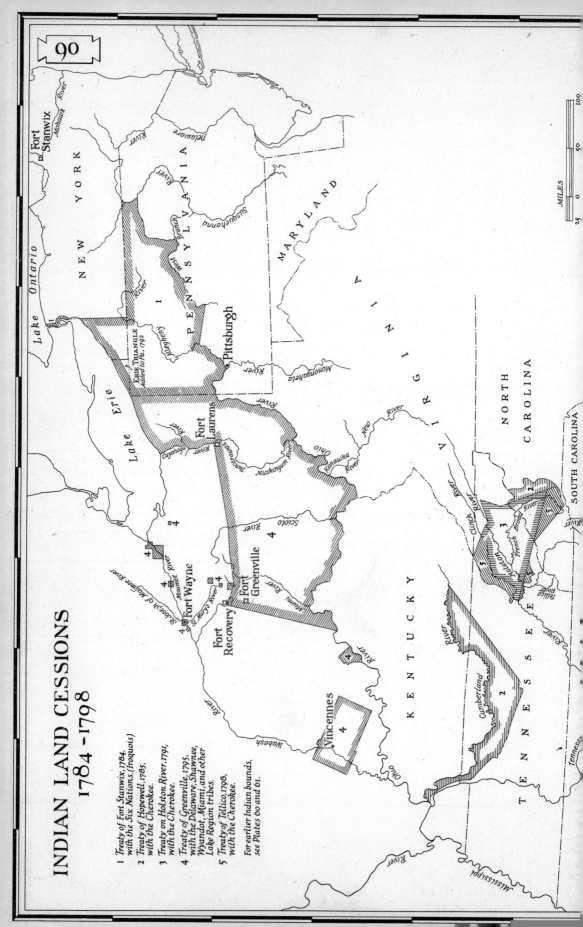

90

INDIAN LAND CESSIONS
1784 - 1798

1 Treaty of Fort Stanwix, 1784,
  with the Six Nations, (Iroquois)
2 Treaty of Hopewell, 1785,
  with the Cherokee.
3 Treaty on Holston River, 1791,
  with the Cherokee.
4 Treaty of Greenville, 1795,
  with the Delaware, Shawnee,
  Wyandot, Miami, and other
  Lake Region tribes.
5 Treaty of Tellico, 1798,
  with the Cherokee.

For earlier Indian bounds,
see Plates 60 and 61.

MILES

Fort
Stanwix

NEW YORK

Lake Ontario

Mohawk River

Delaware River

PENNSYLVANIA

West Branch River

Susquehanna River

MARYLAND

ERIE TRIANGLE
added to Pa. 1792

Allegheny

Pittsburgh

Monongahela River

Lake Erie

Cuyahoga River

Fort
Laurens

Tuscarawas River

Muskingum River

Scioto River

Ohio River

Kanawha River

New River

VIRGINIA

NORTH
CAROLINA

SOUTH
CAROLINA

Clinch River

French Broad River

Holston River

Nollichucky River

Fort Wayne

St. Joseph of Maumee River

Maumee River

St. Mary's River

Fort
Recovery

Fort
Greenville

Miami River

KENTUCKY

Cumberland River

TENNESSEE

Tennessee River

Vincennes

Wabash River

Ohio River

Mississippi River

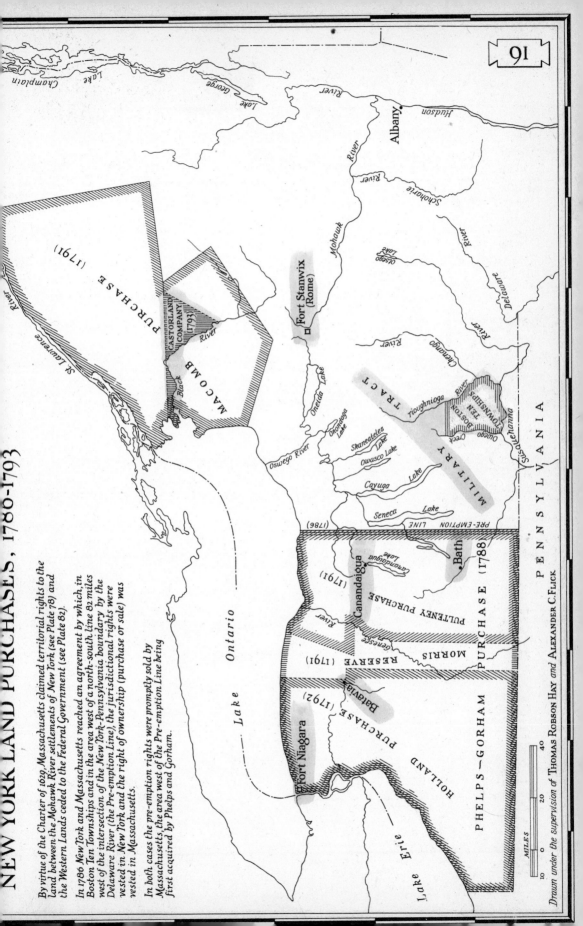

NEW YORK LAND PURCHASES, 1780-1793

By virtue of the Charter of 1629, Massachusetts claimed territorial rights to the land between the Mohawk River settlements of New York (see Plate 78) and the Western Lands ceded to the Federal Government (see Plate 82).

In 1786 New York and Massachusetts reached an agreement by which, in Boston Ten Townships and in the area west of a north-south line 82 miles west of the intersection of the New York-Pennsylvania boundary by the Delaware River (the Pre-emption Line), the jurisdictional rights were vested in New York and the right of ownership (purchase or sale) was vested in Massachusetts.

In both cases the pre-emption rights were promptly sold by Massachusetts, the area west of the Pre-emption Line being first acquired by Phelps and Gorham.

91

Drawn under the supervision of THOMAS ROBSON HAY and ALEXANDER C. FLICK

MILES
10   0   20   40

Lake Champlain

Lake George

Hudson River

Albany.

Schoharie River

Mohawk River

Fort Stanwix (Rome)

Otsego Lake

Delaware River

St. Lawrence River

MACOMB PURCHASE (1791)

CASTORLAND COMPANY (1793)

Black River

Oneida Lake

Onondaga Lake

Oswego River

Skaneateles Lake

Owasco Lake

Cayuga Lake

Seneca Lake

Canandaigua Lake

Genesee River

Chenango River

Tioughnioga River

Otsego Creek

BOSTON TEN TOWNSHIPS

MILITARY TRACT

Susquehanna River

PENNSYLVANIA

PRE-EMPTION LINE

Bath.

PULTENEY PURCHASE (1791)

PHELPS-GORHAM PURCHASE (1788)

Canandaigua

MORRIS RESERVE (1791)

HOLLAND PURCHASE (1792)

Batavia

Fort Niagara

Lake Ontario

Lake Erie

(1786)

PLATE 91

New York Land Purchases

1786–1793

PLATE 92

Indiana and Illinois
Territories
1800–1818

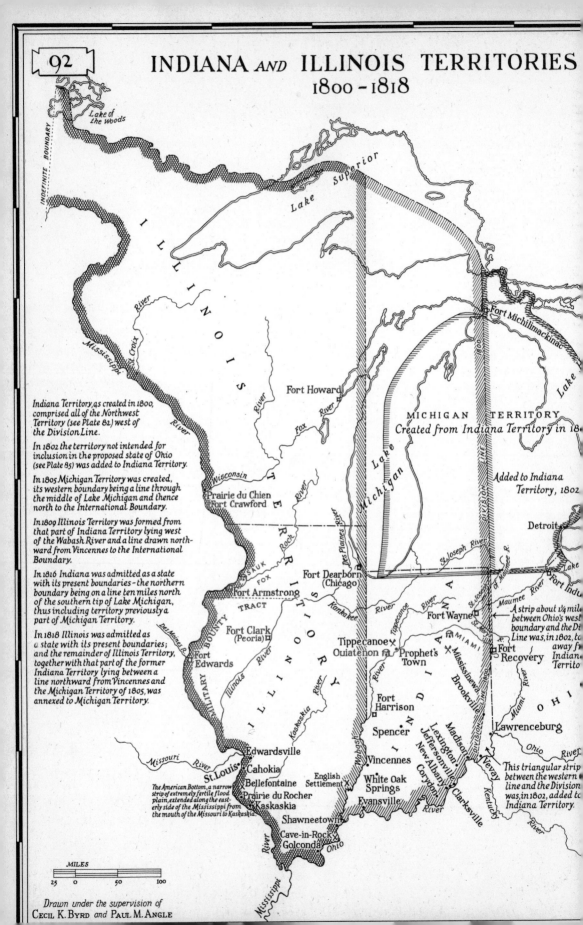

INDIANA AND ILLINOIS TERRITORIES
1800–1818

92

Lake of the Woods

INDEFINITE BOUNDARY

I L L I N O I S

Lake Superior

Mississippi River

St. Croix River

Wisconsin River

Rock River

SAUK

FOX

TRACT

BOUNTY

MILITARY

Des Moines R.

Missouri River

St.Louis
Cahokia
Bellefontaine
Prairie du Rocher
Kaskaskia

The American Bottom, a narrow strip of extremely fertile flood plain, extended along the easterly side of the Mississippi from the mouth of the Missouri to Kaskaskia.

Edwardsville

English Settlement ✕

White Oak Springs

Evansville

Shawneetown

Cave-in-Rock
Golconda

Ohio

Mississippi River

MILES
25 0 50 100

Drawn under the supervision of
CECIL K. BYRD *and* PAUL M. ANGLE

Indiana Territory, as created in 1800, comprised all of the Northwest Territory (see Plate 81) west of the Division Line.

In 1802 the territory not intended for inclusion in the proposed state of Ohio (see Plate 85) was added to Indiana Territory.

In 1805 Michigan Territory was created, its western boundary being a line through the middle of Lake Michigan and thence north to the International Boundary.

In 1809 Illinois Territory was formed from that part of Indiana Territory lying west of the Wabash River and a line drawn north-ward from Vincennes to the International Boundary.

In 1816 Indiana was admitted as a state with its present boundaries – the northern boundary being on a line ten miles north of the southern tip of Lake Michigan, thus including territory previously a part of Michigan Territory.

In 1818 Illinois was admitted as a state with its present boundaries; and the remainder of Illinois Territory, together with that part of the former Indiana Territory lying between a line northward from Vincennes and the Michigan Territory of 1805, was annexed to Michigan Territory.

Fort Howard

Fox River

Prairie du Chien
Fort Crawford

Fort Armstrong

Fort Clark (Peoria)

Fort Edwards

I L L I N O I S   T E R R I T O R Y

Illinois River

Kaskaskia River

Fort Dearborn (Chicago)

Lake Michigan

Des Plaines River

Kankakee River

MICHIGAN   TERRITORY
Created from Indiana Territory in 18..

Added to Indiana Territory, 1802

Detroit

Fort Michilimackinac

Lake Huron

St. Joseph River

Maumee River

Fort Wayne

MIAMI

Fort Recovery

A strip about 1¼ mile between Ohio's west boundary and the Di.. Line was, in 1802, to .. away f.. Indian.. Territo..

Fort Indu..

Lake ..

I N D I A N A

Tippecanoe ✕
Ouiatenon 🏛 Prophet's Town

Tippecanoe River

Wabash River

Mississinewa River

Fort Harrison

Spencer

Vincennes

Lexington
Madison
Jeffersonville
New Albany
Corydon
Clarksville

Brookville

Lawrenceburg

Ohio River

Vevay

Kentucky River

O H I O

This triangular strip between the western .. line and the Division .. was, in 1802, added to Indiana Territory.

St. Joseph River

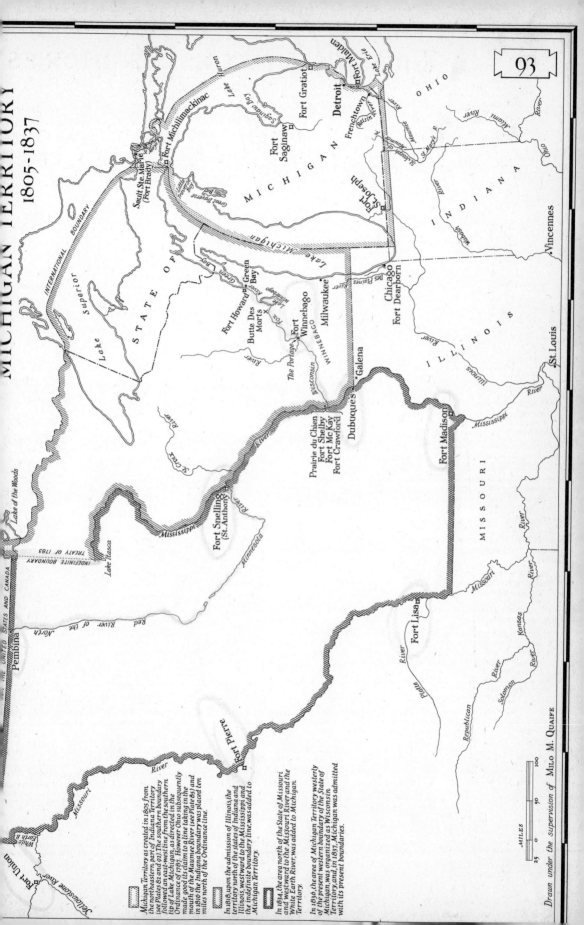

MICHIGAN TERRITORY 1805-1837

OHIO

INDIANA

ILLINOIS

Lake Erie

Fort Malden

Detroit

Frenchtown

Fort Gratiot

Fort Saginaw

Saginaw Bay

Lake Huron

Fort Michillimackinac

Sault Ste. Marie (Fort Brady)

MICHIGAN

Fort St. Joseph

Lake Michigan

STATE OF

Lake Superior

INTERNATIONAL BOUNDARY

Green Bay

Fort Howard

Butte Des Morts

Fort Winnebago

Milwaukee

WINNEBAGO

The Portage

Wisconsin River

Galena

Dubuque's

Chicago
Fort Dearborn

Des Plaines River

Illinois River

St. Louis

Vincennes

Wabash River

Miami River

Ohio River

St. Mary's River

Maumee River

Prairie du Chien
Fort Shelby
Fort McKay
Fort Crawford

Fort Madison

Mississippi River

Fort Snelling (St. Anthony)

St. Croix River

Minnesota River

Lake Itasca

MISSOURI

Missouri River

Kansas River

Solomon River

Republican River

Platte River

Fort Lisa

Fort Pierre

Red River of the North

INDEFINITE BOUNDARY

TREATY OF 1783

Pembina

Lake of the Woods

THE UNITED STATES AND CANADA

White Earth R.

Fort Union

Yellowstone River

Missouri River

Michigan Territory as created in 1805 from the northeastern part of Indiana Territory (see Plates 82 and 91). The southern boundary followed an east-west line from the southern tip of Lake Michigan, as directed in the Ordinance of 1787. However Ohio subsequently made good its claim to a line taking in the mouth of the Maumee River (see Plate 85) and in 1816 the Indiana boundary was placed ten miles north of the Ordinance line.

In 1818, upon the admission of Illinois, the territory north of the states of Indiana and Illinois, westward to the Mississippi and the indefinite boundary line, was added to Michigan Territory.

In 1834, the area north of the State of Missouri and westward to the Missouri River and the White Earth River, was added to Michigan Territory.

In 1836, the area of Michigan Territory westerly of the present western boundary of the State of Michigan, was organized as Wisconsin Territory, and in 1837, Michigan was admitted with its present boundaries.

MILES
25   0   50   100

Drawn under the supervision of MILO M. QUAIFE

PLATE 93

Michigan Territory

1805–1837

PLATE 94

Louisiana Purchase
and the
Trans-Mississippi West

1803 – 1817

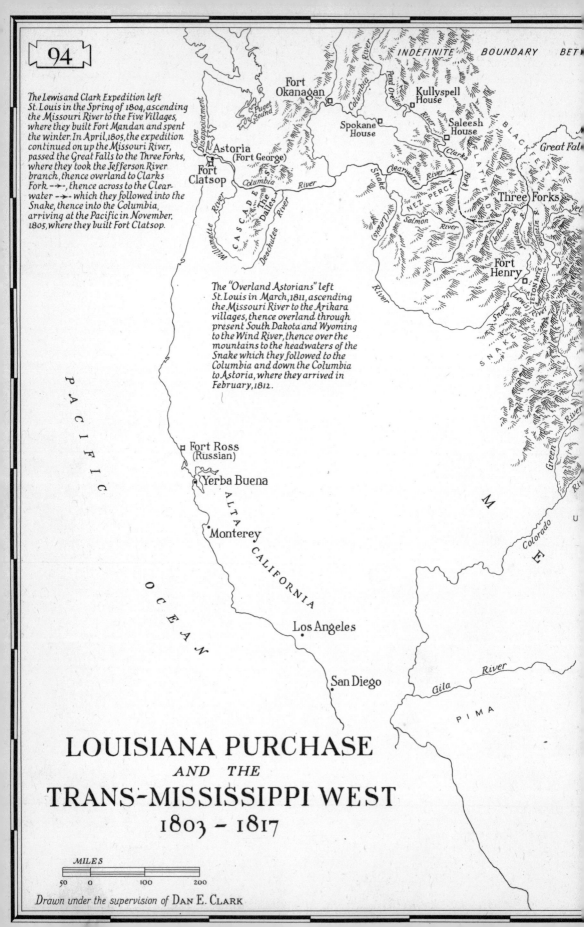

LOUISIANA PURCHASE AND THE TRANS-MISSISSIPPI WEST 1803 – 1817

Drawn under the supervision of DAN E. CLARK

UNITED STATES AND CANADA

Lake of the Woods

INTERNATIONAL BOUNDARY

Lake Superior

Pembina

Red River of the North

Sandy Lake

Leech Lake

HIDATSA

Fort Mandan

Five Villages

MANDAN

SIOUX

el's Fort

Fort Manuel

ARIKARA

Z.M.Pike, leaving St.Louis, in August 1805, with 20 soldiers, ascended the Mississippi and, from a log fort built here, explored the upper reaches of the river.

St.Peters (Minnesota) River

Falls of St.Anthony

Mississippi River

That part of the Louisiana Purchase north and west of the Territory of Orleans was, from 1804 to 1805, known as the District of Louisiana; from 1805 to 1812, as the Territory of Louisiana; in 1812 the name was changed to Missouri Territory

GIARD TRACT

Fort aux Cedres (Loisel's Post)

Missouri

Big Sioux R.

Dubuque's

Credit Island

MISSOURI

North Platte River

South Platte River

Platte River

Council Bluffs

Fort Lisa

Platte River

River

Fort Madison

St.Charles

La Charette

Portage des Sioux

Illinois River

St.Louis

Fort Bellefontaine

Kaskaskia

PAWNEE

KANSAS

Kansas River

Fort Osage (Clark)

Osage River

Ste. Genevieve

KENTUCKY

Z.M.Pike, with a party of soldiers, left Fort Bellefontaine in July 1806, and after exploring the Pawnee country crossed the Sangre de Cristo range where he was arrested by the Spaniards and taken to Chihuahua.

Cape Girardeau

New Madrid

Ohio River

TENNESSEE

PIKES PEAK

ARAPAHO

Arkansas River

Neosho River

Verdigris River

OSAGE River

White River

St.Francis River

Fort Pickering

Cimarron River

River

Chouteau's

Arkansas River

River

Canadian River

KIOWA

COMANCHE

Fort Smith

Ouachita River

Mississippi River

MISSISSIPPI TERRITORY

Fe

Ibuquerque

BOUNDARY OF LOUISIANA

Red River

River

Natchitoches

Walnut Hills

verde

NEW MEXICO

APACHE

Brazos River

Trinity River

Sabine River

NEUTRAL GROUND

(TERRITORY OF ORLEANS)

Natchez

Fort Adams

Pearl River

rnada l Muerto

Colorado River

River

River

Los Adaes

Nacogdoches

LOUISIANA ADMITTED APRIL 30, 1812

ADDED TO LOUISIANA APRIL 14, 1812

New Orleans

Pecos River

SANGRE DE CRISTO RANGE

WESTERN

TEXAS

Champ d'Asile

River

Galveston Island

Barataria Bay

San Antonio

Rio Grande

Nueces River

GALVESTON ISLAND

Gulf of Mexico

hihuahua

COAHUILA

Presidio de Rio Grande

Goliad

PLATE 95

Louisiana Purchase
and the
Trans-Mississippi West

1803–1817

PLATE 96

War of 1812

Lake Region

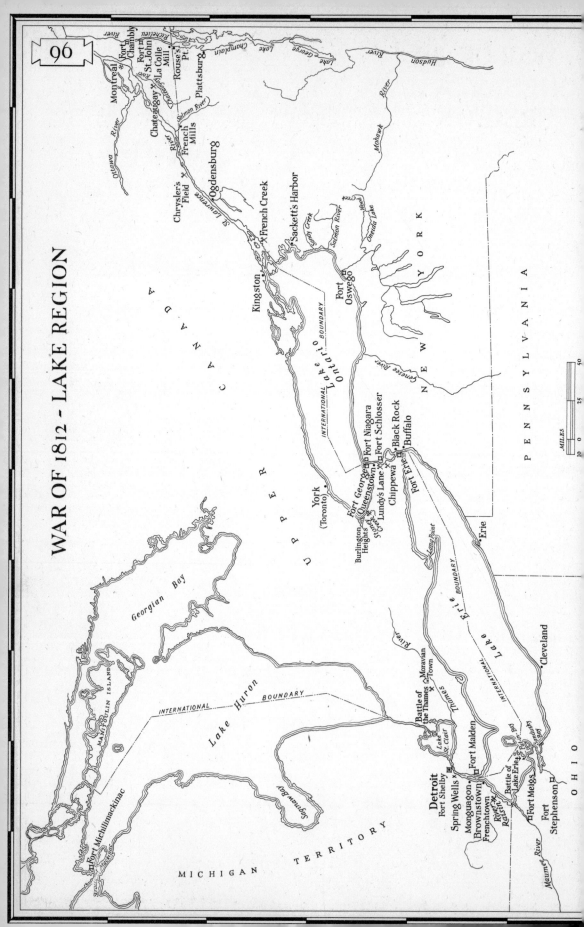

WAR OF 1812 – LAKE REGION

MICHIGAN TERRITORY

Lake Huron

Georgian Bay

MANITOULIN ISLAND

Straits of Mackinac

Fort Michilimackinac

INTERNATIONAL   BOUNDARY

Saginaw Bay

Lake St. Clair

Detroit
Fort Shelby
Spring Wells ×
Monguagon ×
Brownstown ×
Frenchtown
River Raisin ×

Fort Malden

Battle of
the Thames ×
Moravian
Town ×

Thames River

Long Point

Lake Erie

Erie BOUNDARY

INTERNATIONAL

Cleveland

Erie

OHIO

Maumee River

Fort Meigs
Fort Stephenson

Battle of
Lake Erie ×
Put-in-Bay
Sandusky Bay

PENNSYLVANIA

NEW YORK

Lake Ontario

INTERNATIONAL   BOUNDARY

UPPER   CANADA

CANADA

York
(Toronto)

Fort George
Queenstown
Burlington
Heights
Stoney Creek

Lundy's Lane ×
Chippewa ×
Fort Erie

Fort Niagara
Fort Schlosser
Black Rock
Buffalo

Genesee River

Fort
Oswego

Oneida Lake

Wood Creek

Salmon River

Sandy Creek

Sackett's Harbor

French Creek ×

Kingston

St. Lawrence R.

Chrysler's Field ×
Ogdensburg

French Mills

Ottawa River

Montreal

Fort Chambly
Fort St. John
La Colle Mill

Richelieu River

Rouse's Pt.
Plattsburg

Chateaugay ×
Chateaugay River
Salmon River

Lake Champlain

Lake George

Hudson River

Mohawk River

MILES
0   10   25   50

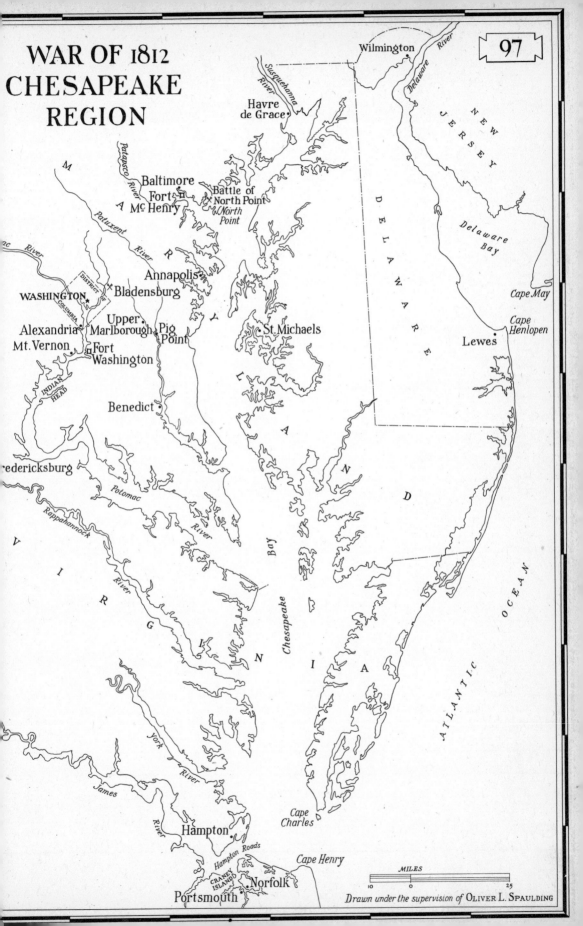

WAR OF 1812 CHESAPEAKE REGION

Wilmington

Havre de Grace

Susquehanna River

Delaware River

NEW JERSEY

DELAWARE

Delaware Bay

Cape May

Cape Henlopen

Lewes

Baltimore
Fort McHenry
Battle of North Point
(*North Point*)

Patapsco River

M A R Y L A N D

Patuxent River

Annapolis
Bladensburg

St. Michaels

WASHINGTON
DISTRICT of COLUMBIA

Alexandria
Mt. Vernon
Upper Marlborough
Pig Point
Fort Washington

INDIAN HEAD

Benedict

redericksburg

Potomac River

Rappahannock River

V I R G I N I A

Chesapeake Bay

ATLANTIC OCEAN

York River

James River

Hampton

CRANEY ISLAND

Portsmouth

Norfolk

Cape Charles

Hampton Roads

Cape Henry

MILES
10   0   25

Drawn under the supervision of OLIVER L. SPAULDING

PLATE 97

War of 1812

Chesapeake
Region

PLATE 98

War of 1812

Gulf Region

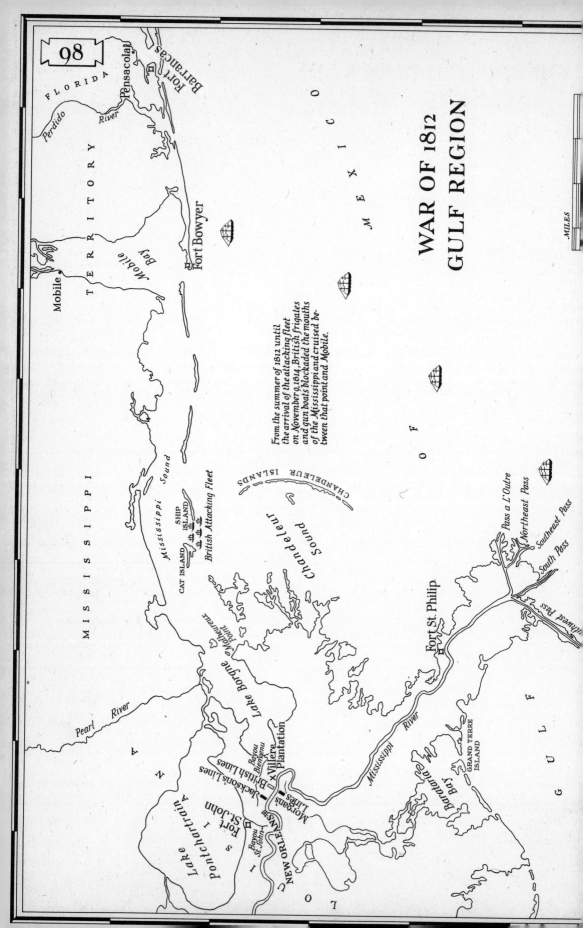

FLORIDA

Pensacola
Fort Barrancas

Perdido River

T E R R I T O R Y

Fort Bowyer

Mobile Bay

Mobile

M I S S I S S I P P I

Mississippi Sound

CAT ISLAND
SHIP ISLAND
British Attacking Fleet

Pearl River

Pontchartrain
Lake Pontchartrain

Fort St. John

Bayou St. John

NEW ORLEANS

Jacksons Lines
British Lines
Morgans Lines

Bayou Bienvenu

Villere Plantation

Chef Menteur Point

Lake Borgne

CHANDELEUR ISLANDS

Chandeleur Sound

Fort St. Philip

Mississippi River

Batavia Bay

GRAND TERRE ISLAND

Pass a L'Outre
Northeast Pass
Southeast Pass
South Pass
Southwest Pass

G   U   L   F

O   F

M   E   X   I   C   O

From the summer of 1812 until
the arrival of the attacking fleet
on November 9, 1814, British frigates
and gun boats blockaded the mouths
of the Mississippi and cruised between that point and Mobile.

WAR OF 1812
GULF REGION

MILES

L   O   U   I   S   I   A   N   A

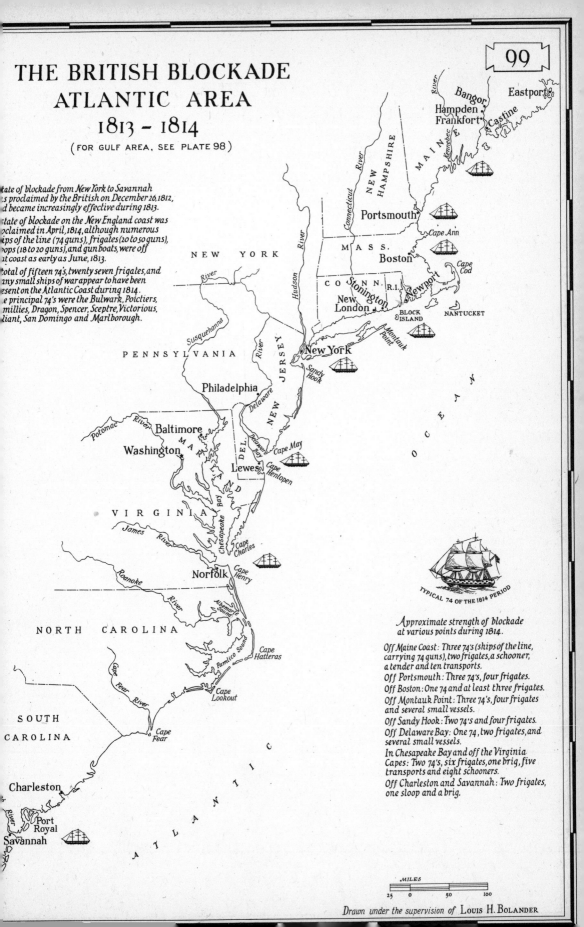

THE BRITISH BLOCKADE ATLANTIC AREA
1813 – 1814
(FOR GULF AREA, SEE PLATE 98)

...tate of blockade from New York to Savannah
...s proclaimed by the British on December 26, 1812,
...d became increasingly effective during 1813.

...tate of blockade on the New England coast was
...oclaimed in April, 1814, although numerous
...ps of the line (74 guns), frigates (20 to 50 guns),
...oops (18 to 20 guns), and gun boats, were off
...t coast as early as June, 1813.

...otal of fifteen 74's, twenty seven frigates, and
...ny small ships of war appear to have been
...esent on the Atlantic Coast during 1814.
...e principal 74's were the Bulwark, Poictiers,
...millies, Dragon, Spencer, Sceptre, Victorious,
...liant, San Domingo and Marlborough.

TYPICAL 74 OF THE 1814 PERIOD

Approximate strength of blockade at various points during 1814.

Off Maine Coast: Three 74's (ships of the line, carrying 74 guns), two frigates, a schooner, a tender and ten transports.

Off Portsmouth: Three 74's, four frigates.

Off Boston: One 74 and at least three frigates.

Off Montauk Point: Three 74's, four frigates and several small vessels.

Off Sandy Hook: Two 74's and four frigates.

Off Delaware Bay: One 74, two frigates, and several small vessels.

In Chesapeake Bay and off the Virginia Capes: Two 74's, six frigates, one brig, five transports and eight schooners.

Off Charleston and Savannah: Two frigates, one sloop and a brig.

MILES
25 0   50   100

Drawn under the supervision of LOUIS H. BOLANDER

PLATE 99

The British Blockade

Atlantic Area

1813–1814

PLATE 100

Boundary Treaties
and
Westward Advance

1818–1836

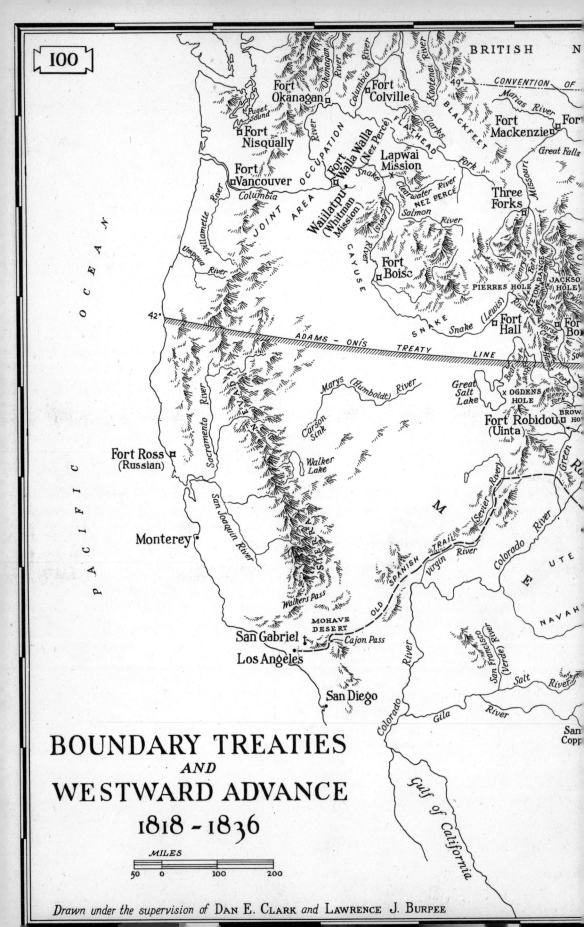

BRITISH N

CONVENTION OF

Marias River

BLACKFEET

49°

Fort Okanagan

Fort Colville

Okanagan River

Columbia River

Kootenai River

Clarks Fork

Fort Mackenzie

Fort

Great Falls

Puget Sound

Fort Nisqually

FLATHEAD

Fort Walla Walla

Lapwai Mission

(Nez Perce)

Snake

Missouri

Fort Vancouver

Columbia

JOINT OCCUPATION AREA

Waiilatpu (Whitman) Mission

Clearwater River

NEZ PERCÉ

Three Forks

Salmon

Umpqua River

Willamette River

CAYUSE

Snake (Lewis) River

River

TETON RANGE

PIERRES HOLE

JACKSON HOLE

Fort Boise

42°

ADAMS - ONÍS TREATY LINE

SNAKE

Snake (Lewis)

Fort Hall

Horse Creek

Fort Bo

For Bo

Marys (Humboldt) River

Great Salt Lake

OGDENS HOLE

Henrys Fork

BROW HO

NEVADA

Carson Sink

Fort Robidou (Uinta)

UTE

Sacramento River

Fort Ross (Russian)

Walker Lake

Sevier River

Green R

Colorado River

San Joaquin River

M

OCEAN

PACIFIC

Monterey

SIERRA

OLD SPANISH TRAIL

Virgin River

E

NAVAH

Walkers Pass

MOHAVE DESERT

Cajon Pass

Colorado River

San Francisco (Verde) River

San Gabriel

Los Angeles

San Diego

Salt River

Colorado

Gila River

San Copp

Gulf of California

BOUNDARY TREATIES
AND
WESTWARD ADVANCE
1818 - 1836

MILES

50   0   100   200

Drawn under the supervision of DAN E. CLARK *and* LAWRENCE J. BURPEE

AMERICA

Assiniboine River

Fort Garry (Winnipeg)

Lake of the Woods

Rainy Lake

BOUNDARY WITH CANADA

Mouse (Souris) River

Pembina (Fort Daer)

Northwest Angle

Rainy River

Pigeon River

Grand Portage

Lake Superior

Fort Union

Missouri River

x The Forks

St. Louis R.

Sault Ste. Marie

Michilimackinac

Fort Clark

River

M I C H I G A N

Red River of the North

Lake Itasca

Fond du Lac

River

Cheyenne River

S I O U X

Minnesota River

Fort Snelling (Fort St. Anthony)

Green Bay

Fox River

Lake Michigan

Fort Pierre (Fort Tecumseh)

T E R R I T O R Y

(Jurisdiction Extended 1834)

Mississippi River

Wisconsin River

Fort Kiowa

Fort Lookout

Prairie du Chien

Wisconsin

Fort Recovery

I L L I N O I S

Fort William (Laramie)

O M A H A

Council Bluffs

Cabanne's Fort Atkinson (Fort Calhoun)

Des Moines River

I N D I A N A

Loup River

A R A P A H O

North Platte River

Platte River

Bellevue

Missouri River

PLATTE PURCHASE 1836

South Platte River

K A N S A S

Blacksnake Hills

Franklin

LONGS PEAK

SOUTH PARK AYOU SALADE

PAWNEE

Fort Leavenworth

River

Fort Osage

Independence

St. Louis

Kaskaskia

PIKES PEAK

Kansas River

Neosho

Osage River

Chouteau's Fort Gibson

Potosi

River

KY.

Bent's Fort

Pawnee Rock

SANTA FE TRAIL

Council Grove

River

O S A G E

MISSOURI (ADMITTED 1821)

TAOS

SANTA FE

Arkansas River

TIMBERS

Verdigris River

Osage River

O Z A R K

MTS.

TENN.

Raton Pass

SANTA FE TRAIL

Cimarron River

A R K A N S A S

River

Arkansas River

C H E R O K E E

White River

Memphis

SANGRE DE CRISTO MTS.

K I O W A

Canadian River

River

Fort Smith

River

Santa Fe

STAKED PLAINS (LLANO ESTACADO)

Coffee's

Fort Towson

T E R R I T O R Y

A R K A N S A S (ADMITTED 1836) 1819

Mississippi River

C O M A N C H E

Red River

ADAMS ONIS TREATY LINE OF

Sabine River

L O U I S I A N A

Natchitoches

Natchez

verde

I

C

Brazos

C R O S S

T E X A S

Trinity River

32°

1819

Fort Jesup

da uerto

A P A C H E

Colorado River

Nacogdoches

Pearl River

aso

Pecos River

River

San Antonio

Red River

River

New Orleans

Rio Grande

Nueces River

G U L F   O F   M E X I C O

ihuahua

PLATE 101

Boundary Treaties
and
Westward Advance

1818–1836

PLATE 102

Green River
and the
Trappers' Rendezvous
1824–1840

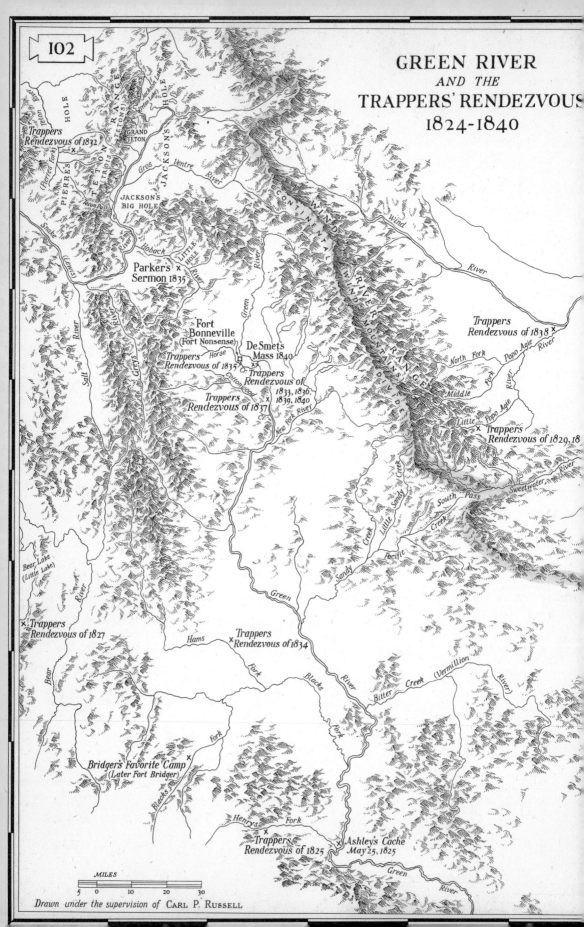

GREEN RIVER
AND THE
TRAPPERS' RENDEZVOUS
1824–1840

*Trappers
Rendezvous of 1832*

TETONS

TETROIS RANGE

Teton Lake

JACKSONS HOLE

HOLE

PIERRE'S HOLE

Pierres Fork

GRAND TETON

Gros Ventre River

JACKSONS BIG HOLE

Teton Pass

Snake (Lewis) River

Hoback

Little Hole

CONTINENTAL

WIND RIVER MOUNTAINS RANGE

Wind River

River

Parker's
Sermon 1835

Green River

Salt River

Fort
Bonneville
(Fort Nonsense)

De Smets
Mass 1840

*Trappers
Rendezvous of 1835*

Horse Cr.

*Trappers
Rendezvous of
1833, 1836,
1839, 1840*

*Trappers of
Rendezvous of 1837*

Cottonwood Cr.

New Fork River

Greys River

DIVIDE

*Trappers
Rendezvous of 1838*

North Fork

Fork

Popo Agie River

Middle

Popo Agie River

Little Popo Agie River

*Trappers
Rendezvous of 1829, 18*

Sandy Creek

Little Sandy Creek

Pacific Creek

South Pass Creek

Sweetwater River

*Bear Lake
(Little Lake)*

Bear River

*Trappers
Rendezvous of 1827*

Green River

Hams

*Trappers
Rendezvous of 1834*

Fork

Blacks River

Bitter Creek (Vermillion River)

Fork

Bridger's Favorite Camp
(Later Fort Bridger)

Fork

Blacks Fork

Henrys Fork

*Trappers
Rendezvous of 1825*

Ashley's Cache
May 25, 1825

Green River

MILES

5 0 10 20 30

Drawn under the supervision of CARL P. RUSSELL

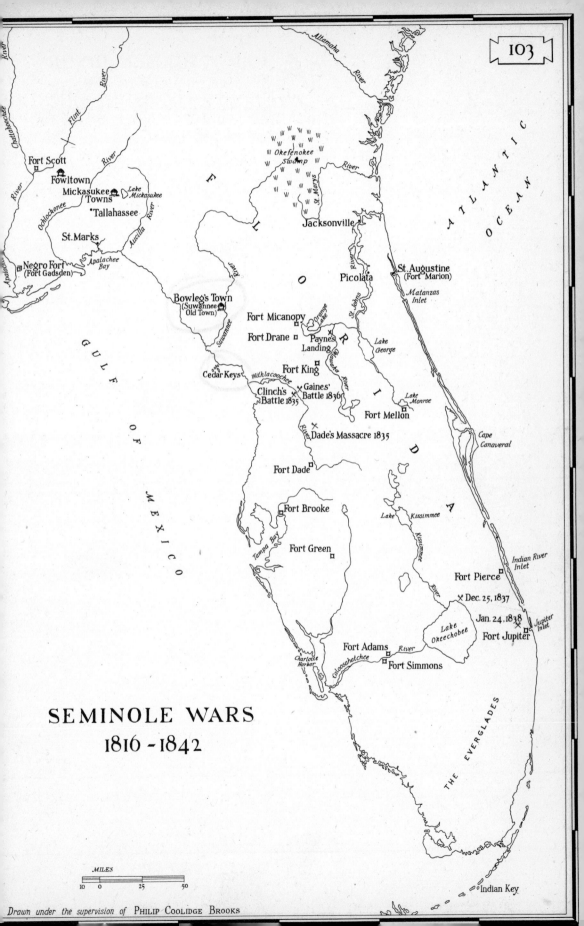

River

Altamaha

River

River

Chattahoochee River

Flint River

Fort Scott

Fowltown

Mickasukee Towns

Lake Mickasukee

*Tallahassee

Ochlochonee River

St. Marks

Aucilla River

Negro Fort (Fort Gadsden)

Apalachee Bay

Apalachicola River

GULF

OF

MEXICO

F L O R I D A

Okefenokee Swamp

St. Marys River

Jacksonville

St. Johns River

Picolata

St. Augustine (Fort Marion)

Matanzas Inlet

Bowleg's Town (Suwannee Old Town)

Fort Micanopy

Orange Lake

Fort Drane

Paynes Landing

Fort King

St. Johns River

Lake George

Suwannee River

Cedar Keys

Withlacoochee

Clinch's Battle 1835

Gaines' Battle 1836

Ocklawaha River

Lake Monroe

Fort Mellon

River

Dade's Massacre 1835

Cape Canaveral

Fort Dade

Fort Brooke

Lake Kissimmee

Tampa Bay

Fort Green

Kissimmee River

Indian River Inlet

Fort Pierce

Dec. 25, 1837

Lake Okeechobee

Jan. 24, 1838

Jupiter Inlet

Fort Jupiter

Fort Adams

River

Charlotte Harbor

Caloosahatchee

Fort Simmons

THE EVERGLADES

ATLANTIC OCEAN

SEMINOLE WARS
1816 – 1842

MILES

10 0   25   50

Indian Key

Drawn under the supervision of PHILIP COOLIDGE BROOKS

PLATE 103

Seminole Wars

1816–1842

PLATE 104

Indian Territory
and
The Southern Plains

1817–1860

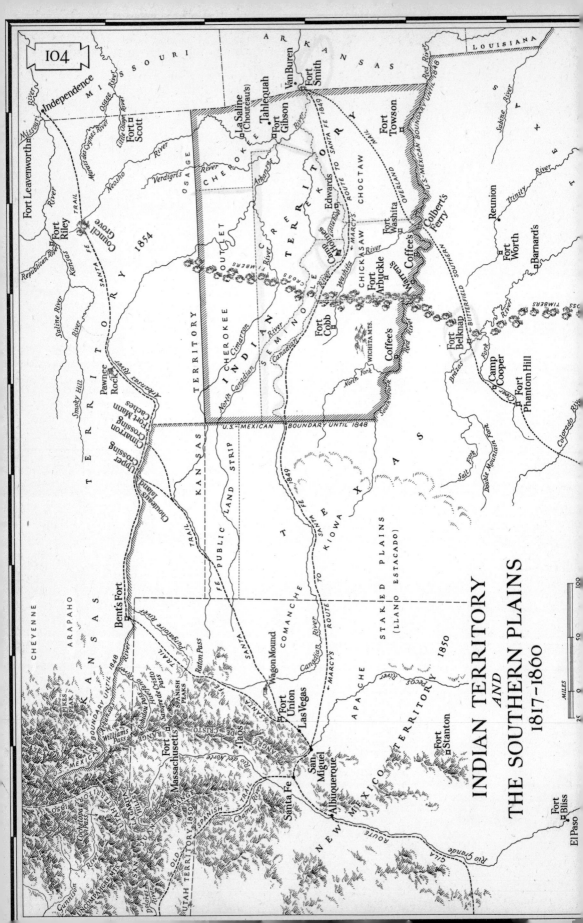

INDIAN TERRITORY
AND
THE SOUTHERN PLAINS
1817–1860

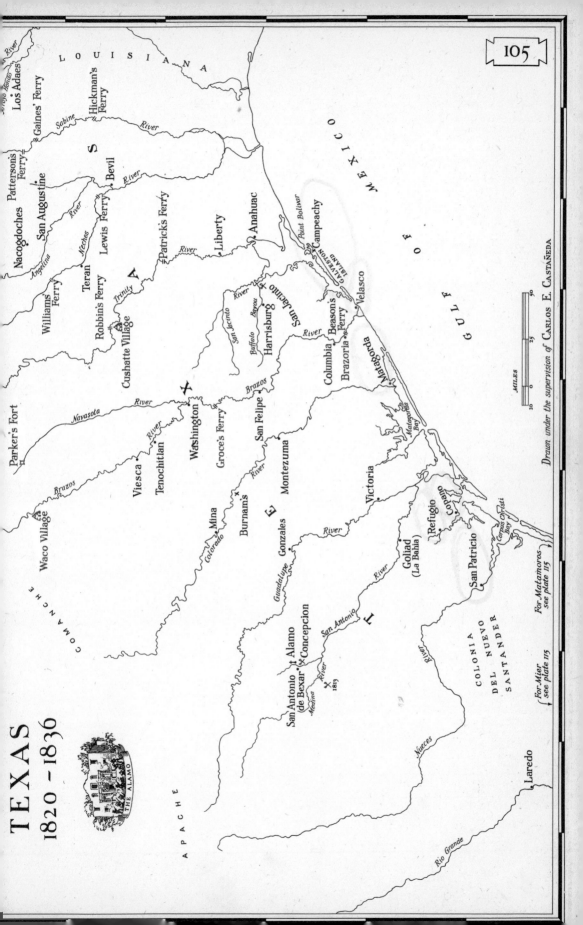

TEXAS
1820-1836

THE ALAMO

LOUISIANA

Arroyo Hondo
Los Adaes
Gaines' Ferry
Patterson's Ferry
Hickman's Ferry
Sabine River
Nacogdoches
San Augustine
Bevil
Lewis Ferry
Williams Ferry
Teran
Robbins Ferry
Neches River
Angelina River
Trinity
Cushatte Village
Patrick's Ferry
Liberty
Anahuac
River
Point Bolivar
Campeachy
GALVESTON ISLAND
Velasco
San Jacinto
River
Harrisburg
Buffalo Bayou
Beason's Ferry
Brazoria
Columbia
Matagorda
Parker's Fort
Navasota River
Washington
Groce's Ferry
San Felipe
Brazos
Viesca
Tenochitlan
Brazos
Waco Village
Mina
Burnam's
Montezuma
Guadalupe
Gonzales
Victoria
Matagorda Bay
Refugio
Copano
San Patricio
Corpus Christi Bay
Goliad
(La Bahia)
River
San Antonio
San Antonio
de Bexar
Alamo
Concepcion
Medina River
1813
River
Nueces
Laredo
Rio Grande
COLONIA
DEL NUEVO
SANTANDER

GULF OF MEXICO

COMANCHE

APACHE

MILES
0 25 50
10 0

Drawn under the supervision of CARLOS E. CASTAÑEDA

For Mier
see plate 115

For Matamoros
see plate 115

PLATE 105

Texas

1820–1836

PLATE 106

Canals

1785–1850

and the
Cumberland Road

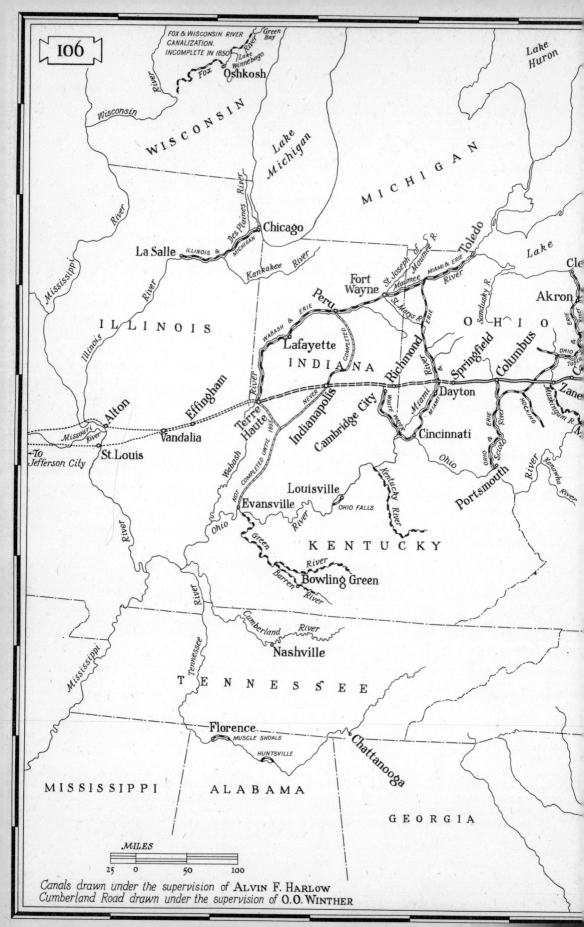

106

FOX & WISCONSIN RIVER
CANALIZATION.
INCOMPLETE IN 1850

Green Bay

Lake Winnebago

Fox River

Oshkosh

Lake Huron

Lake

Wisconsin River

WISCONSIN

Lake Michigan

MICHIGAN

Cle

Mississippi River

Des Plaines River

Chicago

La Salle

ILLINOIS & MICHIGAN

Kankakee River

St. Joseph of Maumee R.

Maumee River

Toledo

MIAMI & ERIE

Akron

Lake

Illinois River

ILLINOIS

Peru

WABASH & ERIE

St. Marys River

ERIE

OHIO

Sandusky R.

Fort Wayne

Miami River &

Springfield

Columbus

ERIE

OHIO & TUSCA

Lafayette

COMPLETED

INDIANA

Richmond

Dayton

Zane

Effingham

Alton

Missouri River

Vandalia

St. Louis

To Jefferson City

Terre Haute

NEVER

WABASH River

NOT COMPLETED UNTIL 1855

Indianapolis

Cambridge City

WHITE WATER

Miami River

MIAMI

Cincinnati

HOCKING

Muskingum R.

ERIE

ERIE & OHIO

Scioto River

Portsmouth

Ohio River

Kanawha River

Evansville

Louisville

OHIO FALLS

Kentucky River

Ohio River

Green River

River

KENTUCKY

Barren River

Bowling Green

Cumberland River

Tennessee River

Nashville

TENNESSEE

Mississippi River

Florence

MUSCLE SHOALS

HUNTSVILLE

Chattanooga

MISSISSIPPI

ALABAMA

GEORGIA

MILES
25 0   50   100

Canals drawn under the supervision of ALVIN F. HARLOW
Cumberland Road drawn under the supervision of O. O. WINTHER

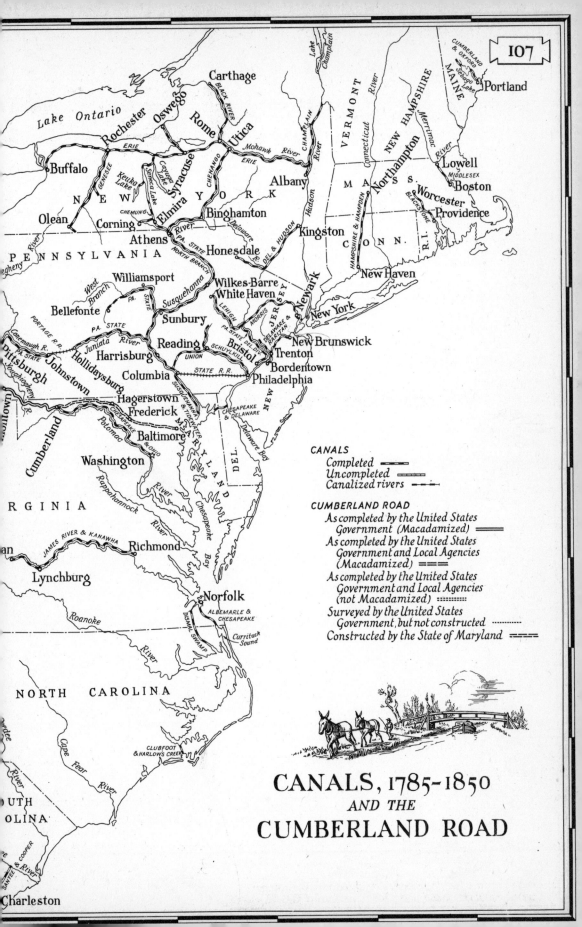

CANALS, 1785–1850
AND THE
CUMBERLAND ROAD

CANALS
Completed ▬▬▬
Uncompleted ▭▭▭
Canalized rivers ▬ ▬ ▬

CUMBERLAND ROAD
As completed by the United States
Government (Macadamized) ══════
As completed by the United States
Government and Local Agencies
(Macadamized) ═══
As completed by the United States
Government and Local Agencies
(not Macadamized) ═════════
Surveyed by the United States
Government, but not constructed ──────────
Constructed by the State of Maryland ═════

PLATE 107

Canals

1785–1850

and the
Cumberland Road

PLATE 108

Railroads

1827–1850

Western Division

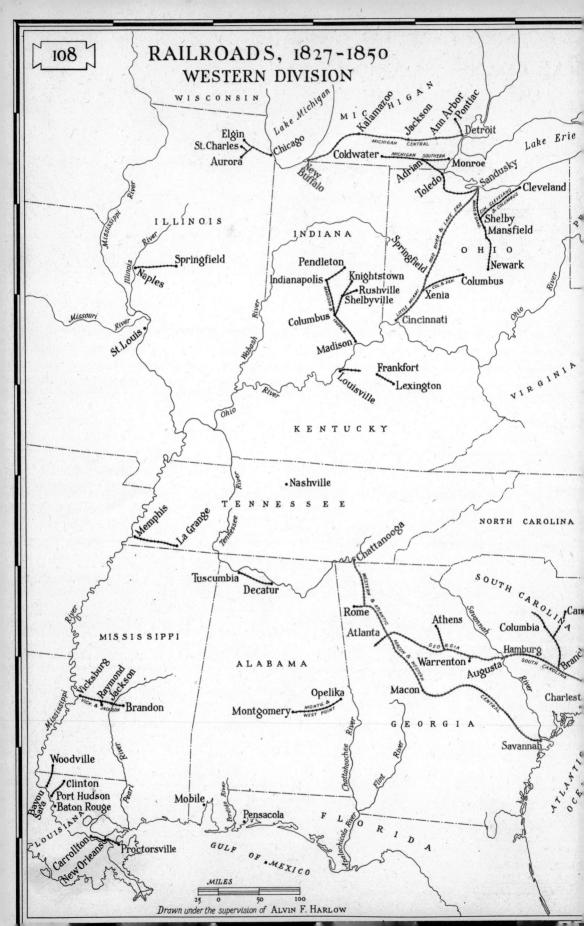

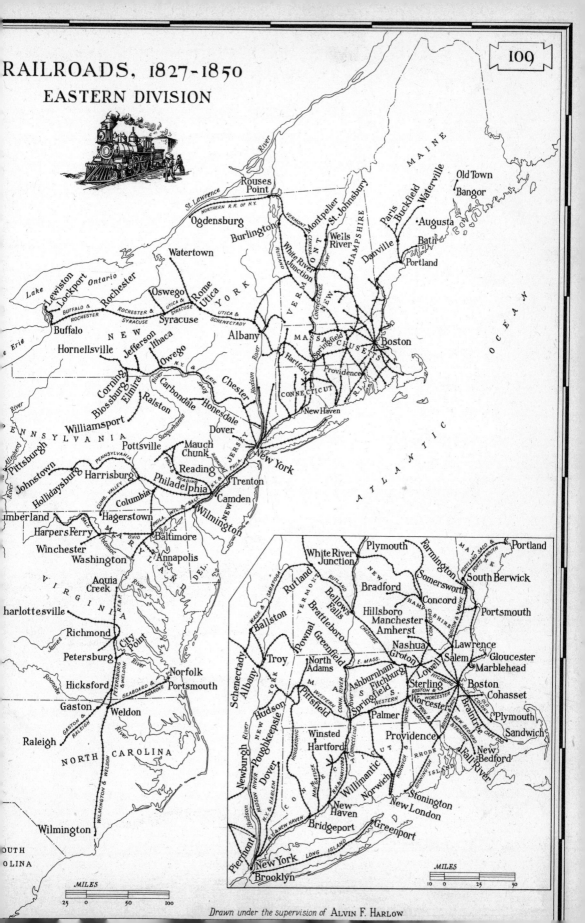

RAILROADS, 1827-1850
EASTERN DIVISION

109

Drawn under the supervision of ALVIN F. HARLOW

PLATE 109

Railroads

1827–1850

Eastern Division

PLATE 110

The
Northeast Boundary

1783–1842

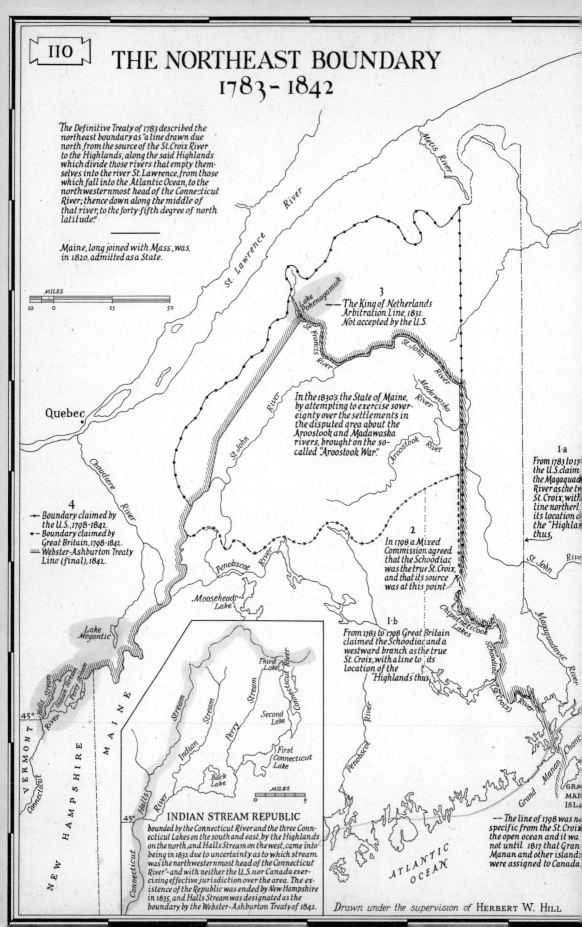

THE NORTHEAST BOUNDARY
1783-1842

The Definitive Treaty of 1783 described the northeast boundary as "a line drawn due north from the source of the St.Croix River to the Highlands; along the said Highlands which divide those rivers that empty themselves into the river St.Lawrence, from those which fall into the Atlantic Ocean, to the northwesternmost head of the Connecticut River; thence down along the middle of that river, to the forty-fifth degree of north latitude."

Maine, long joined with Mass., was, in 1820, admitted as a State.

MILES
10   0   25   50

3
— The King of Netherlands Arbitration Line, 1831. Not accepted by the U.S.

In the 1830's the State of Maine, by attempting to exercise sovereignty over the settlements in the disputed area about the Aroostook and Madawaska rivers, brought on the so-called "Aroostook War."

Quebec

4
— Boundary claimed by the U.S., 1798-1842.
⋆ Boundary claimed by Great Britain, 1798-1842.
▨ Webster-Ashburton Treaty Line (final), 1842.

I·a
From 1783 to 17—
the U.S.claim—
the Magaqua—
River as the tr—
St.Croix, with—
line northerl—
its location o—
the "Highla—
thus,

2
In 1798 a Mixed Commission agreed that the Schoodiac was the true St.Croix, and that its source was at this point.

I·b
From 1783 to 1798 Great Britain claimed the Schoodiac and a westward branch as the true St.Croix, with a line to its location of the "Highlands thus,"

INDIAN STREAM REPUBLIC

MILES
0   5

bounded by the Connecticut River and the three Connecticut Lakes on the south and east, by the Highlands on the north, and Halls Stream on the west, came into being in 1832 due to uncertainty as to which stream was the northwesternmost head of the Connecticut River"-and with neither the U.S. nor Canada exercising effective jurisdiction over the area. The existence of the Republic was ended by New Hampshire in 1835, and Halls Stream was designated as the boundary by the Webster-Ashburton Treaty of 1842.

-- The line of 1798 was n—
specific from the St.Croi—
the open ocean and it wa—
not until 1817 that Gran—
Manan and other islands—
were assigned to Canada

Drawn under the supervision of HERBERT W. HILL

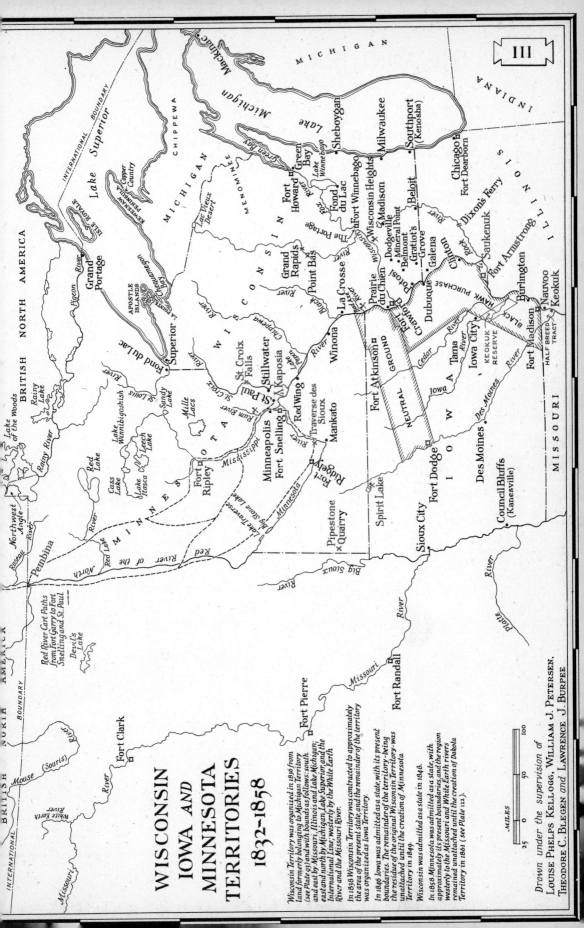

WISCONSIN IOWA AND MINNESOTA TERRITORIES 1832-1858

Wisconsin Territory was organized in 1836 from land formerly belonging to Michigan Territory (see Plate 93) and with bounds as follows: south and east by Missouri, Illinois and Lake Michigan; east and north by Michigan, Lake Superior and the International Line; westerly by the White Earth River and the Missouri River.

In 1838 Wisconsin Territory was contracted to approximately the area of the present state, and the remainder of the territory was organized as Iowa Territory.

In 1846 Iowa was admitted as a state with its present boundaries. The remainder of the territory being the residue of the original Wisconsin Territory was unattached until the creation of Minnesota Territory in 1849.

Wisconsin was admitted as a state in 1848.

In 1858 Minnesota was admitted as a state, with approximately its present boundaries, and the region westerly to the Missouri and White Earth rivers remained unattached until the creation of Dakota Territory in 1861 (see Plate 112).

Drawn under the supervision of
LOUISE PHELPS KELLOGG, WILLIAM J. PETERSEN,
THEODORE C. BLEGEN and LAWRENCE J. BURPEE

MILES
25 0 50 100

PLATE 111

Wisconsin
Iowa and Minnesota
Territories

1832–1858

PLATE 112

The
Unorganized Territory
and Oregon Country

1836–1848

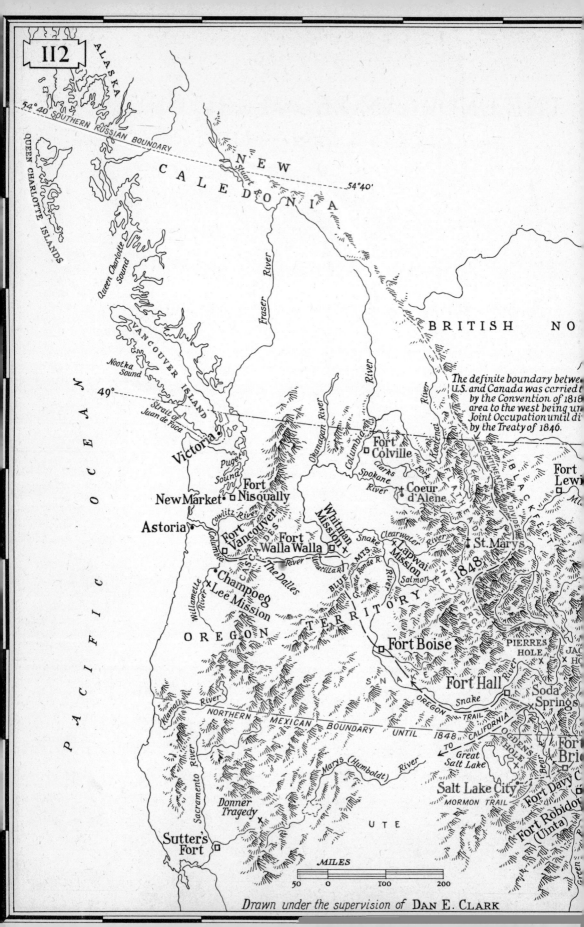

112

ALASKA

54° 40' SOUTHERN RUSSIAN BOUNDARY

QUEEN CHARLOTTE ISLANDS

NEW CALEDONIA

54°40'

Queen Charlotte Sound

Stuart River

Fraser River

VANCOUVER ISLAND

Nootka Sound

BRITISH NO

The definite boundary betwe
U.S. and Canada was carried t
by the Convention of 1818
area to the west being un
Joint Occupation until di
by the Treaty of 1846.

49°

Strait of Juan de Fuca

Victoria

Puget Sound

Okanagan River

Columbia River

Fort Colville

Kootenay River

Clarks Fork

Spokane River

CONTINENTAL DIVIDE

BLACKFEET

Fort Lewi

New Market

Fort Nisqually

Coeur d'Alene

PACIFIC OCEAN

Astoria

Cowlitz River

Fort Vancouver

CASCADES

Columbia River

Fort Walla Walla

The Dalles

River

Matilla R.

Whitman Mission

Snake

BLUE MTS.

Grande Ronde R.

Clearwater River

Lapwai Mission

Salmon River

NEZ PERCE

St. Marys

1848

Champoeg
Lee Mission

Willamette River

OREGON   TERRITORY

Klamath River

River

NORTHERN   MEXICAN   BOUNDARY   UNTIL   1848

Fort Boise

PIERRES HOLE

JA
HO

OREGON   TRAIL   CALIFORNIA

Fort Hall

Soda Springs

Snake

OGDEN'S HOLE

Bear

Fort
Brie

Donner Tragedy

Marys (Humboldt) River

TO

Great Salt Lake

Salt Lake City

Fort Davy C.

MORMON TRAIL

Fort Robido
(Uinta)

UTE

Green

Sacramento River

Sutter's Fort

MILES

50   0   100   200

Drawn under the supervision of DAN E. CLARK

THE UNORGANIZED TERRITORY
AND OREGON COUNTRY
1836-1848

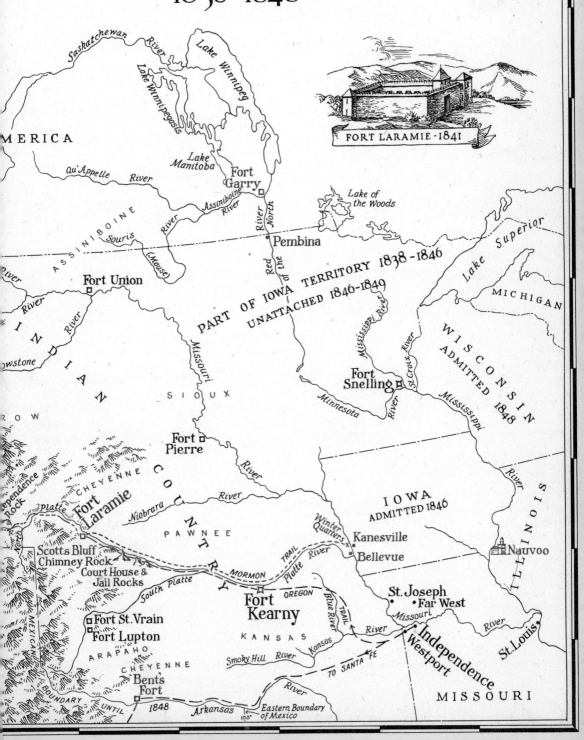

FORT LARAMIE - 1841

AMERICA

Saskatchewan River

Lake Winnipeg

Lake Winnipegosis

Qu'Appelle River

Lake Manitoba

Fort Garry

River North

Lake of the Woods

ASSINIBOINE

Souris (Mouse) River

Assiniboine River

Red River of the

Pembina

Lake Superior

MICHIGAN

Fort Union

PART OF IOWA TERRITORY 1838-1846

UNATTACHED 1846-1849

Mississippi River

St. Croix River

WISCONSIN ADMITTED 1848

River

INDIAN

Yellowstone River

Missouri River

SIOUX

Fort Snelling

Minnesota River

Mississippi

CROW

Fort Pierre

River

Independence Rock

CHEYENNE

COUNTRY

Fort Laramie

Niobrara River

PAWNEE

River

IOWA ADMITTED 1846

River

ILLINOIS

Platte

Scotts Bluff
Chimney Rock
Court House &
Jail Rocks

South Platte

MORMON

Platte River

Winter Quarters

Kanesville

Bellevue

TRAIL

Nauvoo

Fort Kearny

OREGON

TRAIL

Blue River

St. Joseph
Far West

Fort St. Vrain
Fort Lupton

KANSAS

Smoky Hill River

Kansas River

River

Missouri

Independence
Westport

River

St. Louis

MEXICAN

ARAPAHO

CHEYENNE

Bents Fort

BOUNDARY UNTIL 1848

Arkansas River

Eastern Boundary of Mexico

TO SANTA FE

100°

MISSOURI

PLATE 113

The
Unorganized Territory
and Oregon Country

1836–1848

PLATE 114

The
Clash with Mexico
and New Boundaries

1836–1848

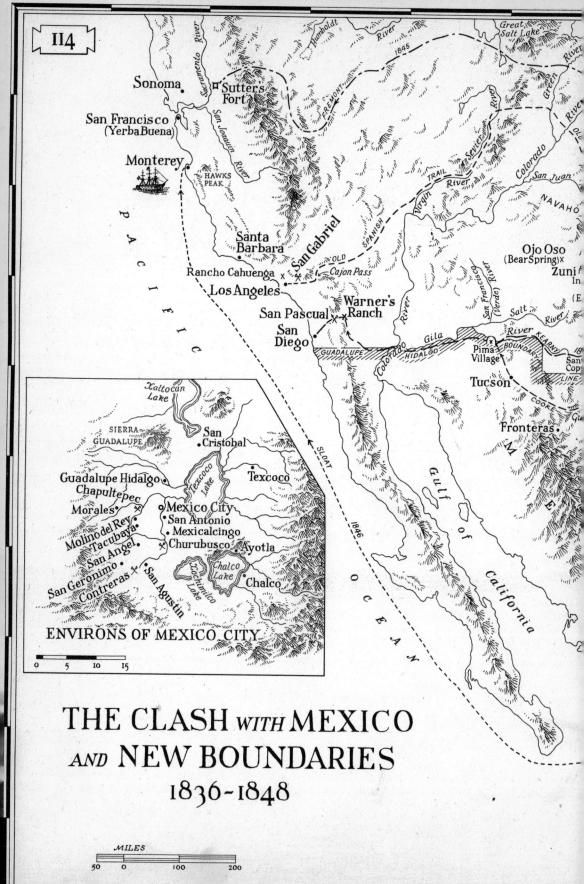

114

Sonoma · · Sutter's Fort · · San Francisco (Yerba Buena) · Monterey · HAWK'S PEAK

Humboldt River 1845 · Great Salt Lake · FREMONT · Sevier River · Green River · San Joaquin River · Sacramento River · PACIFIC · SPANISH TRAIL · OLD · Virgin River · Colorado · San Juan · NAVAHO

Santa Barbara · San Gabriel · Rancho Cahuenga × · Cajon Pass · Los Angeles · San Pascual × Warner's Ranch · San Diego · GUADALUPE HIDALGO · Colorado River · Gila · HIDALGO · San Francisco (Verde) River · Salt River · River KEARNY · BOUNDARY · LINE · COOKE · Pima Village · Tucson · Ojo Oso (Bear Spring) × · Zuni In. (E · San Cop · Fronteras · M · E

Gulf of California

SLOAT · 1846

OCEAN

ENVIRONS OF MEXICO CITY

Xaltocan Lake · SIERRA GUADALUPE · San Cristobal · Texcoco Lake · Texcoco · Guadalupe Hidalgo · Chapultepec · Morales · Mexico City · San Antonio · Molino del Rey · Tacubaya · Mexicalcingo · San Angel · Churubusco × · Ayotla · San Geronimo · Contreras × · San Agustin · Xochimilco Lake · Chalco Lake · Chalco

0   5   10   15

THE CLASH WITH MEXICO AND NEW BOUNDARIES 1836-1848

MILES
50   0   100   200

Drawn under the supervision of CARL COKE RISTER

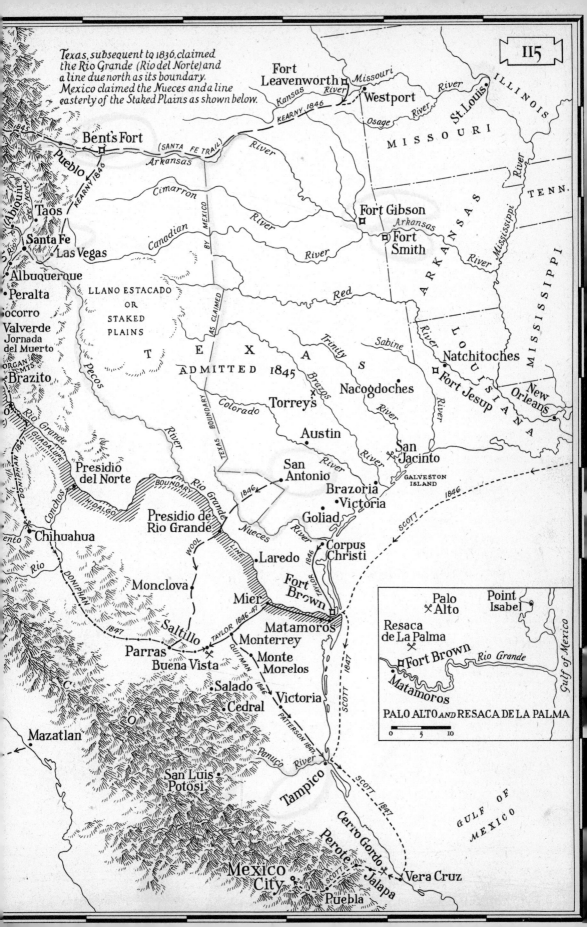

Texas, subsequent to 1836, claimed
the Rio Grande (Rio del Norte) and
a line due north as its boundary.
Mexico claimed the Nueces and a line
easterly of the Staked Plains as shown below.

Fort
Leavenworth
Missouri
Westport
River
Kansas   *River*
KEARNY 1846
Osage   *River*
St. Louis
ILLINOIS
MISSOURI
TENN.

Bent's Fort
(SANTA FE TRAIL)
Pueblo
River
Arkansas
KEARNY 1846
1845

Cimarron
Canadian
River
River

Fort Gibson
Arkansas
Fort
Smith
ARKANSAS
River   *Mississippi*   *River*

Taos
Santa Fe
Las Vegas

BY MEXICO

LLANO ESTACADO
OR
STAKED
PLAINS

Red
River

Sabine
River
LOUISIANA

Albuquerque
Peralta
Socorro
Valverde
Jornada
del Muerto
ORGAN MTS.
Brazito

Pecos

T E X A S
ADMITTED 1845

AS CLAIMED

Trinity
River
Brazos
Torrey's
Nacogdoches
River
Natchitoches
Fort Jesup
New
Orleans

Rio Grande
GUADALUPE
1847

Presidio
del Norte
Conchos
DONIPHAN

BOUNDARY
HIDALGO
Rio Grande
Presidio de
Rio Grande
1846
Colorado
River
TEXAS BOUNDARY

Austin
San
Antonio
River
River
San
Jacinto
GALVESTON
ISLAND
1846

Chihuahua
Rio

Monclova
WOOL
Nueces
River
Laredo

Brazoria
Victoria
Goliad
Corpus
Christi
SCOTT
1846

DONIPHAN

LINE
TAYLOR 1846-47

Saltillo
Mier
Fort
Brown

Parras
Buena Vista
Monterrey
Monte
Morelos
QUITMAN

Matamoros

SCOTT 1847

Palo
Alto
Point
Isabel

Resaca
de La Palma
Fort Brown
Rio Grande

Salado
Cedral

River
1846
Victoria

SCOTT 1847
PATTERSON 1846

Matamoros

PALO ALTO *AND* RESACA DE LA PALMA
0   5   10

Gulf of Mexico

Mazatlan

San Luis
Potosí

Tampico
Panuco   *River*
SCOTT 1847

GULF OF
MEXICO

MEXICO

Mexico
City
Cerro
Gordo
Perote
Jalapa
SCOTT
Vera Cruz
Puebla

PLATE 115

The
Clash with Mexico
and New Boundaries

1836–1848

PLATE 116

California
and the
Sierra Nevada Region

1833–1860

CALIFORNIA
AND THE
SIERRA NEVADA REGION
1833-1860

OREGON

Crescent City

Klamath Lake

KLAMATH MOUNTAINS

MT. SHASTA

Klamath River

Pit River

LASSENS ROUTE

Humboldt River

CALIFORNIA TRAIL

HASTINGS CUTOFF

Pyramid Lake

Humboldt Sink

Sacramento River

Carson Sink

PONY EXPRESS

Downieville

Donner Tragedy

Truckee River

Fort Churchill

Marysville Buttes

Marysville

Nevada City

Virginia City

Comstock Lode

Carson City

Genoa

Coloma

Bear River

American River

Lake Tahoe

Walker Lake

Fort Ross

Sutter's Fort

Sacramento

Placerville

Mokelumne River

Cosumnes River

Sonoma

Benicia

Stockton

Sonora

Stanislaus River

UTAH TERRITORY

San Francisco (Yerba Buena)

Oakland

Tuolumne River

Merced River

San Jose

Mariposa

Santa Cruz

San Juan

HAWKS PEAK

Monterey

San Joaquin River

Kings River

Owens Lake

DEATH VALLEY

Tulare Lake

NEW MEX

Kern River

Walkers Pass

San Luis Obispo

Kern Lake

Colorado River

OLD SPANISH TRAIL

MOHAVE DESERT

Cajon Pass

SAN MIGUEL

Santa Barbara

San Fernando

San Gabriel

San Bernardino

SANTA ROSA

SANTA CRUZ

Ventura

Rancho Cahuenga

Los Angeles

San Juan Capistrano

Warner's Ranch

SANTA CATALINA

GILA TRAIL

San Pascual

Fort Yuma

San Diego

MEXICO

BAJA CALIFORNIA

Gulf of California

PACIFIC OCEAN

MILES

25 0 50 100

Drawn under the supervision of JOHN W. CAUGHEY

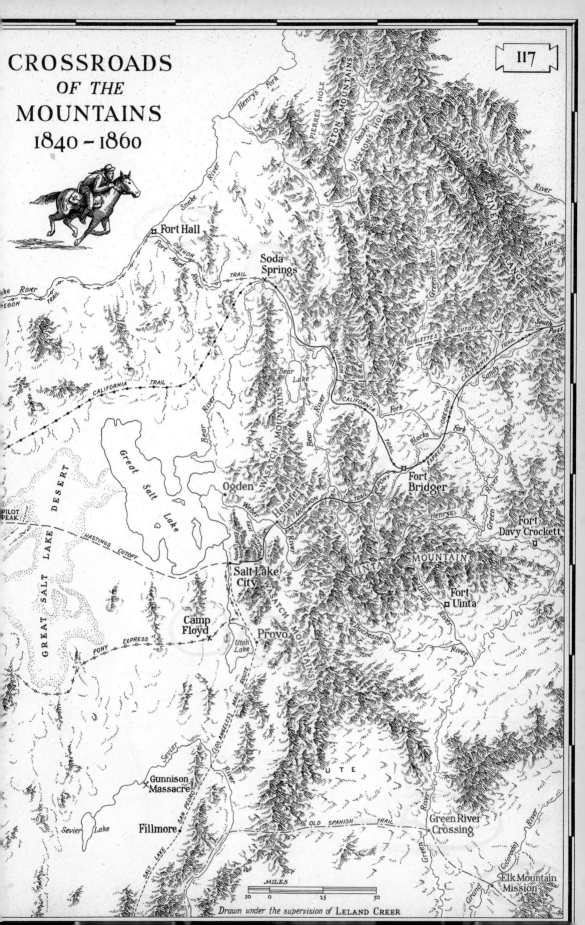

CROSSROADS
OF THE
MOUNTAINS
1840 – 1860

Henrys Fork

PIERRES HOLE

TETON MOUNTAINS

JACKSONS HOLE

Snake River

WIND RIVER RANGE

Wind River

Popo Agie River

Snake River

Port Neuf River

OREGON TRAIL

☐ Fort Hall

Soda Springs

TRAIL

Green River

Horse Creek

South Pass

SUBLETTES CUTOFF

CALIFORNIA TRAIL

CALIFORNIA TRAIL

Bear Lake

OREGON TRAIL

Hams Fork

Sandy

Blacks Fork

Fork

Bear River

Bear River

PONY EXPRESS TRAIL

Fort Bridger

Snake River Trail

Oregon Trail

Henrys Fork

Green River

Fort Davy Crockett

Ogden

WASATCH MOUNTAINS

Weber River

Henefer

MORMON

1849 Conn

Echo

UINTA MOUNTAINS

Great Salt Lake

Salt Lake City

WASATCH MOUNTAINS

Fort Uinta

PILOT PEAK

HASTINGS CUTOFF

Duchesne

Uinta River

GREAT SALT LAKE DESERT

Camp Floyd

Utah Lake

Provo

PONY EXPRESS

River

UTE

Sevier River

(LOS ANGELES) MAIL ROUTE

Gunnison Massacre

SAN PEDRO

Green River Crossing

Sevier Lake

Fillmore

OLD SPANISH TRAIL

Green River

(Colorado) River

Grand

Elk Mountain Mission

MILES
10 0   25   50

Drawn under the supervision of LELAND CREER

PLATE 117

Crossroads
of the
Mountains

1840–1860

PLATE 118

Westward Advance

1849–1860

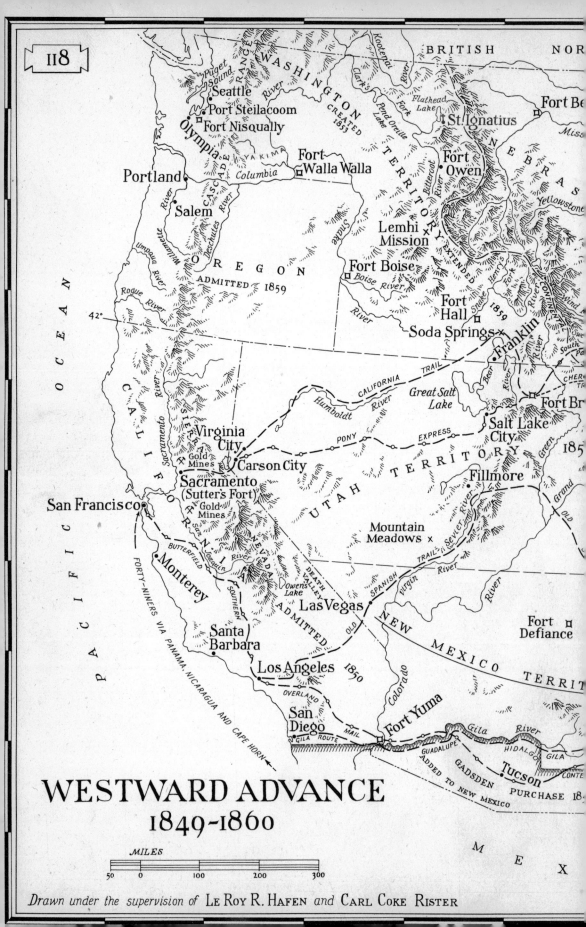

WESTWARD ADVANCE
1849-1860

Drawn under the supervision of LE ROY R. HAFEN *and* CARL COKE RISTER

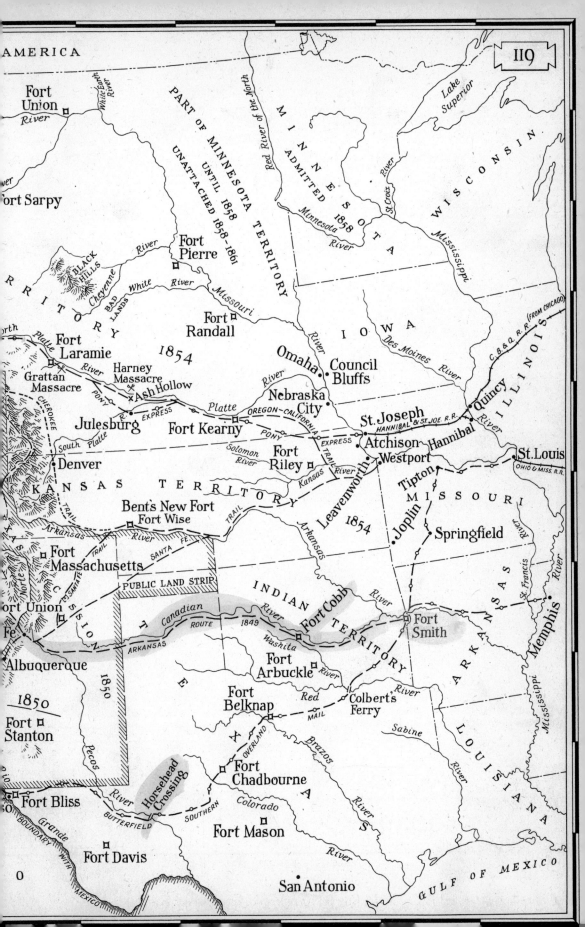

Fort
Union
River

rt Sarpy

Fort Sarpy

White Earth River

PART OF MINNESOTA TERRITORY
UNTIL 1858
UNATTACHED 1858-1861

Red River of the North

MINNESOTA
ADMITTED
1858

Lake Superior

WISCONSIN

St. Croix River

Minnesota River

Mississippi

BLACK HILLS
Cheyenne River
BAD LANDS
White River
Missouri River

Fort
Pierre

Fort
Randall

1854

IOWA

Des Moines River

C.B.&Q.R.R. (FROM CHICAGO)

ILLINOIS

TERRITORY

North
Platte River
Fort
Laramie

Grattan
Massacre

Harney
Massacre
Ash Hollow

PONY

Julesburg

R. R.
EXPRESS

South Platte

Denver

KANSAS

Fort Kearny

Platte
OREGON–CALIFORNIA

PONY

Solomon River

Fort
Riley

Kansas River

Omaha

Council
Bluffs

River

Nebraska
City

EXPRESS

St. Joseph
HANNIBAL & ST. JOE. R.R.

Atchison

Westport

TRAIL

TERRITORY

Leavenworth

1854

Hannibal

Quincy

River

St. Louis
OHIO & MISS. R.R.

Tipton

MISSOURI

Joplin

Springfield

CHEROKEE

TRAIL

TEXAS

Bent's New Fort
Fort Wise

TRAIL

Arkansas River

Arkansas

SANTA FE

PUBLIC LAND STRIP

SANTA FE

Fort
Massachusetts

Fort Union
Fe.

Albuquerque

ARKANSAS

SION

N

ROUTE 1849

Canadian
1849

INDIAN

River

Fort Cobb

River

St. Francis River

Memphis

ARKANSAS

Fort
Smith

Mississippi River

1850

Fort
Stanton

Pecos

1850

Washita

Fort Arbuckle

River

Red
MAIL

Colbert's
Ferry

TERRITORY

Fort
Belknap

X

OVERLAND

Fort
Chadbourne

Brazos River

Sabine

LOUISIANA

River

Fort Bliss

River

Horsehead
Crossing

BUTTERFIELD

SOUTHERN

Colorado River

A
S

Fort Mason

Gulf of Mexico

Grande

BOUNDARY WITH MEXICO

Fort Davis

San Antonio

GULF OF MEXICO

0

PLATE 119

Westward Advance

1849–1860

PLATE 120

Pikes Peak
Region

1858–1860

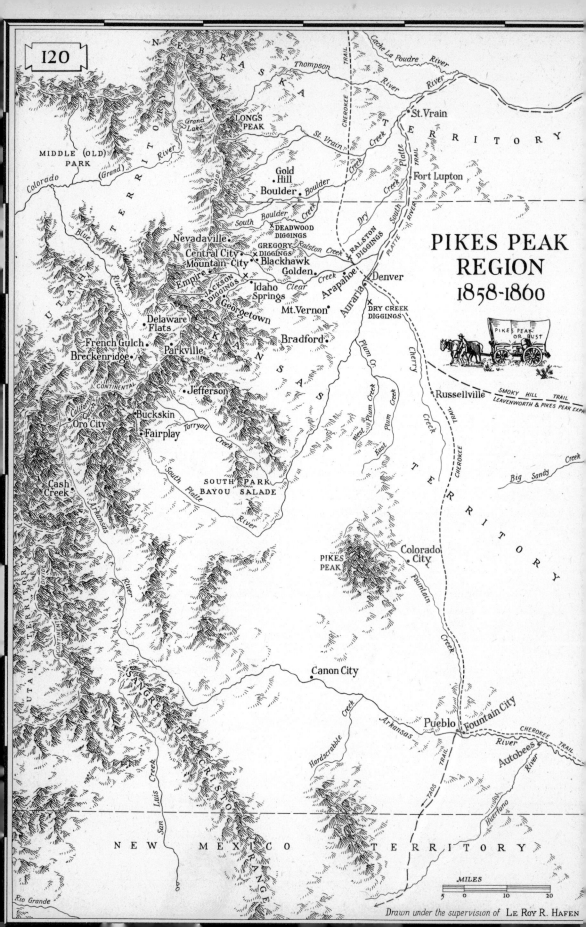

PIKES PEAK REGION 1858-1860

PIKES PEAK OR BUST

NEBRASKA

Thompson River

Cache La Poudre River

Grand Lake

LONG'S PEAK

St. Vrain

St. Vrain River

Fort Lupton

Gold Hill

Boulder

Boulder Creek

Cherokee Trail

Platte River

South Platte River

Dry Creek

MIDDLE (OLD) PARK

Colorado (Grand) River

UTAH TERRITORY

South Boulder Creek

DEADWOOD DIGGINGS

Nevadaville

Central City

Mountain City

GREGORY DIGGINGS

Blackhawk

Golden

Ralston Creek

RALSTON DIGGINGS

Blue River

Empire

JACKSON DIGGINGS

Idaho Springs

Georgetown

Clear Creek

Arapahoe

Denver

Auraria

DRY CREEK DIGGINGS

Delaware Flats

Mt. Vernon

French Gulch

Breckenridge

Parkville

Bradford

KANSAS TERRITORY

CONTINENTAL

Jefferson

Buckskin

Tarryall Creek

Fairplay

Cherry Creek

Russellville

SMOKY HILL TRAIL

LEAVENWORTH & PIKES PEAK EXPR.

CHEROKEE TRAIL

California Gulch

Oro City

Cash Creek

Arkansas River

SOUTH PARK BAYOU SALADE

South Platte River

West Plum Creek

Plum Cr.

East Plum Creek

Big Sandy Creek

PIKES PEAK

Colorado City

Fountain Creek

SANGRE DE CRISTO RANGE

Canon City

San Luis Creek

Hardscrabble Creek

Arkansas River

Pueblo

Fountain City

Autobees

CHEROKEE TRAIL

TAOS TRAIL

Huerfano River

Rio Grande

NEW MEXICO TERRITORY

MILES
5   0   10   20

Drawn under the supervision of LE ROY R. HAFEN

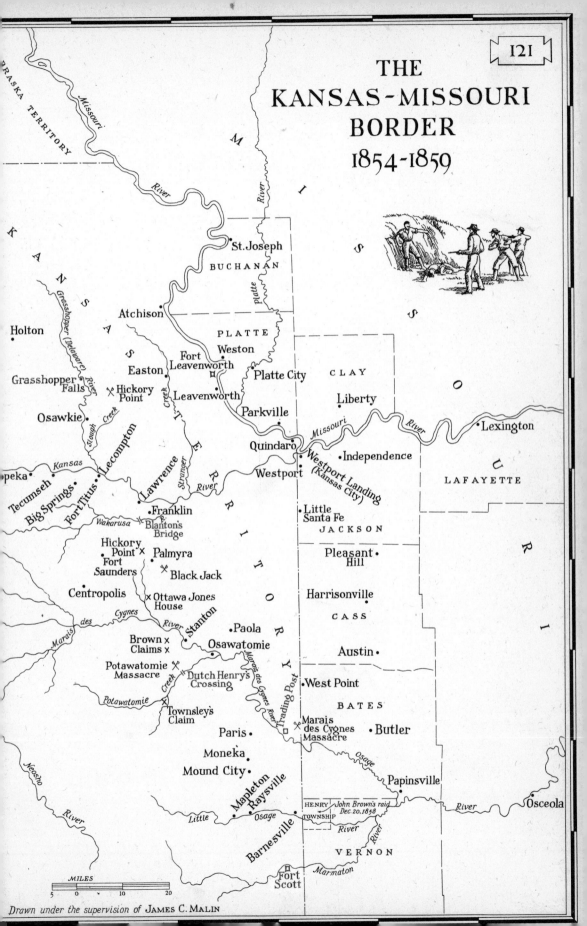

THE KANSAS-MISSOURI BORDER
1854-1859

NEBRASKA TERRITORY

Missouri River

M I S S O U R I

KANSAS

St. Joseph

BUCHANAN

Platte River

Holton

Atchison

PLATTE

Weston

Fort Leavenworth

Easton

Grasshopper Falls

Hickory Point

Leavenworth

Platte City

CLAY

Osawkie

Lecompton

Liberty

Parkville

Topeka

Kansas

Tecumseh

Big Springs

Fort Titus

Lawrence

Stranger River

Quindaro

Westport Landing (Kansas City)

Westport

Independence

Lexington

LAFAYETTE

Franklin

Blanton's Bridge

Wakarusa

Little Santa Fe

JACKSON

Hickory Point

Palmyra

Fort Saunders

Black Jack

Pleasant Hill

Centropolis

Ottawa Jones House

des Cygnes River

Stanton

Harrisonville

CASS

Brown Claims

Paola

Osawatomie

Austin

Potawatomie Massacre

Dutch Henry's Crossing

Trading Post

West Point

Marais des Cygnes River

BATES

Potawatomie Creek

Townsley's Claim

Paris

Marais des Cygnes Massacre

Butler

Moneka

Mound City

Mapleton

Raysville

Osage River

Papinsville

Osceola

Neosho River

Marais des Cygnes

HENRY TOWNSHIP

John Brown's raid Dec. 20, 1858

Barnesville

Little Osage River

V E R N O N

Fort Scott

Marmaton

MILES
5   0   10   20

Drawn under the supervision of JAMES C. MALIN

PLATE 121

The Kansas-Missouri Border

1854–1859

PLATE 122

The
United States

March 4, 1861

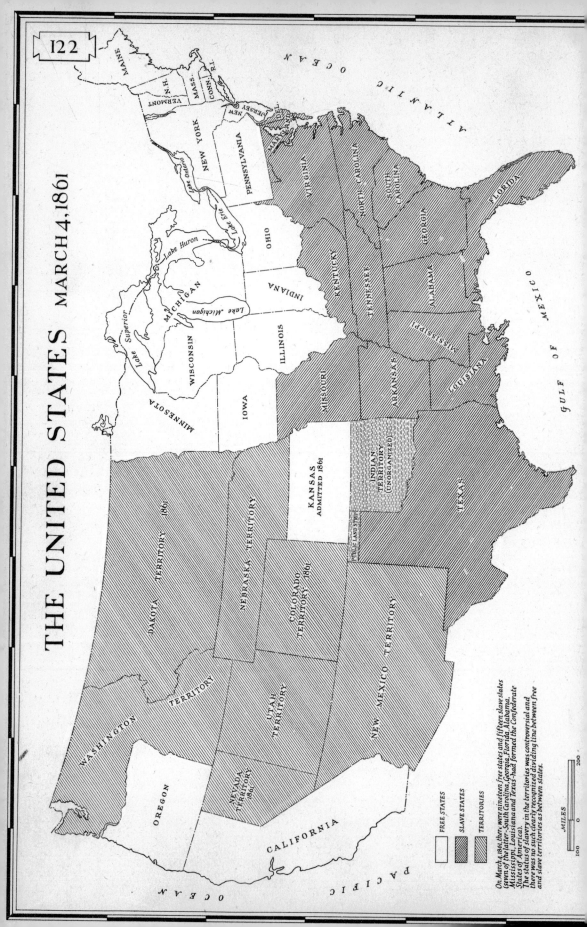

122

THE UNITED STATES MARCH 4, 1861

ATLANTIC OCEAN

MAINE
N.H.
VERMONT
MASS.
CONN. R.I.
NEW YORK
NEW JERSEY
PENNSYLVANIA
MARYLAND
DELAWARE
VIRGINIA
NORTH CAROLINA
SOUTH CAROLINA
FLORIDA
GEORGIA
OHIO
KENTUCKY
TENNESSEE
ALABAMA
INDIANA
MISSISSIPPI
MICHIGAN
ILLINOIS
WISCONSIN
IOWA
MINNESOTA
MISSOURI
ARKANSAS
LOUISIANA
Lake Ontario
Lake Erie
Lake Huron
Lake Michigan
Lake Superior

GULF OF MEXICO

KANSAS
ADMITTED 1861
INDIAN TERRITORY
(UNORGANIZED)
PUBLIC LAND STRIP
TEXAS
DAKOTA TERRITORY 1861
NEBRASKA TERRITORY
COLORADO TERRITORY 1861
WASHINGTON TERRITORY
UTAH TERRITORY
NEW MEXICO TERRITORY
NEVADA TERRITORY 1861
OREGON
CALIFORNIA

PACIFIC OCEAN

On March 4, 1861, there were nineteen free states and fifteen slave states
(seven of the latter—South Carolina, Georgia, Florida, Alabama,
Mississippi, Louisiana and Texas—had formed the Confederate
States of America).
The status of slavery in the territories was controversial and
there was no such clearly recognized dividing line between free
and slave territories as between states.

FREE STATES
SLAVE STATES
TERRITORIES

MILES
100   0   200

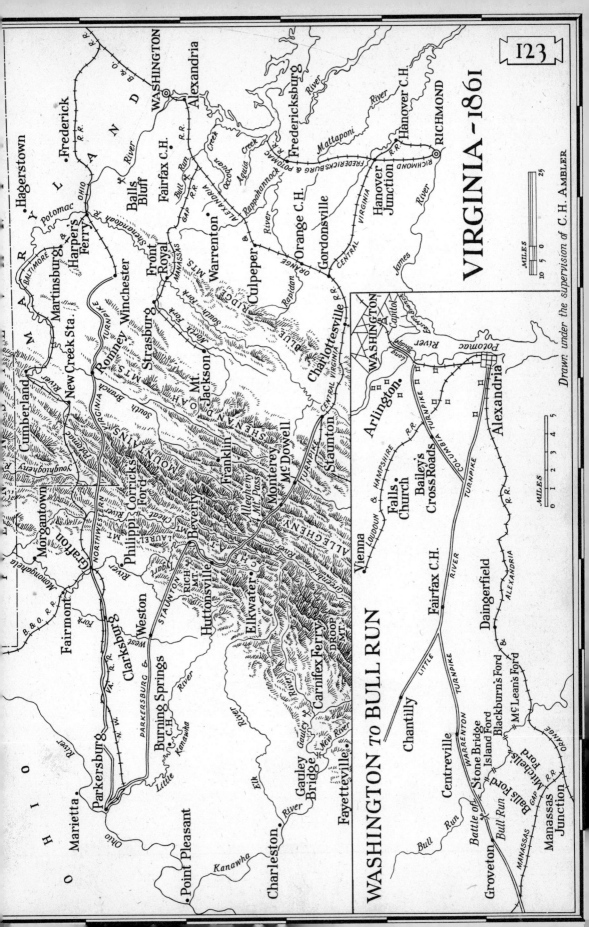

VIRGINIA – 1861

Drawn under the supervision of C. H. AMBLER

WASHINGTON TO BULL RUN

123

PLATE 123

Virginia

1861

PLATE 124

Civil War

1861–1865

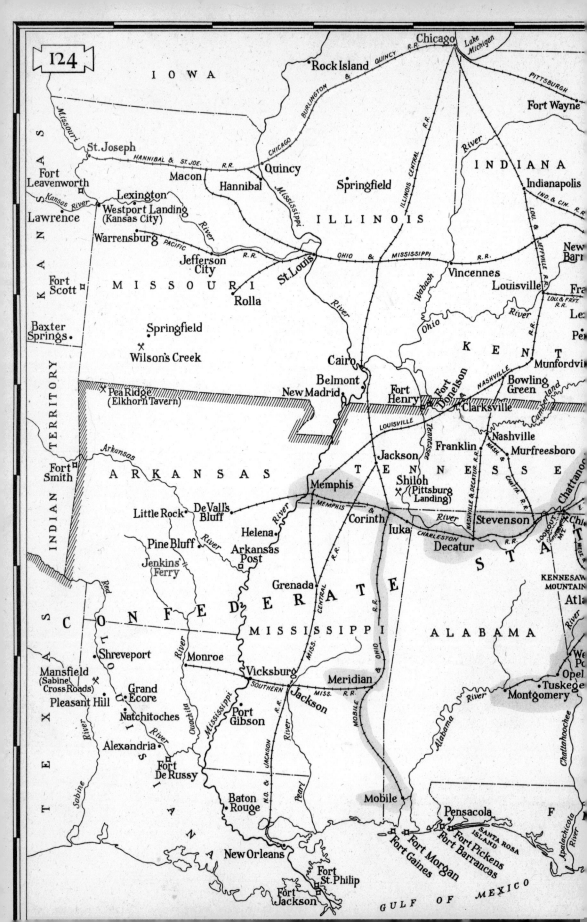

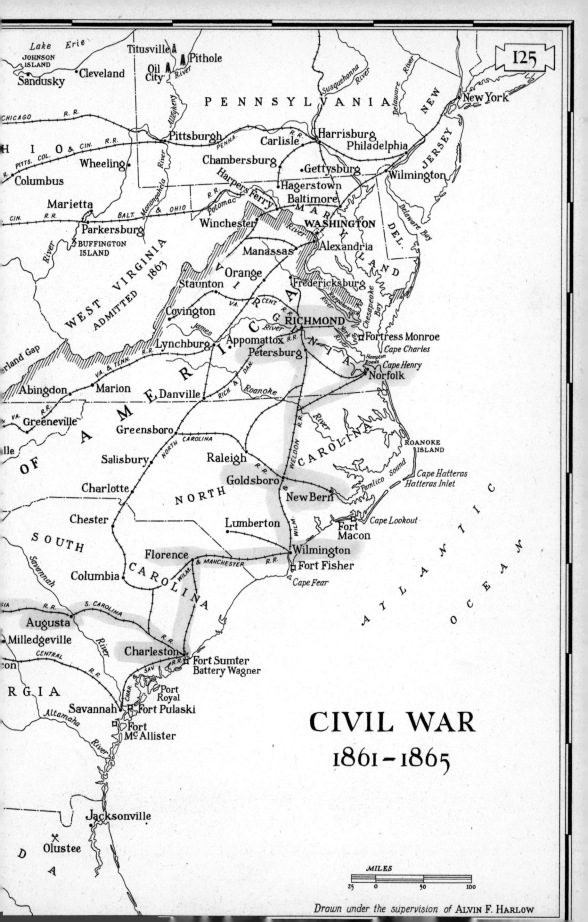

Lake Erie
JOHNSON ISLAND
Sandusky • Cleveland
Titusville • Pithole
Oil City
CHICAGO R.R.
OHIO & CIN. R.R.
PITTS. COL. R.R.
Columbus
Wheeling
Pittsburgh
PENNA. R.R.
Chambersburg
PENNSYLVANIA
Susquehanna River
Harrisburg
Carlisle
Philadelphia
Gettysburg
Hagerstown
Wilmington
NEW JERSEY
Delaware River
New York

Marietta
CIN. R.R.
Parkersburg
BUFFINGTON ISLAND
BALT. & OHIO
Harpers Ferry
Potomac River
Winchester
Baltimore
MARYLAND
WASHINGTON
DEL.
Delaware Bay

WEST VIRGINIA ADMITTED 1863
Monongahela River
Staunton
Manassas
Orange
Alexandria
Covington
James River
Fredericksburg
Rappahannock River
Chesapeake Bay
VA. CENT. R.R.
RICHMOND
York River
Fortress Monroe
Cape Charles
Lynchburg
Appomattox
Petersburg
Hampton Roads
Cape Henry
VA. & TENN. R.R.
Abingdon
Marion
Danville
RICH. & DAN. R.R.
Roanoke River
Norfolk
erland Gap
Greeneville
OF
Greensboro
NORTH CAROLINA
CAROLINA
Roanoke River
ROANOKE ISLAND
VA.
AMERICA
Salisbury
Raleigh
WELDON R.R.
Pamlico Sound
Cape Hatteras
Hatteras Inlet
Charlotte
NORTH
Goldsboro
New Bern
lle
Chester
Lumberton
WILM. & WELDON R.R.
Fort Macon
Cape Lookout

SOUTH
Savannah River
CAROLINA
Florence
WILM. & MANCHESTER R.R.
Wilmington
Columbia
S. CAROLINA R.R.
Fort Fisher
Cape Fear
ATLANTIC OCEAN
GIA
Augusta
Milledgeville
CENTRAL R.R.
on
Charleston
CHAR. R.R.
SAV. R.R.
Fort Sumter
Battery Wagner
RGIA
Altamaha River
Savannah
Port Royal
Fort Pulaski
Fort McAllister

Jacksonville
D
Olustee
A

CIVIL WAR
1861–1865

MILES
25   0   50   100

Drawn under the supervision of ALVIN F. HARLOW

PLATE 125

Civil War

1861–1865

PLATE 126

Missouri Region

1861–1864

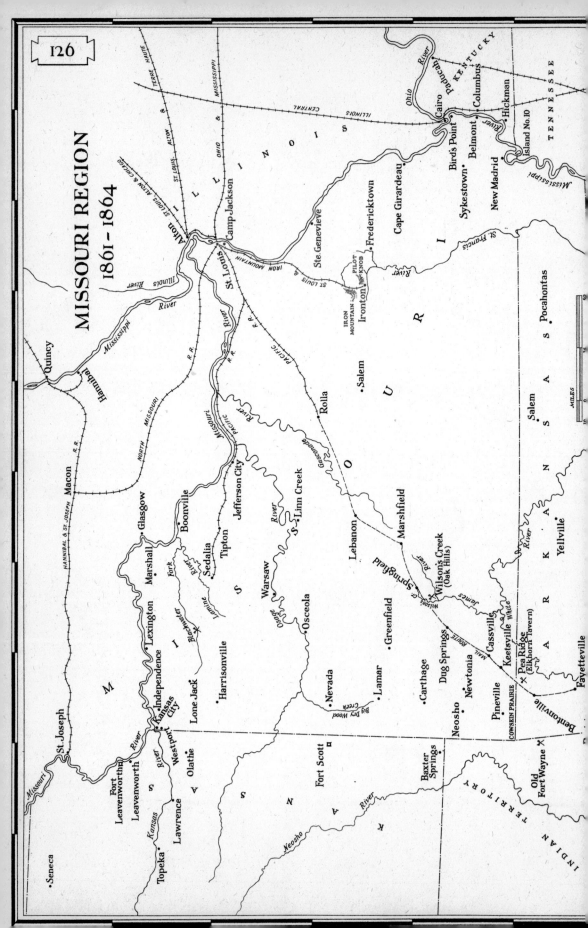

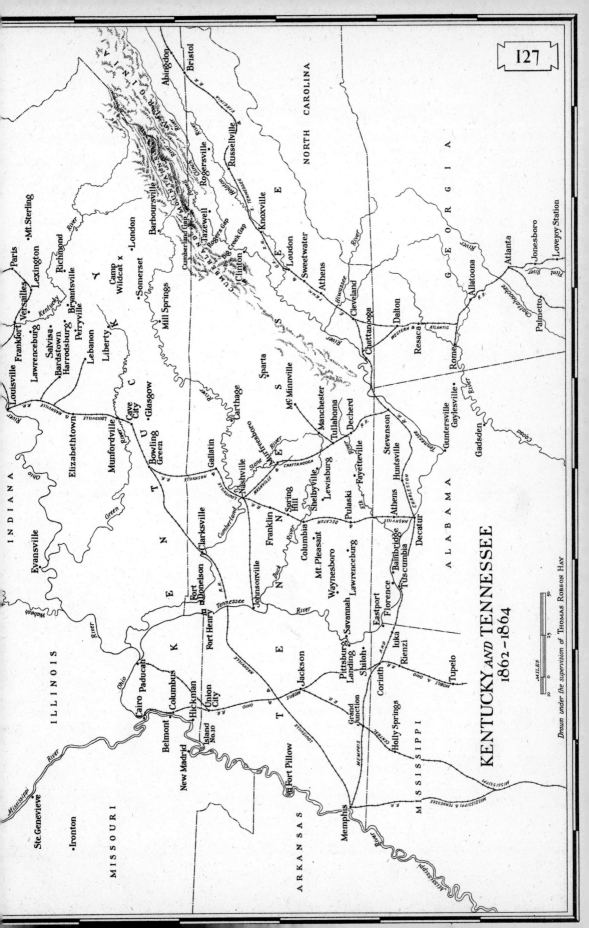

KENTUCKY *and* TENNESSEE
1862–1864

Drawn under the supervision of THOMAS ROBSON HAY

127

PLATE 127

Kentucky and Tennessee

1862–1864

PLATE 128

Virginia, Maryland
and
Pennsylvania

1862–1863

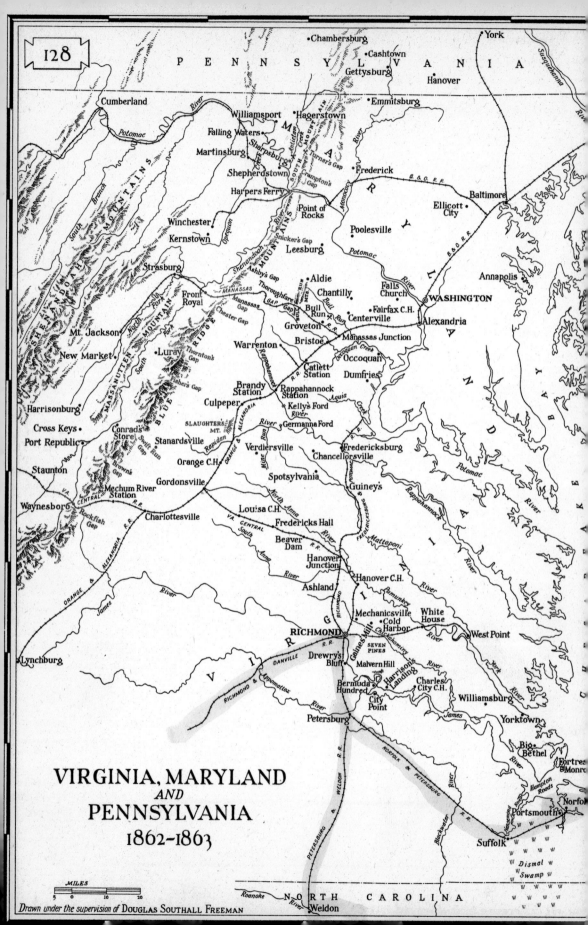

VIRGINIA, MARYLAND
AND
PENNSYLVANIA
1862-1863

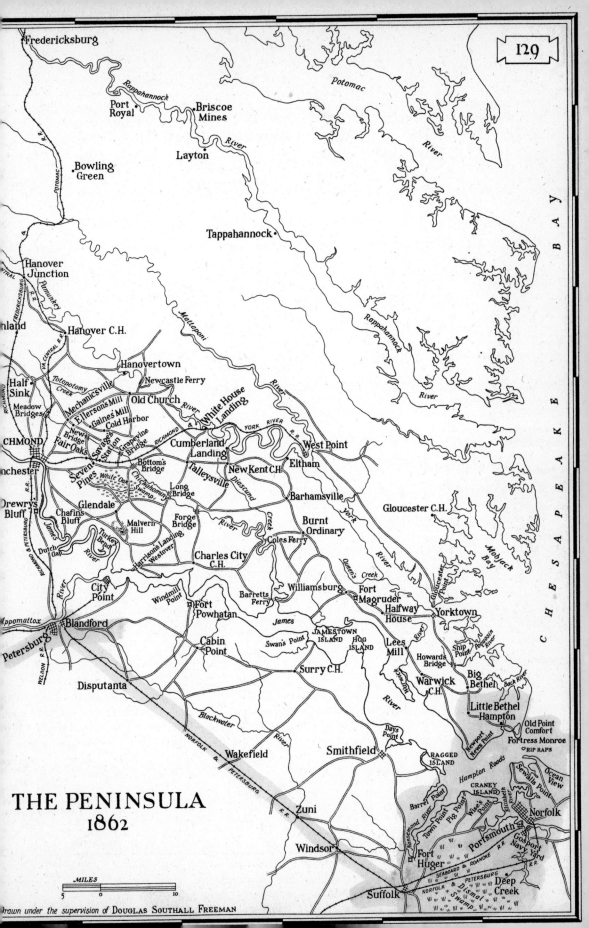

THE PENINSULA
1862

MILES
5 0 10

Drawn under the supervision of DOUGLAS SOUTHALL FREEMAN

PLATE 129

The Peninsula

1862

PLATE 130

Trans-Mississippi

1861–1865

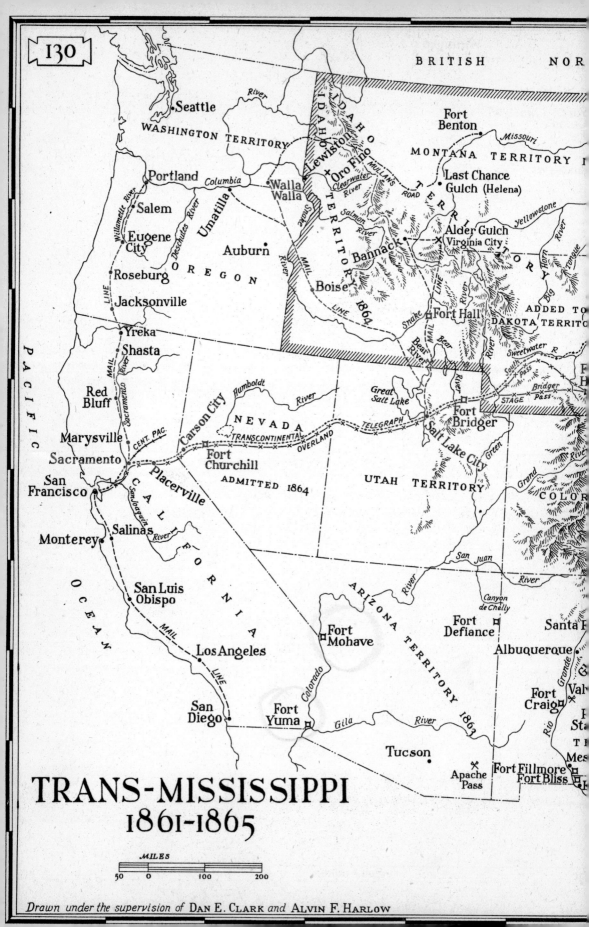

130

BRITISH   NOR

Seattle

WASHINGTON TERRITORY

River

Fort
Benton

Missouri

MONTANA TERRITORY

IDAHO

Lewiston

Oro Fino

Clearwater River

Last Chance
Gulch (Helena)

Portland

Columbia

Walla
Walla

Deschutes River

Umatilla

Snake

Willamette River

Salem

OREGON

Eugene
City

Auburn

River

Boise

Bannack

Alder Gulch
Virginia City

Yellowstone River

TERRITORY

Roseburg

Jacksonville

MAIL

LINE 1864

Salmon River

MULLANS ROAD

LINE

TERRITORY

Fort Hall

ADDED TO
DAKOTA TERRITO

Big Horn River

Tongue

Yreka

Shasta

Red
Bluff

MAIL

Sacramento River

Humboldt

River

Great
Salt Lake

NEVADA

Snake

Bear

Bear
River

River

Sweetwater R.

South Pass

Bridger Pass

Marysville

CENT. PAC.

Carson City

TRANSCONTINENTAL

TELEGRAPH

Fort
Bridger

Salt Lake City

STAGE

Sacramento

Placerville

Fort
Churchill

OVERLAND

ADMITTED 1864

UTAH TERRITORY

Green

COLOR

San
Francisco

C. San Joaquin

CALIFORNIA

River

PACIFIC

OCEAN

Monterey

Salinas

River

San Juan

River

San Luis
Obispo

ARIZONA TERRITORY

River

Canyon
de Chelly

Fort
Defiance

Santa F

Los Angeles

MAIL

Fort
Mohave

Colorado

Albuquerque

Fort
Craig

Val

LINE

TH

San
Diego

Fort
Yuma

Gila

River

R

Sta

Tucson

Mes

Rio Grande

Apache
Pass

Fort Fillmore
Fort Bliss

TRANS-MISSISSIPPI
1861-1865

MILES

50   0   100   200

Drawn under the supervision of DAN E. CLARK *and* ALVIN F. HARLOW

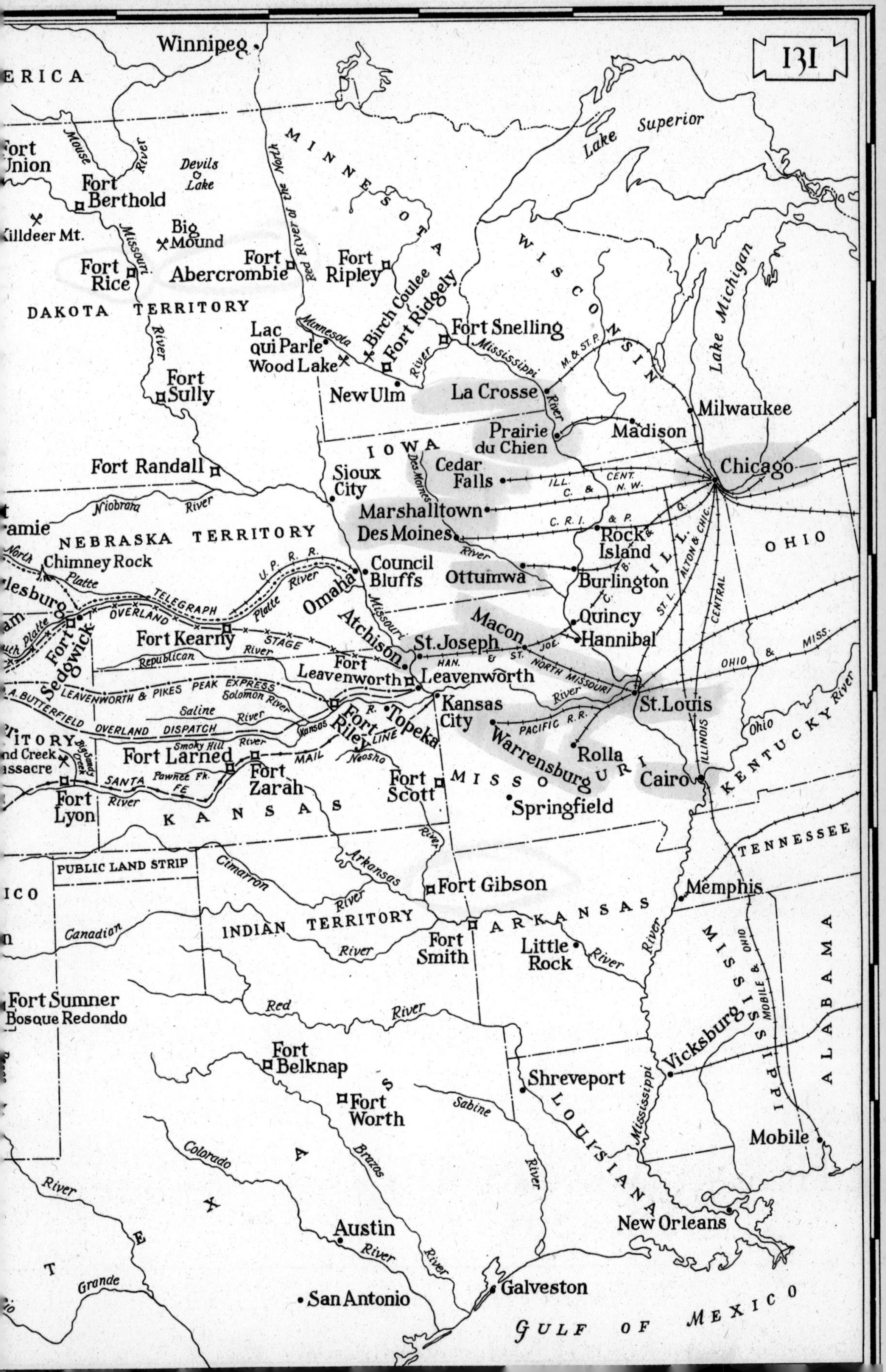

Winnipeg
MINNESOTA
WISCONSIN
Lake Superior
Lake Michigan
Devils Lake
Fort Union
Fort Berthold
Killdeer Mt.
Big Mound
Fort Rice
Fort Abercrombie
Fort Ripley
DAKOTA TERRITORY
Birch Coulee
Fort Ridgely
Fort Snelling
Lac qui Parle
Wood Lake
New Ulm
La Crosse
Prairie du Chien
Madison
Milwaukee
Fort Sully
Fort Randall
IOWA
Cedar Falls
Sioux City
Chicago
Marshalltown
Des Moines
Rock Island
Council Bluffs
Ottumwa
Burlington
NEBRASKA TERRITORY
Chimney Rock
Omaha
Atchison
Quincy
Hannibal
Macon
St. Joseph
Fort Kearny
Fort Sedgwick
Fort Leavenworth
Leavenworth
OHIO
St. Louis
Kansas City
Topeka
Fort Riley
Rolla
Warrensburg
Cairo
Fort Larned
Fort Zarah
Fort Lyon
Fort Scott
MISSOURI
Springfield
KANSAS
KENTUCKY
TENNESSEE
PUBLIC LAND STRIP
Fort Gibson
Memphis
INDIAN TERRITORY
ARKANSAS
Fort Smith
Little Rock
Fort Sumner
Bosque Redondo
Fort Belknap
Fort Worth
Shreveport
Vicksburg
MISSISSIPPI
ALABAMA
LOUISIANA
TEXAS
Mobile
New Orleans
Austin
Galveston
San Antonio
GULF OF MEXICO
Missouri River
Mississippi River
Platte River
Red River
Arkansas River
Canadian River
Cimarron River
Brazos River
Colorado River
Sabine River
Rio Grande
Niobrara River
Republican River
Solomon River
Saline River
Smoky Hill River
Santa Fe
TELEGRAPH
OVERLAND STAGE
LEAVENWORTH & PIKES PEAK EXPRESS
BUTTERFIELD OVERLAND DISPATCH
MAIL LINE
U. P. R. R.
ILL. CENT.
C. & N. W.
C. R. I. & P.
HAN. & ST. JOE.
NORTH MISSOURI
PACIFIC R.R.
OHIO & MISS.
ILLINOIS CENTRAL
MOBILE & OHIO
M. & ST. P.

PLATE 131

Trans-Mississippi

1861–1865

PLATE 132

Chickamauga
and
Chattanooga

1863

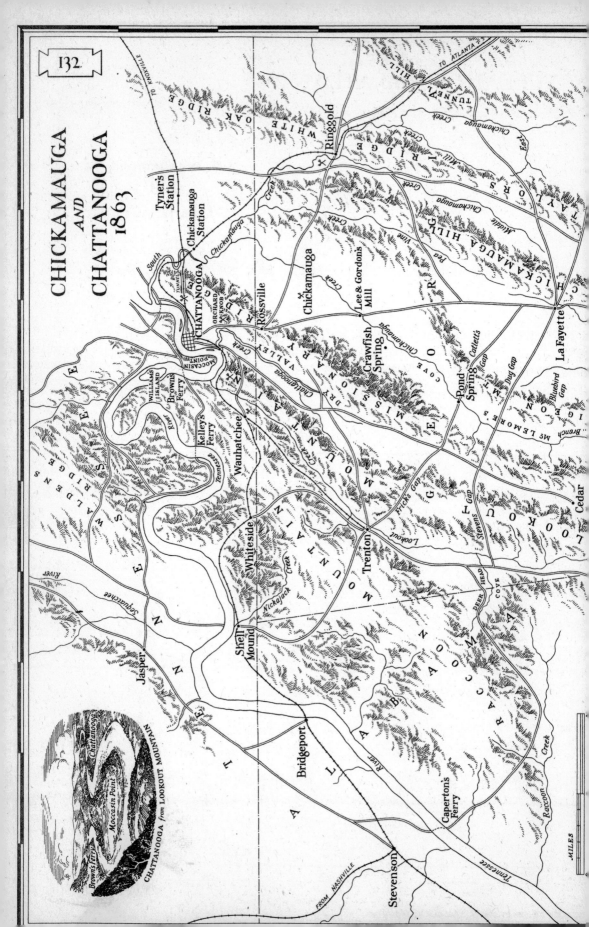

132

CHICKAMAUGA
AND
CHATTANOOGA
1863

TO KNOXVILLE

TO ATLANTA

WHITE OAK RIDGE

Ringgold

TUNNEL HILL

East Chickamauga Creek

Chickamauga Creek

Mill Creek

Tyners Station

Chickamauga Station

South Chickamauga Creek

Chickamauga Creek

TUNNEL

CHATTANOOGA

ORCHARD KNOB

Rossville

Chickamauga

Vine Creek

Chickamauga Creek

Lee & Gordons Mill

Pea Vine Creek

Middle Chickamauga Creek

HICKAMAUGA HILL

TAYLORS RIDGE

La Fayette

MOCCASIN POINT

Chattanooga Creek

RIDGE

Crawfish Spring

Cove Chickamauga

Pond Spring

Catlett's

Dug Gap

Bluebird Gap

Pigeon Gap

"Branch" Mc LEMORE'S

Cedar

WILLIAMS ISLAND

Browns Ferry

MISSIONARY VALLEY

DRY VALLEY

Tennessee River

Kelleys Ferry

Wauhatchee

MISSIONARY RIDGE

O
G
E

Fricks Gap

Stevens Gap

Lookout Gap

DEER HEAD COVE

LOOKOUT MT

WALDENS RIDGE

Whiteside

Raccoon Creek

Kickajack Creek

Trenton

M
O
U
N
T
A
I
N

A
L
A
B
A
M
A

RACCOON

River

Sequatchee River

Jasper

Shell Mound

TENNESSEE

Bridgeport

Capertons Ferry

Raccoon Creek

Tennessee River

Stevenson

FROM NASHVILLE

Browns Ferry

Moccatin Point

Chattanooga

CHATTANOOGA From LOOKOUT MOUNTAIN

MILES

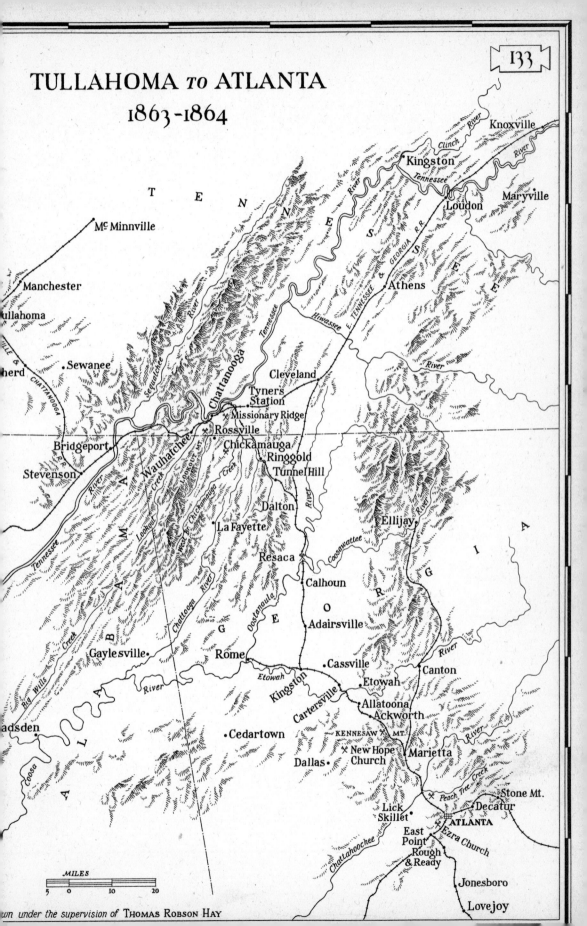

TULLAHOMA *TO* ATLANTA
1863-1864

Knoxville

McMinnville

Manchester

Tullahoma

Kingston

Maryville

Loudon

Sewanee

Tennessee River

Athens

Cleveland

Tyner's Station

Missionary Ridge

Chattanooga

× Rossville

Bridgeport

Chickamauga

Ringgold

Tunnel Hill

Stevenson

Wauhatchee

Dalton

Ellijay

La Fayette

Resaca

Calhoun

Adairsville

Gaylesville

Rome

Cassville

Canton

Etowah

Cedartown

Kingston

Cartersville

Allatoona

Ackworth

KENNESAW × MT.

× New Hope Church

Dallas

Marietta

Lick Skillet

× Peach Tree Creek

Decatur

Stone Mt.

ATLANTA

East Point

Ezra Church

Rough & Ready

Jonesboro

Lovejoy

Chattahoochee

T E N N E S S E E

A L A B A M A

G E O R G I A

E. TENNESSEE & GEORGIA R.R.

Clinch River

Hiwassee River

Coosawattee

Oostanaula River

Etowah River

Chattooga River

Coosa River

Big Wills Creek

Lookout Creek

West Br. Chickamauga

MILES
5 0 10 20

wn under the supervision of THOMAS ROBSON HAY

PLATE 133

Tullahoma
to Atlanta

1863–1864

PLATE 134

Memphis
to the Gulf

1862–1863

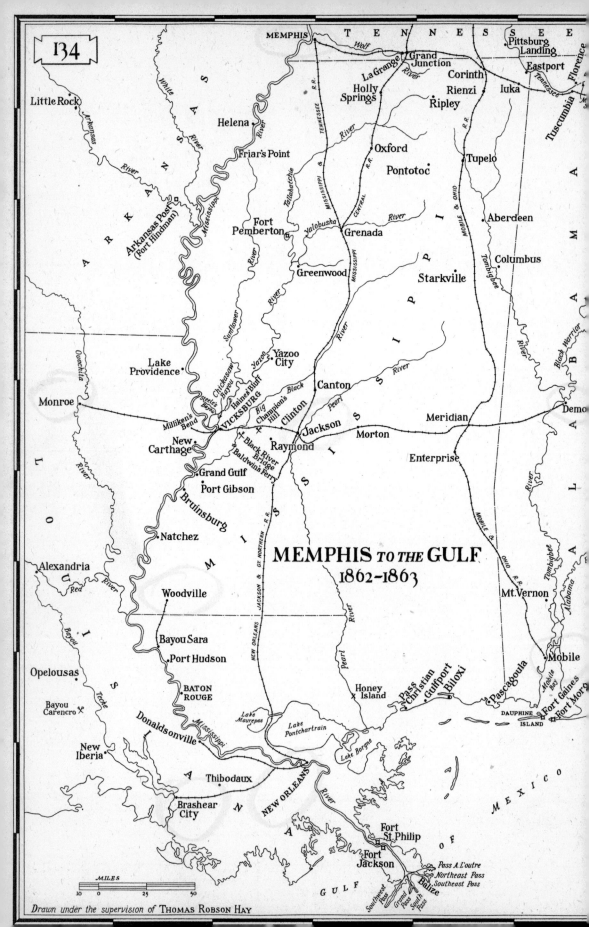

MEMPHIS TO THE GULF
1862-1863

Drawn under the supervision of THOMAS ROBSON HAY

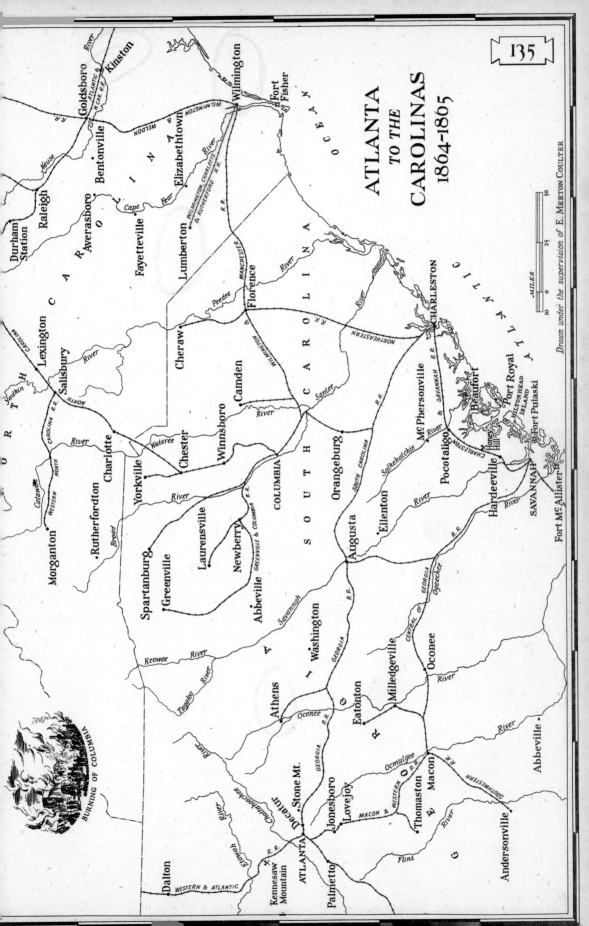

135

ATLANTA TO THE CAROLINAS 1864–1865

Drawn under the supervision of E. MERTON COULTER

MILES

BURNING OF COLUMBIA

PLATE 135

Atlanta to the Carolinas

1864–1865

PLATE 136

Virginia

1864–1865

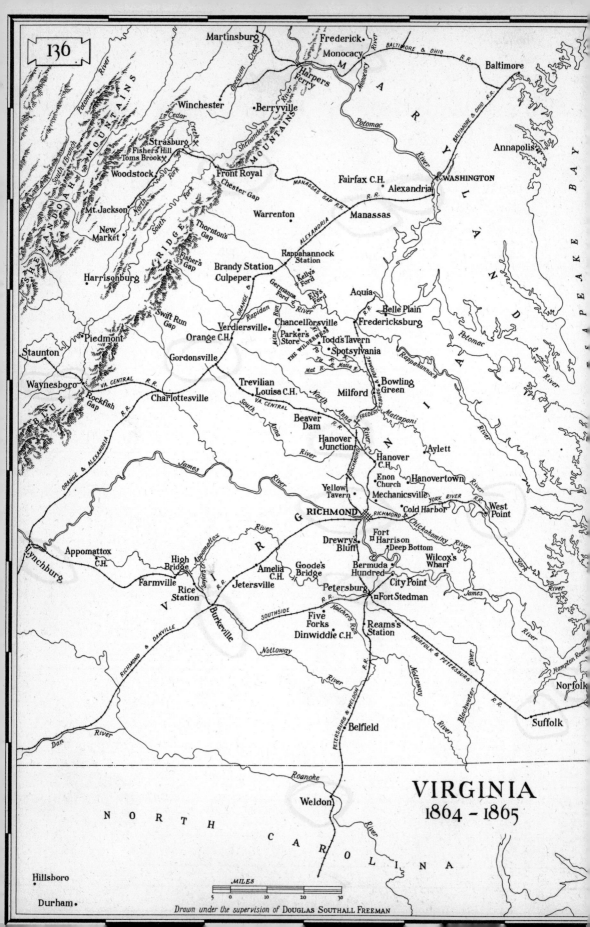

VIRGINIA
1864 - 1865

Drawn under the supervision of DOUGLAS SOUTHALL FREEMAN

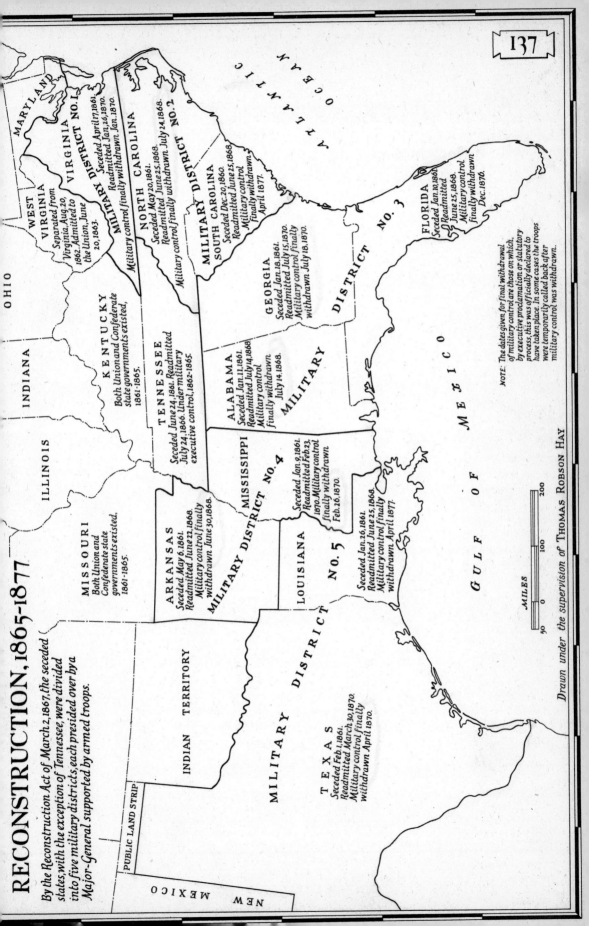

RECONSTRUCTION, 1865–1877

PLATE 137

Reconstruction

1865–1877

PLATE 138

Cow Country, Railroads
and Indian Troubles

1865–1885

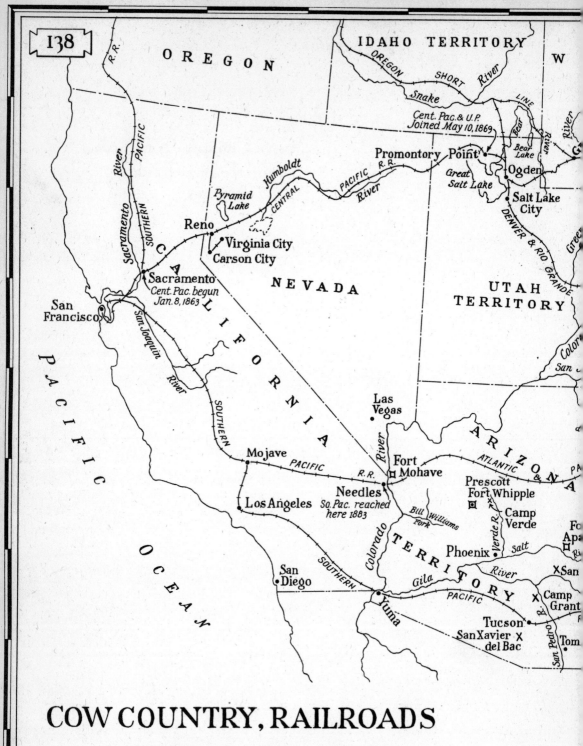

138

IDAHO TERRITORY W

OREGON

Cent. Pac. & U.P.
Joined May 10, 1869

Promontory Point

Ogden

Salt Lake City

Pyramid Lake

Reno

Virginia City
Carson City

Sacramento
Cent. Pac. begun
Jan. 8, 1863

San Francisco

NEVADA

UTAH TERRITORY

CALIFORNIA

Las Vegas

ARIZONA

Mojave

PACIFIC R.R.

Los Angeles

Needles
So. Pac. reached
here 1883

Fort Mohave

Prescott
Fort Whipple

Camp Verde

Phoenix

PACIFIC OCEAN

San Diego

Yuma

SOUTHERN

Tucson
San Xavier
del Bac

Camp Grant

Tom.

TERRITORY

COW COUNTRY, RAILROADS

AND INDIAN TROUBLES

1865–1885

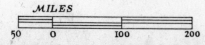

MILES
50   0   100   200

Drawn under the supervision of ALVIN F. HARLOW *and* CARL COKE RISTER

N G

Platte Bridge

ER R.

Fort Halleck

PACIFIC R. R.

North Platte R.

Fort Laramie

U.P. reached here Nov. 1867

Cheyenne

Fort Collins

Greeley

Thornburgh Fight

COLORADO

ADMITTED 1876

Gunnison R.

Uncompahgre River

Del Norte

T. & S. F. reached here 1880

Santa Fe

gate

Albuquerque

MEXICO TERRITORY

Fort Stanton

ilver ity

A. T. & S. F. R. R.

Fort Bliss

eming

El Paso

So. Pac. building eastward reached here 1881.

Fort Quitman

Fort Davis

SOUTHERN

Rio

X I C O

DAKOTA TERRITORY

NEBRASKA

ADMITTED 1867

Ogallala

River

UNION Platte River PACIFIC

Grand Island

Fort Kearny

Fort Sedgwick

Julesburg

Republican River

Denver

South Platte

Beecher Island

KANSAS

PACIFIC

K. P. railhead Oct. 1867 R. R.

Hays City

Fort Hays

Smoky Hill River

Fort Wallace

Pawnee Fork

Fort Larned

Pueblo

Arkansas R. R.

Dodge City

ATCHISON TOPEKA & SANTA FE

PUBLIC LAND STRIP

North Canadian

Adobe Walls X

Tascosa

Canadian

Amarillo

Fort Bascom

GOODNIGHT-LOVING

Fort Sumner

Pecos

CATTLE TRAIL

Horsehead Crossing

TEXAS & PACIFIC

Colorado

Fort Concho

Bandera

WESTERN CATTLE TRAIL

Abilene

Ellsworth

Newton

Wichita

Caldwell

Hunnewell

Camp Supply

River

Fort Cobb

Fort Sill

Doan's Store

Red

Wichita Falls

Fort Griffin

Brazos

River

INDIAN

FLINT HILLS

Arkansas

Fort Gibson

Muskogee

Fort Reno

Fort Smith

TERR.

CHISHOLM CATTLE TRAIL

SHAWNEE

Denison

M.K.&T. reached here 1871

Texarkana

Dallas

Fort Worth

T E X A S

R. R.

Austin

INT. &

San Antonio

Missouri River

IOWA

Council Bluffs

C. R. I. & P. R. R.

C.R.I.&P. reached here 1869

Omaha

MISSOURI

St. Joseph

ST. JOE. & G. I.

Seneca

Junction City

HANNIBAL & ST. JOE. R. R.

Kansas City

Topeka

M. P. R. R.

Kansas River

K. & T. EAST TRAIL

Baxter Springs

ARKANSAS

MISSOURI TRAIL

NOR.

Marshall

GT.

Houston

GULF OF MEXICO

Fort Clark

Eagle Pass

Nueces River

Rio Grande

Laredo

Corpus Christi

PLATE 139

Cow Country, Railroads
and Indian Troubles

1865-1885

PLATE 140

Red River Region

1865–1885

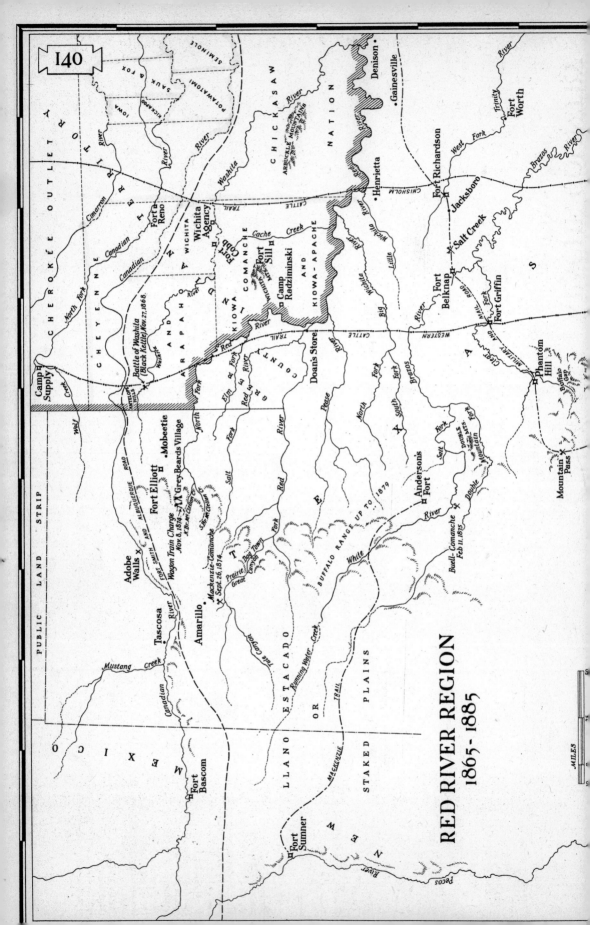

RED RIVER REGION
1865 - 1885

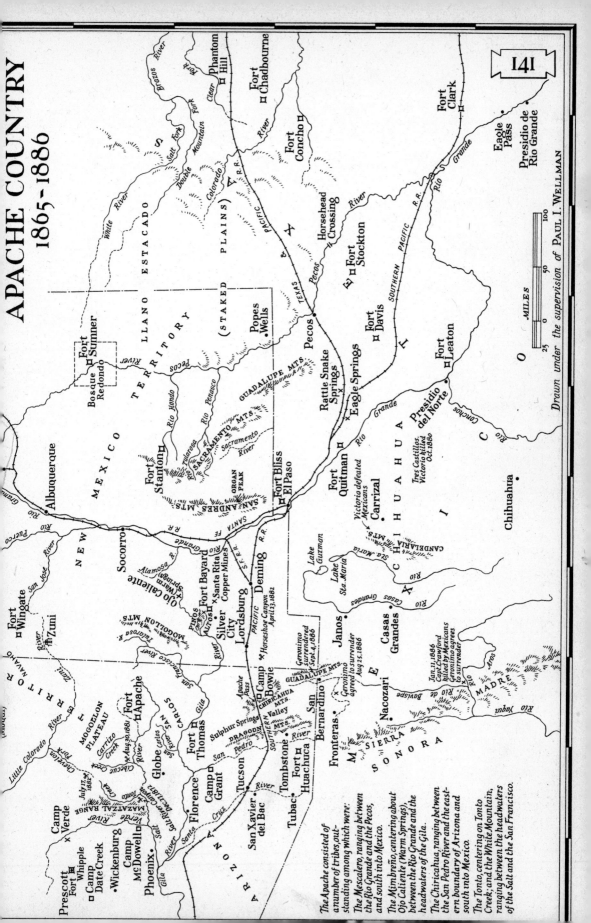

PLATE 141

Apache Country

1865–1886

PLATE 142

Sioux-Cheyenne
Country

1865–1890

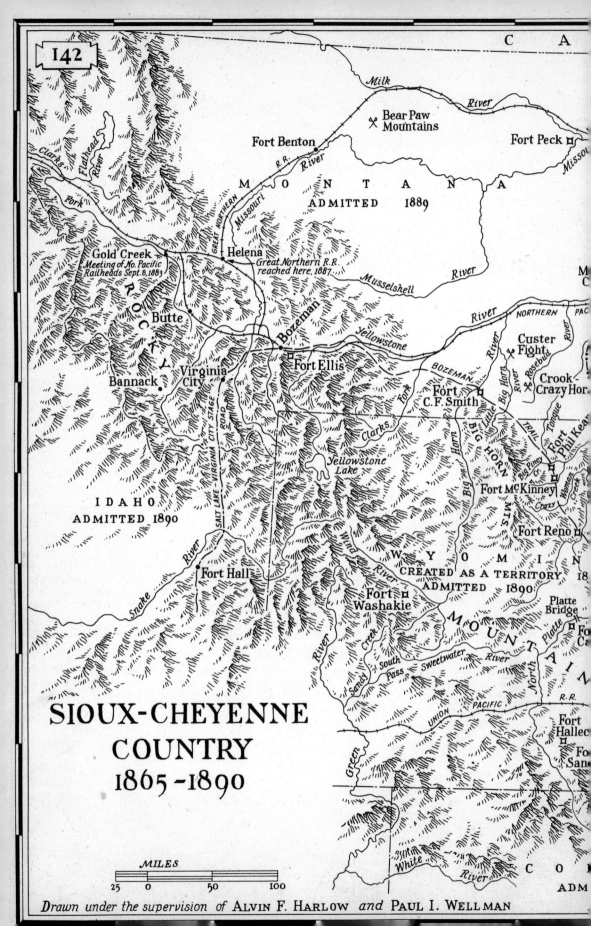

142

C A

Milk   River

Bear Paw
Mountains

Fort Peck

Fort Benton

Missour

R. R.   River

M O N T A N A

GREAT NORTHERN

ADMITTED 1889

Missouri River

Flathead River

Clarks Fork

Gold Creek
Meeting of No. Pacific
Railheads Sept. 8, 1883

Helena
Great Northern R.R.
reached here, 1887

Musselshell   River

M

NORTHERN   PAC

Butte

ROCKY

Bozeman

Yellowstone

River

Custer
Fight

Crook-
Crazy Hor.

Fort Ellis

BOZEMAN

Rosebud River

Torque

Virginia
City

Clarks   Fork

Fort
C. F. Smith

Little Big Horn

Big Horn

TRAIL

Fort
Phil Kear

Bannack

Big Horn MTS.

Big Piney Cr.

Fort McKinney

Mantua Creek

Crazy

SALT LAKE—VIRGINIA CITY STAGE ROAD

Yellowstone
Lake

I D A H O
ADMITTED 1890

Wind   River

Fort Reno

W Y O M I N
CREATED AS A TERRITORY 18
ADMITTED 1890

Snake   River

Fort Hall

Fort
Washakie

Platte
Bridge

Fo
Ca

MOUNTAIN

Sands   Creek

South
Pass   Sweetwater   River

North   Platte

R. R.

UNION   PACIFIC

Fort
Hallec

SIOUX-CHEYENNE
COUNTRY
1865–1890

Green   River

Fo
San

C O
ADM

MILES

25   0   50   100

White   River

Drawn under the supervision of ALVIN F. HARLOW *and* PAUL I. WELLMAN

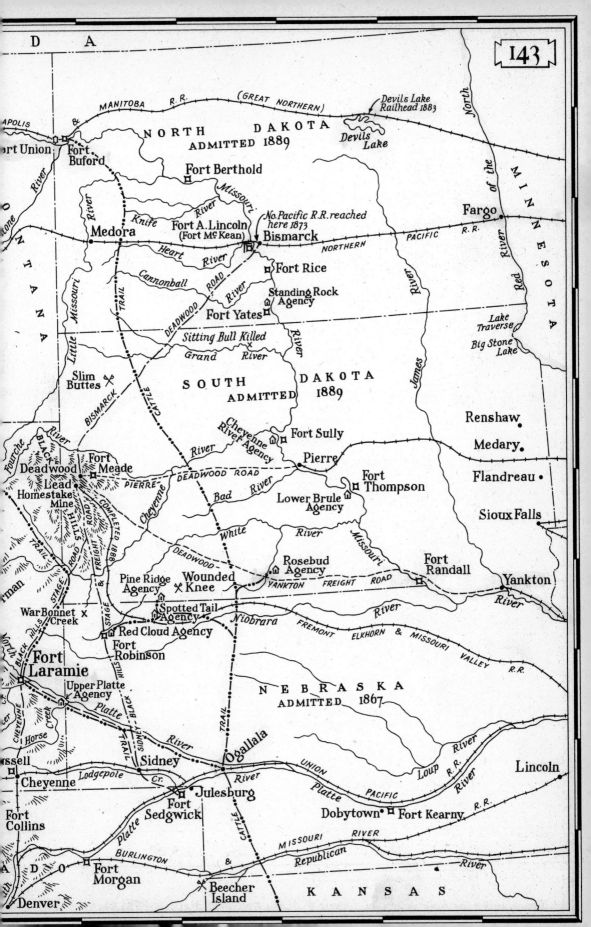

D A

MANITOBA R.R. (GREAT NORTHERN)

Devils Lake
Railhead 1883

NORTH DAKOTA
ADMITTED 1889

Devils
Lake

North

of the

MINNESOTA

APOLIS

ort Union
Fort
Buford

River

Fort Berthold

Missouri

River

Fargo

Medora

Knife

River

River

Fort A. Lincoln
(Fort McKean)

No. Pacific R.R. reached
here 1873

Red River

Lake
Traverse

MONTANA

Little Missouri

TRAIL

Heart

River

Cannonball

River

Bismarck

Fort Rice

Standing Rock
Agency

PACIFIC

NORTHERN

River

R.R.

Big Stone
Lake

DEADWOOD

ROAD

Fort Yates

Sitting Bull Killed
×

Grand

River

River

James

BISMARCK

Slim
Buttes ×

SOUTH DAKOTA
ADMITTED 1889

Renshaw

Medary

Fourche

River

BLACK

Cheyenne
River Agency

River

Fort Sully

CATTLE

DEADWOOD ROAD

Pierre

Fort
Thompson

Flandreau

Deadwood

Fort
Meade

PIERRE

Bad

River

Lower Brule
Agency

Sioux Falls

Lead
Homestake
Mine

BLACK HILLS

Cheyenne

White

River

Missouri

River

Rosebud
Agency

Fort
Randall

Yankton

man

STAGE ROAD & FREIGHT ROAD

COMPLETED 1888

DEADWOOD

Pine Ridge
Agency

Wounded
× Knee

YANKTON FREIGHT ROAD

War Bonnet ×
Creek

STAGE

Spotted Tail
Agency

Niobrara

FREMONT

River

ELKHORN & MISSOURI VALLEY R.R.

Yankton

River

North Platte

Black Hills

Red Cloud Agency

Fort
Robinson

Fort
Laramie

SIDNEY BLACK HILLS TRAIL

Upper Platte
Agency

Cheyenne

Platte

Horse Creek

River

NEBRASKA
ADMITTED 1867

TRAIL

Sidney

River

Ogallala

UNION

Loup River

R.R.

River

Lincoln

ssell

Cheyenne

Lodgepole

Cr.

River

PACIFIC

Platte

R.R.

Fort
Collins

Julesburg

Fort
Sedgwick

CATTLE

Dobytown

Fort Kearny

O

Platte

River

BURLINGTON

MISSOURI

River

&

Republican

River

Fort
Morgan

Beecher
Island

KANSAS

Denver

PLATE 143

Sioux-Cheyenne
Country

1865–1890

PLATE 144

Red Cloud's Country

1865–1876

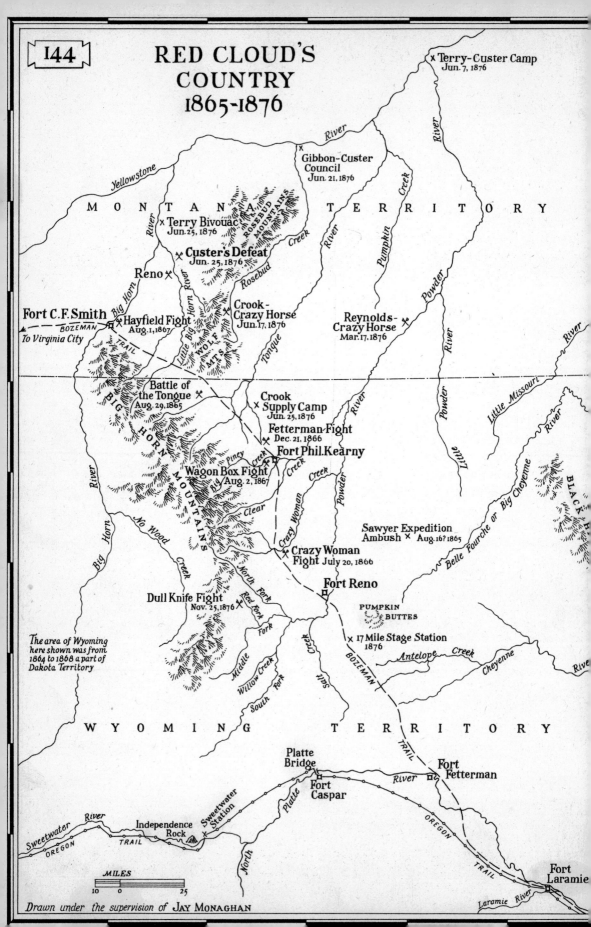

RED CLOUD'S COUNTRY 1865-1876

144

Terry-Custer Camp
Jun. 7, 1876

Gibbon-Custer
Council
Jun. 21, 1876

River

MONTANA TERRITORY

Yellowstone

Rosebud Creek

Pumpkin Creek

Terry Bivouac
Jun. 25, 1876

ROSEBUD MOUNTAINS

Custer's Defeat
Jun. 25, 1876

Reno

Crook-
Crazy Horse
Jun. 17, 1876

Rosebud Creek

Powder River

Reynolds-
Crazy Horse
Mar. 17, 1876

Fort C.F. Smith
Hayfield Fight
Aug. 1, 1867

Little Big Horn River

WOLF MT'S.

BOZEMAN TRAIL

To Virginia City

Big Horn River

Tongue River

Little Powder River

Little Missouri River

Battle of
the Tongue
Aug. 29, 1865

BIG HORN MOUNTAINS

Crook
Supply Camp
Jun. 25, 1876

Piney Creek

Fetterman Fight
Dec. 21, 1866

Fort Phil. Kearny

Wagon Box Fight
Aug. 2, 1867

Clear Creek

Powder Creek

Crazy Woman Creek

BLACK HILLS

Belle Fourche or Big Cheyenne River

No Wood Creek

Sawyer Expedition
Ambush × Aug. 16? 1865

Big Horn River

Crazy Woman
Fight July 20, 1866

Fort Reno

The area of Wyoming
here shown was from
1864 to 1868 a part of
Dakota Territory

Dull Knife Fight
Nov. 25, 1876

North Fork

Red Fork

PUMPKIN BUTTES

17 Mile Stage Station
1876

Antelope Creek

Cheyenne River

Middle Fork

Willow Creek

South Fork

Salt Creek

BOZEMAN TRAIL

WYOMING TERRITORY

Platte
Bridge

Fort
Caspar

Platte River

Fort Fetterman

Sweetwater
Station

North Platte

OREGON TRAIL

Sweetwater River

Independence
Rock

OREGON TRAIL

Fort
Laramie

Laramie River

MILES
10 0 25

Drawn under the supervision of JAY MONAGHAN

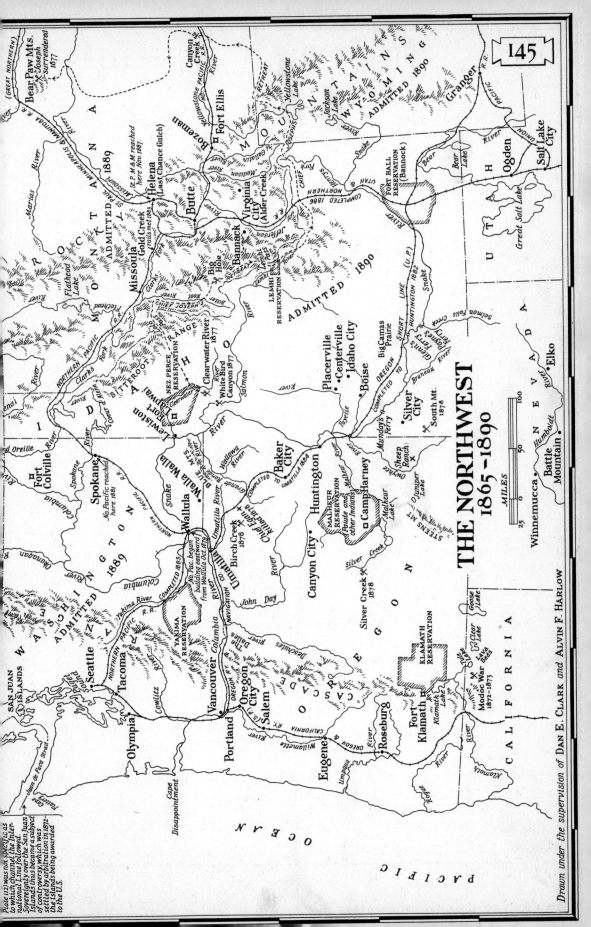

THE NORTHWEST 1865-1890

MILES

25   0   50   100

Drawn under the supervision of Dan E. Clark and Alvin F. Harlow

PACIFIC OCEAN

WASHINGTON ADMITTED 1889

MONTANA ADMITTED 1889

IDAHO ADMITTED 1890

WYOMING ADMITTED 1890

OREGON

NEVADA

CALIFORNIA

UTAH

Plate 112) was not specific as to which channel the International Line followed. Sovereignty over the San Juan Islands thus became a subject of controversy which was settled by arbitration in 1872—the islands being awarded to the U.S.

Bear Paw Mts. Joseph surrendered 1877

Helena (Last Chance Gulch)

Butte

Bozeman

Fort Ellis

Virginia City (Alder Creek)

Bannack

Missoula Gold Creek

Big Hole

Yellowstone Lake

Jackson Lake

Granger

Ogden

Salt Lake City

Great Salt Lake

Fort Hall Reservation (Bannock)

Bear Lake

Nez Perce Reservation

Fort Lapwai

Lewiston

Clearwater River 1877

White Bird Canyon 1877

Lemhi Reservation

ADMITTED 1890

Placerville

Centerville

Idaho City

Boise

Big Camas Prairie

Glenn's Ferry 1877

Silver City

South Mt. 1878

Salmon Falls

Winnemucca

Battle Mountain

Elko

Fort Colville

Spokane

No Pacific reached here 1881

Wallula

Walla Walla

Baker City

Huntington

Camp Harney

Malheur Reservation Paiute and other Indians

Malheur Lake

Harney Lake

Sheep Ranch

Steens Mt.

Canyon City

Silver Creek 1878

Birch Creek 1878

Umatilla Reservation

Seattle

Tacoma

Olympia

Vancouver

Oregon City

Portland

Salem

Eugene

Roseburg

Fort Klamath

Klamath Reservation

Modoc War Lava Beds 1872-1873

Clear Lake

Goose Lake

San Juan Islands

Cape Disappointment

Juan de Fuca Strait

ROCKY MOUNTAINS

BITTERROOT RANGE

CHIEF JOSEPH RANGE

BLUE MTS.

CASCADE RANGE

PLATE 145

The Northwest

1865–1890

PLATE 146

Indian Territory
and the
State of Oklahoma

1885–1907

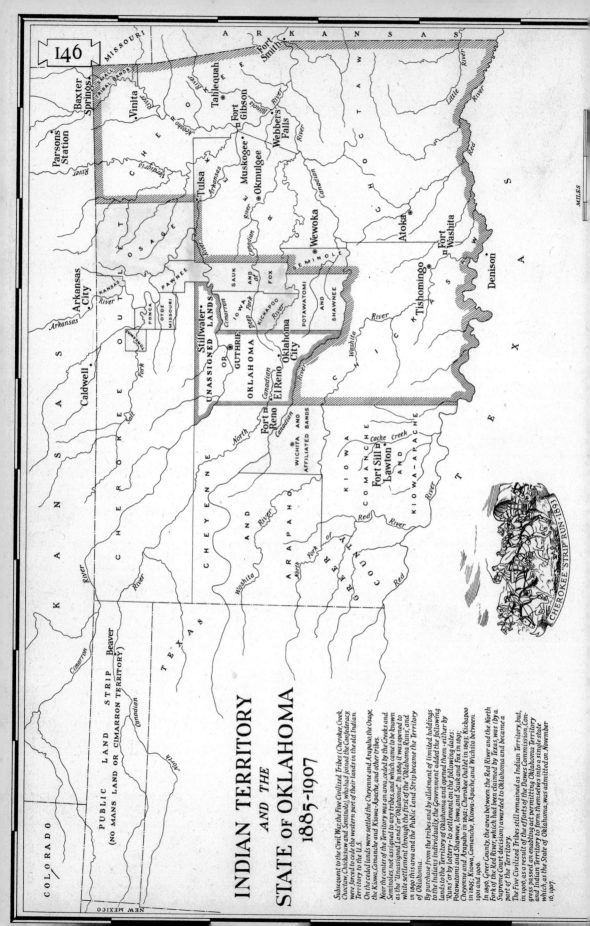

COLORADO

NEW MEXICO

K A N S A S

MISSOURI

A R K A N S A S

ARKANSAS

Parsons' Station

Baxter Springs

Vinita

SMALL TRIBAL BANDS

Fort Smith

Tahlequah

C H E R O K E E

Fort Gibson

Webber's Falls

Illinois River

Little River

Red River

Arkansas City

KANSAS

Caldwell

River

C H E R O K E E   O U T L E T

O S A G E

Grand or Neosho R.

Verdigris River

Tulsa

Muskogee

Okmulgee

C R E E K

Canadian

C H O C T A W

Atoka

Fort Washita

Denison

Arkansas

Salt Fork

PONCA

OTOE MISSOURI

TONKAWA

PAWNEE

Cimarron River

Arkansas River

SAUK AND FOX

IOWA AND of

KICKAPOO

Deep Fork

POTAWATOMI

SEMINOLE

Wewoka

SHAWNEE AND

C H I C K A S A W

Tishomingo

Washita River

Stillwater

UNASSIGNED LANDS

GUTHRIE

OKLAHOMA OR

Oklahoma City

El Reno

Fort Reno

Canadian

North Canadian

WICHITA AND AFFILIATED BANDS

Red River

River

KIOWA

COMANCHE

Cache Creek

Fort Sill

Lawton

KIOWA-APACHE

AND

T E X A S

G R E E R   C O U N T Y

North Fork of Red River

Washita

C H E Y E N N E

A N D

A R A P A H O

River

North

Canadian

Beaver

PUBLIC LAND STRIP

(NO MANS LAND OR CIMARRON TERRITORY)

Cimarron

Canadian

North

MILES

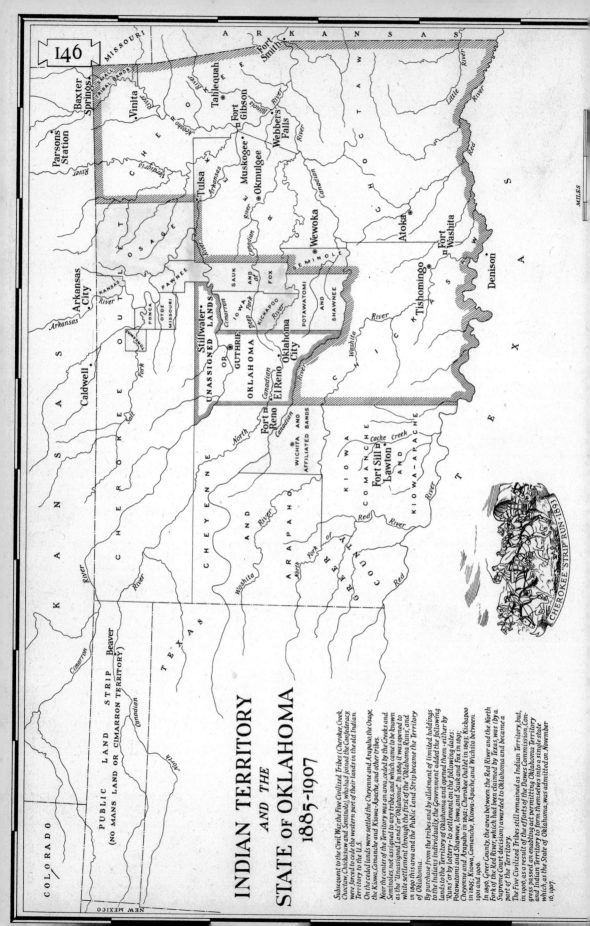
CHEROKEE "STRIP" RUN 1893

INDIAN TERRITORY
AND THE
STATE of OKLAHOMA
1885-1907

Subsequent to the Civil War, the Five Civilized Tribes (Cherokee, Creek, Choctaw, Chickasaw and Seminole), who had joined the Confederacy, were forced to cede the western part of their lands in the old Indian Territory to the U.S.

On the ceded lands were settled the Cheyenne and Arapaho, the Osage, the Kiowa, Comanche and Kiowa-Apache, and other tribes.

Near the center of the Territory was an area, ceded by the Creeks and Seminoles, not assigned to any tribes, and which came to be known as the "Unassigned Lands" or "Oklahoma". In 1889 it was opened to white settlement through the first of the "Oklahoma Runs", and in 1890 this area and the Public Land Strip became the Territory of Oklahoma.

By purchase from the tribes and by allotment of limited holdings to the Indians individually, the Government added the following lands to the Territory of Oklahoma and opened them - either by "Runs" or by lottery - to settlement on the following dates: Potawatomi and Shawnee, Iowa, and Sauk and Fox in 1891; Cheyenne and Arapaho in 1892; Cherokee Outlet in 1893; Kickapoo in 1895; Kiowa, Comanche, Kiowa-Apache, and Wichita between 1901 and 1906.

In 1896, Greer County, the area between the Red River and the North Fork of the Red River, which had been claimed by Texas, was (by a Supreme Court decision) awarded to Oklahoma and became a part of the Territory.

The Five Civilized Tribes still remained as Indian Territory but, in 1906, as a result of the efforts of the Dawes Commission, Congress passed an enabling act permitting Oklahoma Territory and Indian Territory to form themselves into a single state which, as the State of Oklahoma, was admitted on November 10, 1907.

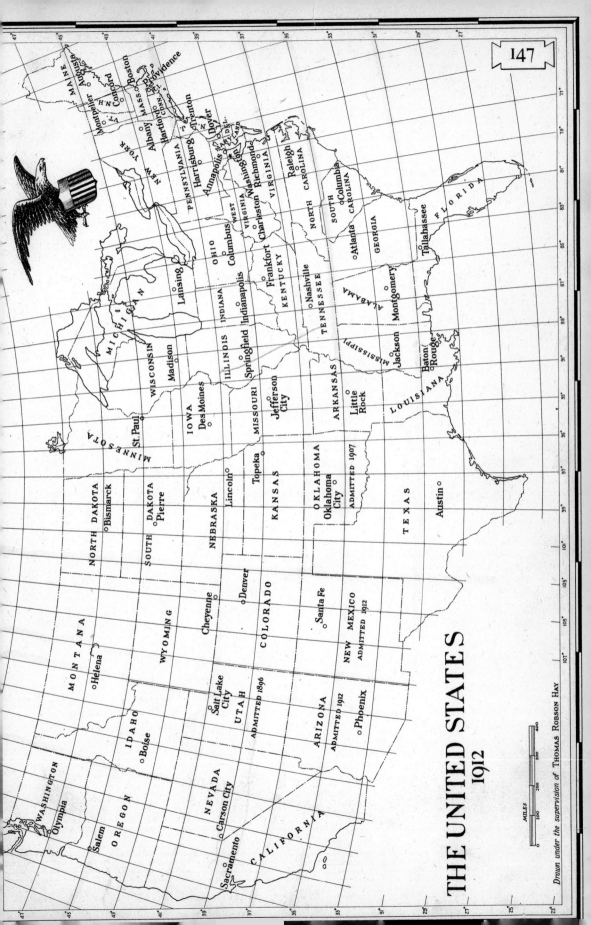

THE UNITED STATES
1912

Drawn under the supervision of THOMAS ROBSON HAY

147

PLATE 147

The United States

1912

Index

This Index is designed to serve two main purposes. First, it enables the user of the *Atlas* to turn, quickly and definitely, to the map or maps on which a given location is shown.

Second, it serves as a cross reference, enabling the user of the work to follow, from map to map, the development of areas in succeeding periods of our history. Thus, the advance of the frontier may be visualized; or the evolution of a Territory, in its changing extents, may be followed through to the final creation of the State; or the migrations and removals of the various Indian tribes may be traced.

In the indexing of historical locations some inconsistencies are inevitable. An Indian village of the time of DeSoto can scarcely be listed as being in a present-day state. On the other hand, Harpers Ferry was important historically long before the existence of the state of West Virginia; Vincennes was a French frontier post sixty years before the Territory of Indiana was formed; yet, for the purposes of an index, it would be confusing to identify these places other than in their present states. Again, as between towns which have had a continuing existence and those which have disappeared or which are not direct descendants of existing towns of the same name, a distinction in the form of listing is desirable—although the basis for decision is often very slight indeed.

Also, there is the matter of spellings, accents and possessives. No uniformity existed, nor is it the province of an atlas of American history to establish uniformity, but rather, in each case, to follow the form most used over the greatest period of time, and, where distinct variations occur, to list those variations with a reference to the form used.

Thus, without departing too greatly from consistency, the editors, in compiling the following Index, have endeavored to so list each location that it may be readily found in the Index—from which the user will turn to the proper map, where the status of the place, during the period of the map, will be amply evident.

A

Boswyck (N. Y.), 20
Botetourt County, Va., 63
Botetourt C. H. (Va.), 63
Bottom's Bridge (Va.), 129
Boulder, Colo., 120
Boulder Creek, 120
Bound Brook, N. J., 23, 71
Boundaries: With Canada, 82, 92, 93, 94–95, 100–101, 110, 111, 112–113, 145; with Mexico, 94–95, 100–101, 104, 112–113, 114–115, 118; with Spanish Florida, 82, 88–89; with Spanish Louisiana, 82
Bourbon County (Ga.), 88
Bourgmont Expedition (1714–1724), 36
Bowie, Camp (Ariz.), 141
Bowlegs Town (Fla.), 89, 103
Bowling Green, Ky., 106, 124, 127
Bowling Green, Va., 129, 136
Bowyer, Fort, 88, 98
Boydton Plank Road. *See* Hatcher's Run
Bozeman, Mont., 142, 145
Bozeman Trail, 142–143, 144
Braddock's Defeat, 43, 57
Braddock's Grave, 57
Braddock's Road, 43, 57
Bradford (Colo.), 120
Bradford, Mass., 26
Bradford, N. H., 109
Brady, Fort, 93
Braintree, Mass., 16, 26, 109
Branchville, S. C., 108
Brandon, Miss., 108
Brandy Station (Va.), 128, 136
Brandywine Creek, 21, 71
Branford, Conn., 17, 26, 79
Brashear City (La.), 134
Brasseaux, Ruisseau de, 46
Brattleboro, Vt., 55, 109
Brazito (N. Mex.), 115
Brazoria, Tex., 105, 115
Brazos River, 6, 33, 36, 53, 95, 101, 104, 105, 115, 119, 131, 139, 140, 141
Breakneck Mountain, 73
Breckenridge, Colo., 120

Breed's Hill, 65
Breton, Cape, 39
Breuckelen, N. Y., 20
Brewerton, Fort, 78
Briar Creek, 74
Briar Creek, Battle of, 74
Bridgeport, Ala., 132, 133
Bridgeport, Conn., 109
Bridgeport, N. J., 23
Bridger, Fort, 112, 117, 118, 130
Bridger's Camp (Wyo.), 102
Bridger's Pass (Wyo.), 130, 139
Bridgeton, N. J., 23, 25
Bridgewater, Mass., 26
Bridgman's Fort, 38
Briscoe Mines (Va.), 129
Bristoe (Va.), 128
Bristol, Maine, 15
Bristol, Pa., 25, 107
Bristol, R. I., 18
Bristol, Tenn.-Va., 127
Broad River (Ga.), 89
Broad River (at Port Royal, S. C.), 9
Broad River (a tributary of the Santee River), 24, 47, 56, 59, 61, 74, 75, 135
Broad River, First, 59
Bronx River, 70
Brooke, Fort, 103
Brookfield, Mass., 26, 38, 55
Brookhaven, N. Y., 17
Brookline, Mass., 64, 65
Brooklyn, N. Y., 20, 70, 109
Brooklyn Heights, N. Y., 70
Brookville, Ind., 92
Brown, Fort, 115
Brown Claims (Kans.), 121
Brown's Bank, 83
Brown's Ferry (Tenn.), 132
Brown's Gap (Va.), 128
Browns Hole, 100, 112
Brownstown (Mich.), 96
Bruinsburg (Miss.), 134
Brule River, 33
Bruneau River, 145
Brunswick, Maine, 38, 66

⌈ **C** ⌉

〔 **G** 〕

[J]

Loramie Creek, 40, 41, 47, 85
Loramie Creek-St. Marys River Portage, 40, 41
Loramie's Store (Ohio), 41, 85
Lordsburg, N. Mex., 141
Los Adaes (La.), 36, 53, 95, 105
Los Angeles, Calif., 52, 94, 100, 114, 116, 118, 130, 138
Loudon, Fort (Pa.), 43, 47
Loudon, Tenn., 127, 133
Loudoun, Fort (Tenn.), 56, 59, 76
Loudoun, Fort (Va.), 58
Loudoun and Hampshire Railroad, 123
Louisa C. H. (Va.), 128, 136
Louisa River (Kentucky River), 61
Louisburg, Fort, 39
Louisiana (French, 1699–1763), 37; (Spanish), 47; (1764), 49; (Spanish), 50, 53, 77, 82; (Territory), 88; (Purchase), 94–95; (District of), 95; (Admitted, 1812), 95; (State of), 98, 101, 105, 108, 115, 122, 124, 131, 134, 137, 147
Louisville, Ga., 89
Louisville, Ky., 62, 63, 84, 106, 108, 124, 127
Louisville and Frankfort Railroad, 124
Louisville and Jeffersonville Railroad, 124
Louisville and Nashville Railroad, 124, 127
Loup, Rivière du, 67
Loup River (Nebr.), 101, 143
Lovejoy, Ga., 127, 133, 135
Lovewell's Fight, 38
Lowell, Mass., 26, 107, 109
Lower Brule Agency (S. Dak.), 143
Lower Landing (Niagara River), 42
Loyal, Fort, 38
Loyal Hannon (Pa.), 43, 57
Loyalhanna Creek, 43, 57
Lumberton, N. C., 125, 135
Lundy's Lane, Battle of, 96
Lupton, Fort, 113, 120
Luray, Va., 128
Lygonia (Maine), 15
Lynchburg, Va., 107, 125, 128, 136
Lynch's Ferry, (Va.), 55

Lynn, Mass., 16, 26
Lynnhaven Roads, 81
Lyon, Fort, 131

M

Mabila, 7
Machault, Fort, 43
Machegonne (Maine), 15
Machot (Va.), 12
Mackenzie, Fort, 100
Mackenzie-Comanche Battle (Sept. 26, 1874), 140
Mackenzie Trail, 140
Mackinac, Mich., 111
Mackinac, Straits of, 96
Mackinac Island, 30
Macomb Purchase (1791), 91
Macon, Fort, 125
Macon, Ga., 108, 125, 135
Macon, Mo., 124, 126, 131
Macon and Western Railroad, 108, 124–125, 135
Mad River and Lake Erie Railroad, 108
Madawaska River, 110
Madeket, 26
Madison, Fort (Iowa). See Fort Madison
Madison, Ind., 92, 108
Madison, Wis., 111, 131, 147
Madison and Indianapolis Railroad, 108
Madison River, 94, 145
Magaguadavic River, 110
Magdalen Islands, 39, 83
Magruder, Fort, 129
Mahicans, The, 20
Mahoning Creek, 57
Maidenhead (N. J.), 23
Maine, 26, 55, 66, 82, 99, 107, 109; (Admitted, 1820), 110; (State of), 122, 147
Malden, Fort, 93
Malheur Reservation (Oreg.), 145
Malheur River, 145
Malheureux Point, 98
Maliseet, The, 39
Mallet Brothers Expedition (1739–1740), 36

Missouri, Kansas and Texas Railroad, 139
Missouri, The, 146
Missouri-Kansas Border (1854–1859), 121
Missouri Pacific Railroad, 139
Missouri Region (1861–1864), 126
Missouri River, 31, 33, 36, 37, 40, 47, 48, 52–53, 77, 92, 93, 94–95, 100–101, 104, 106, 108, 111, 112–113, 115, 118–119, 121, 124, 126, 130–131, 139, 142–143, 145
Mitchell's Ford (Va.), 123
Mobeetie, Tex., 140
Mobile, Ala., 34, 37, 47, 50, 76, 77, 88, 98, 108, 124, 131, 134
Mobile and Ohio Railroad, 124, 127, 131, 134
Mobile Bay, 50, 76, 98, 134
Mobjack Bay, 129
Moccasin Gap, 56, 59, 62, 76
Moccasin Point, 132
Modoc War (1872–1873), 145
Mogollon Mountains, 141
Mogollon Plateau, 141
Mohave, Fort, 130, 138
Mohave, The, 52
Mohave Desert, 52, 100, 116
Mohawk, The, 27, 38, 44, 72, 78
Mohawk River, 20, 22, 27, 38, 44, 47, 55, 67, 72, 78, 90, 91, 96, 107
Mohawk River, Carrying Place to Wood Creek, 38, 72
Mohegan (Conn.), 17
Mojave, Calif., 138
Mokelumne River, 116
Molino del Rey (Mex.), 114
Mölndal, 21
Monclova, Mex., 115
Moneka (Kans.), 121
Monguagon (Mich.), 96
Monguagon, Pointe, 46
Monhegan Island, 15, 83
Monmouth C. H. (N. J.), 71
Monmouth Purchase (1665), 23
Monocacy (Md.), 136

Monocacy River, 128, 136
Monongahela River, 40, 41, 43, 47, 55, 56, 57, 61, 63, 66, 77, 86, 90, 107, 108, 109, 123, 125
Monroe, Fortress, 125, 128, 129
Monroe, Lake, 103
Monroe, La., 124, 134
Monroe, Mich., 108
Montana (Territory, 1864), 130; (1865–1876), 144; (Admitted, 1889), 142–143, 145; (State of), 147
Montauk Point, 79, 80, 83, 99
Monte Morelos, Mex., 115
Monterey, Calif., 52, 94, 100, 114, 116, 118, 130
Monterey, Va., 123
Monterrey, Mex., 115
Montezuma (Tex.), 105
Montgomery, Ala., 108, 124, 147
Montgomery, Fort, 73
Montgomery and West Point Railroad, 108, 124
Montgomery's Route (1775), 67
Montpelier, Vt., 82, 109, 147
Montreal, Canada, 22, 29, 38, 40, 44, 66, 67, 72, 96
Moores Creek, 68
Moores Creek Bridge, Battle of, 68, 74
Moosa, Fort, 34, 51
Moosehead Lake, 67, 110
Moqui (Ariz.), 141
Moqui, The, 52
Morales (Mex.), 114
Moratuc, 10
Moratuc (Roanoke) River, 10
Moravian Town (Canada), 96
Moravian Towns (Pa.), 47
Morgan, Fort (Ala.), 124, 134
Morgan, Fort (Colo.), 143
Morganton, N. C., 135
Morgantown, W. Va., 57, 123
Mormon Trail, 112–113, 117
Morris Canal, 107
Morris Island, 69
Morris Reserve (1791), 91

┗ **N** ┛

Nootka Sound, 112
Norembega River, 29
Norfolk, Va., 24, 55, 66, 74, 80, 81, 97, 99, 107, 109, 125, 128, 129, 136
Norfolk and Petersburg Railroad, 128, 129, 136
Norridgewock, Maine, 67
Norridgewock Fight, 38
North Adams, Mass., 109
North Anna River, 128, 136
North Battery (Boston), 65
North Bridge (Concord), 64
North Canadian River, 104, 139, 140, 146
North Cape, 39, 83
North Carolina, 24, 55, 56, 59, 61, 66, 68, 74, 75, 82, 84, 89, 90, 99, 106–107, 109, 122, 125, 127, 128, 135, 136, 137, 147
North Carolina Railroad, 125, 135
North Castle (N. Y.), 80
North Dakota (Admitted, 1889), 143; (State of), 147. *See also* Dakota Territory
North Missouri Railroad, 126, 131
North Park. *See* New Park
North Platte River, 36, 95, 101, 113, 119, 131, 139, 142–143, 144
North Point, 97
North Point, Battle of, 97
North River (Hudson River), 20, 70
North River (Va.), 58
North Toe River, 75
Northampton, Mass., 26, 38, 55, 107
Northeast Boundary (1783–1842), 110
Northeast Pass (Mississippi Delta), 98, 134
Northeast River, 68
Northeastern Railroad, 135
Northern Neck (Va.), 24
Northern Pacific Railroad, 142–143, 145
Northern Railroad of New York, 109
Northfield, Mass., 26, 38
Northwest Angle, 101, 111
Northwest Territory, 82
Northwestern Virginia Railroad, 123
Northwestern Virginia Turnpike, 123
Norwalk, Conn., 17, 26, 79
Norwich, Conn., 17, 26, 109

Norwich (Vt.), 55
Norwich and Worcester Railroad, 109
Nottoway River, 136
Nova Scotia, 39, 83
Nueces River, 53, 95, 101, 105, 115, 139
Number 4 (N. H.), 38, 44, 55
Nya Elfsborg, 21
Nya Göteborg, 21
Nya Korsholm, 21
Nya Vasa, 21

O

Oak Hills, Battle of, 126
Oakfuskee (Ala.), 56, 76
Oakland, Calif., 116
Oblong, The, 27
Ocale, 7
Occoquan, Va., 128
Occoquan Creek, 123, 128
Occupasspatuxet (R. I.), 18
Ocean View (Va.), 129
Ochlockonee River, 24, 34, 103
Ochus, 7
Ocmulgee River, 7, 24, 34, 47, 56, 76, 89, 135
Oconee, Ga., 135
Oconee River, 7, 24, 47, 56, 74, 76, 89, 135
Ocute, 7
Ogallala, Nebr., 139, 143
Ogden, Utah, 117, 138, 145
Ogdens Hole, 100, 112
Ogdensburg, N. Y., 96, 109
Ogeechee River, 24, 34, 35, 74, 76, 89, 135
Ohio (Admitted, 1803), 85; (State of), 92, 93, 96, 106, 108, 122, 123, 124–125, 131, 147
Ohio, Forks of the (1754–1759), 43
Ohio, The Upper (1753–1779), 57
Ohio and Erie Canal, 106
Ohio and Mississippi Railroad, 119, 124, 126, 131
Ohio Company of Associates Purchase, 85, 86
Ohio Company of Virginia, 57

Pl 339

Q

S

South River (N. C.), 68
South Toe River, 75
Southampton, N. Y., 17, 20, 26, 79
Southeast Pass (Mississippi Delta), 98, 134
Southern Mississippi Railroad, 124
Southern Pacific Railroad, 138, 141, 145
Southold, N. Y., 17, 20, 26, 79
Southport (Wis.), 111
Southside Railroad, 136
Southwest Pass (Mississippi Delta), 49, 98, 134
Southwest Point (Tenn.), 84
Southwest Territory (Territory South of the River Ohio), 82
Southwestern Railroad, 135
Sowams (R. I.), 18
Spanish Fort (Ga.), 34
Spanish Peaks, 104
Spanish Trail. *See* Old Spanish Trail
Sparta, Tenn., 127
Spartanburg, S. C., 135
Spencer, Ind., 92
Spirit Lake, 111
Spokane, Wash., 145
Spokane House (Wash.), 94
Spokane River, 112, 145
Spotswood, N. J., 23, 71
Spotswood Expedition, 24, 58
Spotsylvania, Va., 74, 128, 136
Spotted Tail Agency (Nebr.), 143
Spring Hill, Tenn., 127
Spring Wells (Mich.), 96
Springfield, Ill., 108, 124, 147
Springfield, Mass., 17, 26, 55, 109
Springfield, Mo., 119, 124, 126, 131
Springfield, N. J., 71
Springfield (N. Y.), 55, 78
Springfield, Ohio, 106, 108
Sta. Maria, Lake, 141
Sta. Maria, Rio, 141
Stadaconé, 29
Staked Plains, 101, 104, 115, 140, 141
Stalnakers (Va.), 56, 59, 61, 63
Stamford, Conn., 17, 26, 79
Stanardsville, Va., 128

Standing Rock Agency (N. Dak.), 143
Stanislaus River, 116
Stanton, Fort, 104, 119, 130, 139, 141
Stanton (Kans.), 121
Stanwix, Fort, 44, 55, 61, 72, 78, 90, 91
Stanwix, Fort, Treaty of (1768), 60, 78
Stanwix, Fort, Treaty of (1784), 90
Starkville, Miss., 134
Starved Rock, 33, 48
Staten Island, 20, 23, 70, 71, 80
Staunton, Va., 47, 55, 56, 58, 61, 63, 74, 123, 125, 128, 136
Staunton River, 56, 59, 61, 63, 74
Stedman, Fort, 136
Steele's Bayou, 134
Steens Mountain, 145
Stephenson, Fort, 96
Sterling, Mass., 109
Sterling Iron Works (N. Y.), 27
Steuben, Fort, 85
Stevens Gap (Ga.), 132
Stevenson, Ala., 124, 127, 132, 133
Stewarts Crossing, 57
Stillwater, Minn., 111
Stillwater, N. Y., 72
Stillwater, Okla, 146
Stockton, Calif., 116
Stockton, Fort, 141
Stoddert, Fort, 88
Stone Arabia (N. Y.), 72
Stone Bridge (Va.), 123
Stone Mountain, Ga., 133, 135
Stone River, 127
Stoney Creek, Battle of, 96
Stonington, Conn., 26, 99, 109
Stonington Railroad, 109
Stono River, 69
Stony Brook, 64, 65
Stony Point, N. Y., 73, 78, 80
Strandviken, 21
Stranger Creek, 121
Strasburg, Va., 58, 123, 128, 136
Stratford, Conn., 17, 26, 79
Strawberry Bank (N. H.), 15
Strother, Fort, 89

[T]

⌷ W ⌷

X

Y